A Different View of Cur.
and Assessment for Severe,
Complex and Profound Learning
Disabilities

A Different View of Curriculum and Assessment links a theoretical pedagogical model with a sympathetic practical model of curriculum and assessment difference for those with PMLD, CLD and SLD.

Split into two parts, this accessible resource combines theoretical explanations with first-hand accounts of how this works in educational establishments through the analysis of evidence-based practice carried out in a number of English special (specialist) schools. The expert authors challenge the notion that a national, or common-core-standards, curriculum, however expertly differentiated, is fit-for-purpose for the PMLD, CLD and SLD populations in any country. *A Different View* offers cogent and reasoned arguments for considering that, irrespective of age, such learners learn differently to their neuro-typical, conventionally developing peers. If they learn differently, this book shows how we should be teaching them differently.

Reflecting the centrality of process over product, this book will clearly explain how each individual learner might be enabled and facilitated to become the best they can be and do the best they can do in order to fully realise their potential as equal and independent citizens.

Peter Imray is a freelance trainer, advisor and writer in the area of special educational needs and Associate Lecturer at the University of Birmingham. His previous books include *Inclusion is Dead: Long Live Inclusion* (Routledge, 2017) and *Curricula for Teaching Children and Young People with Severe or Profound and Multiple Learning Difficulties* (Routledge, 2013).

Lila Kossyvaki is Associate Professor in Severe, Profound and Multiple Learning Disabilities (SLD/PMLD) at the University of Birmingham.

Mike Sissons began his career as carer for adults with profound learning disabilities and has subsequently worked for over 30 years as a teacher and senior leader in special schools.

Connecting Research with Practice in Special and Inclusive Education
Series edited by Philip Garner

This new series represents a commitment to supporting the emergence of applied research in Special and Inclusive Education. It comprises an authoritative collection of books which examine in depth the key issues being experienced in the field, both currently and into the future. These have been selected to illustrate both national and international dimensions of a chosen theme in Special and Inclusive Education. Each book has been commissioned from leading writers each of whom has substantial experience in their topic and who is also recognised for their capacity to connect a body of systematic evidence to the needs of a practitioner audience. Authors contributing to the series are often practitioners or practitioner-researchers themselves.

On Educational Inclusion
An Exploration of Meanings, History, and Issues
Edited by James M Kauffman

Establishing Pathways to Inclusion
Investigating the Experiences and Outcomes for Students with Special Educational Needs
Richard Rose and Michael Shevlin

Contemporary Approaches to Behaviour and Mental Health in the Classroom
Weaving Together Theory, Practice, Policy and Educational Discourse
Emma Clarke

Inclusive Education at the Crossroads
Exploring effective special needs provision in global contexts
Philippa Gordon-Gould and Garry Hornby

A Different View of Curriculum and Assessment for Severe, Complex and Profound Learning Disabilities
Edited by Peter Imray, Lila Kossyvaki and Mike Sissons

A Different View of Curriculum and Assessment for Severe, Complex and Profound Learning Disabilities

Edited by
Peter Imray, Lila Kossyvaki and
Mike Sissons

Routledge
Taylor & Francis Group

LONDON AND NEW YORK

Designed cover image: © Getty Images

First published 2024
by Routledge
4 Park Square, Milton Park, Abingdon, Oxon OX14 4RN

and by Routledge
605 Third Avenue, New York, NY 10158

Routledge is an imprint of the Taylor & Francis Group, an informa business

© 2024 selection and editorial matter, Peter Imray, Lila Kossyvaki and Mike Sissons; individual chapters, the contributors

The right of Peter Imray, Lila Kossyvaki and Mike Sissons to be identified as the authors of the editorial material, and of the authors for their individual chapters, has been asserted in accordance with sections 77 and 78 of the Copyright, Designs and Patents Act 1988.

British Library Cataloguing-in-Publication Data
A catalogue record for this book is available from the British Library

ISBN: 978-1-032-43860-3 (hbk)
ISBN: 978-1-032-43859-7 (pbk)
ISBN: 978-1-003-36913-4 (ebk)

DOI: 10.4324/9781003369134

Typeset in Galliard
by Apex CoVantage, LLC

Contents

Contributors

Editors

Peter Imray is a freelance trainer, advisor and writer in the area of special educational needs with over 30 years teaching experience and Associate Lecturer at the University of Birmingham. His current interests centre on supporting schools to embed specifically written (not National Curriculum) curricula for learners of all ages with PMLD, SLD and ASD. Peter has written numerous articles, and his last book, written with Andrew Colley and titled *Inclusion is Dead: Long Live Inclusion*, was a polemic against the dominant inclusive ideology of a common school and/or class and/or curriculum for those with SLD and PMLD. It was published by Routledge in May 2017.

Dr Lila Kossyvaki (BEd, MEd, PGCHE, PhD, CPsychol) is Associate Professor in Severe, Profound and Multiple Learning Disabilities (SLD/PMLD) at the University of Birmingham. As part of this role, Lila teaches students at postgraduate level and conducts research as well as supervising students at doctoral and post-doctoral level. Lila has published several research papers, book chapters and a research monograph. She has presented her work at conferences and workshops in the UK and around the world.

Mike Sissons began his career as a carer for adults with profound learning disabilities and has subsequently worked for over 30 years as a teacher and senior leader in special schools. He has coordinated and delivered outreach support for pupils with severe and complex learning disabilities in mainstream schools and has also worked as a member of a multidisciplinary team providing assessment and teaching for communication aid users. All his roles have included a large component of training. Mike is the author of MAPP (*Mapping and Assessing Personal Progress*), written as a response to the need to recognise progress and inform planning for pupils with profound, complex and severe learning disabilities.

Practitioners

Julia Barnes is a senior teacher and Sensory Pathway Manager at Ravenscliffe High School in the north of England and is studying for an educational doctorate at University of Birmingham. Her thesis is exploring the human-touch experiences of three teenage participants with PMLD whilst in their educational setting. Julia is influenced by anthropology and feminist philosophy as she strives for social justice for people who are marginalised or voiceless. Creative methodologies are deployed to explore their perspectives in her research. Her teaching also uses creativity to promote flourishing for all.

Lana Bond has been specialising in SEND for over 15 years, working across numerous specialist schools in London. She is currently a teacher and Head of Communication at Woodlands Primary Specialist School in Harrow, responsible for implementing and embedding Intensive Interaction into the school curriculum. Lana has achieved a MEd (Dist) in Severe, Profound and Complex Learning Disabilities and has contributed to publications such as *The Routledge Companion to Severe, Profound and Multiple Learning Difficulties* and *The Intensive Interaction Classroom Guide*. She is also the co-creator of *Sensory Stories for All*, a range of inclusive books to be enjoyed by all children.

Gillian Carver was Head Teacher at St Ann's Specialist School in Ealing for 21 years, having retired in December 2022 after a teaching career in London schools spanning 43 years. She has worked in Special Education for the past 38 years, has an adult son with Down's Syndrome and remains passionate about preventing the marginalisation of children, young people and adults with complex, profound and severe learning disabilities. Curriculum innovation, the relentless quest to accord young people agency, meaningful pragmatic support to families, ambition and generally 'daring to be different' continue to be the hallmarks of St Ann's everyday practice.

Andrew Colley is the author of a number of books and articles about teaching and learning with young people with PMLD, including *Inclusion is Dead: Long Live Inclusion* (Routledge, 2017) with Peter Imray and *Enhancing Wellbeing and Independence: for young people with PMLD* (Routledge, 2022) with Julie Tilbury. He has taught in special schools in Essex and Cambridgeshire, has master's degrees in education from the Universities of Birmingham and Cambridge, was Senior Lecturer in Special Education at The University of East London and an occasional lecturer at the University of Suffolk.

Martin Goodwin is a department lead and teacher of pupils with PMLD at Mary Elliot Academy in Birmingham, England (part of the Thrive Education Partnership). Martin's specialisms include communication, interaction and play, pedagogical approaches, curriculum, assessment and specific areas such as sex and relationships, policy and non-directive advocacy/participation approaches. Martin is an editor of PMLD Link and has taught as a visiting lecturer/regional tutor on the University of Birmingham S/PMLD course. Martin has authored articles, co-wrote *Communicate with Me – A Resource to Enable Effective Communication and Involvement of People with a Learning Disability* (Routledge, 2015) and contributed to the *PMLD Essential and Core Standards* and the Equals Pre-Formal Curriculum.

Timmy Holdsworth has worked at St Ann's Specialist School in Ealing, west London in various teaching roles since 2009 and was appointed Head-teacher in 2023. He believes in making young people feel as secure and safe as they can be by enabling them to have as much control over their lives as possible. Timmy has played a key part in developing the school's 'Learning to Be' and 'Learning to Do' approaches with students with complex learning disabilities (CLD), both of which focus upon developing the students' regulating skills and enabling them to develop meaning and purpose within the various communities they inhabit.

Katie Lyon is Headteacher at Kingsbury Specialist Primary School in West Lancashire, England. She has been teaching since gaining her BEd (Hons) in Primary Education at Leeds Metropolitan University. Katie has over 25 years teaching experience in both mainstream and special education, holding teaching and senior leadership positions in both sectors. Over the last 12 years, she has worked in special education, 8 years as a senior leader. Katie has delivered talks for Equals, Evidence for Learning and Hirstwood Training at national conferences and delivered online training programmes promoting the *Leadership of Personalised Teaching and Learning*.

Diego Gazquez Navarro is a specialist teacher for deafblind students and Communication and Interaction Lead at Linden Lodge School, a specialist school for sensory-impaired children and young people in south London. He has a master's degree in education from Kingston University and has taught people with moderate, severe and profound and multiple learning disabilities at schools in London for over 25 years. In 2021, he received a London Teacher of the Year Award from Inspire KM Charity Team for Raising Aspirations.

Aimee Robinson is Assistant Head Teacher at Priory Woods School and Arts College in Middlesbrough, England. She has been teaching for 10 years since gaining her PGCE in Early Primary Education at York St John University. Aimee began her teaching career as a NQT in Special Education, working as a middle leader for the past 7 years before becoming part of the senior leadership team in September 2022. Aimee has worked with Equals and schools across the UK in developing teaching and learning and designing curriculum pathways to ensure all young people with complex additional needs can succeed and acquire skills for life beyond school.

Nathan Taylor is Assistant Headteacher at JFK Specialist School in Newham, east London. Nathan has been teaching for 27 years, with 16 years senior leadership experience in specialist schools across England. Nathan is a music graduate from Bretton Hall, College of Leeds University, and has an MA in Special Education Needs from the University of East London. He is currently a doctoral student at Leeds Beckett University, undertaking a critical analysis of assessment for children and young people with profound and multiple learning disabilities, incorporating embodied and creative methodologies.

Trish Turner is Headteacher at Brackenfield Specialist School in Derbyshire, England, home of the East Midlands SEND Training Hub. She has been teaching for over 20 years since gaining her BSc (Hons) in Design Technology at Nottingham Trent University. She has worked in Special Education as a senior leader for the past 12 years. Through the SEND Training Hub and her work as a Trustee of Equals, Trish works nationally with schools, universities, ITT (Initial Teacher Trainer) providers and Local Authorities, developing school leadership practice and curriculum to prepare young people with complex additional needs for adulthood.

James Waller is Headteacher at Sunningdale School, Tyne and Wear, England. He has worked with young people with severe and complex learning disabilities since 2001. James contributes to a number of national bodies relating to specialist education, including Equals and the National SEND Forum. He has developed and delivered workshops on a variety of topics related to teaching those with SLD, PMLD and CLD on behalf of regional and national organisations, including Local Authorities. James contributes to the delivery of National Professional Qualifications, has led a bespoke specialist Initial Teacher Education programme via SENhub and has co-developed Early Career Framework SEND materials nationally.

Jo Williams is Deputy Headteacher at Dee Banks School in Chester, England, an all-age school catering for pupils with severe, complex and profound learning disabilities. She has been teaching for 20 years and has worked in special education for the past 16 years, with 8 years of senior leadership experience. Through her work as an Equals Trustee, Jo works with other schools and contributes to the development of specialist curriculum and assessment approaches to support learners with complex needs.

Foreword

I moved from a career as a classroom teacher in 1987 to the higher education sector, specifically that of teacher education. My interest in those days was in finding ways to best support marginalised learners. As a practitioner, I was especially involved with students who were excluded from mainstream schools, a preoccupation which has remained with me ever since.

When I joined a teacher education department within a university, I rapidly became aware that mine was a rather limited experience of 'special educational needs'. I was at once surrounded by others whose focus was far more diverse and, I have no doubt, considerably better informed about the complexities of ensuring grounded provision than my own rather limited perspectives.

It was a joy to have new vistas opened to me. A major feature of teacher education all those years ago was the $2+2$ 'Bachelor of Education' degree, which prepared student-teachers as specialists in supporting children and young people with severe or profound and multiple learning difficulties (then termed 'SLD' and 'PMLD'). I was immersed in a field of which I'd previously had relatively little awareness. The experience was uplifting, enabling and rather humbling.

I was astonished by the amount of research-related material that was emerging from what I'd hitherto believed was such a narrow area of study. I became an avid reader of texts from those who were already icons in the field or who were to go on to contribute much to our sum of knowledge concerning learners who have most often been amongst the most isolated, poorly resourced and marginalised within the formal school system.

Thus, I recall the impressions made on me by writers such as Tina Tilstone, Judy Sebba, Jean Ware, Ann Lewis, Rob Ashdown, Juliet Goldbart, Dave Hewitt and Melanie Nind and many others. I was exposed to an Aladdin's cave of riches, illustrated, for instance, by Lewis's paper on young children's attitudes to SLD (Lewis and Lewis, 1987). Or Nind and Hewett's (1988) piece on interaction as curriculum. Or, as my exposure to this complex territory widened, Golbart's book specifically addressing the needs of students with PMLDs. The impact of my discovery of such a goldmine was indelible, as were the career-defining ideas they were instrumental in pointing me towards.

But what was particularly striking was the emphasis given to investigating the curricular provision for learners with SLD and PMLD. I was pitched into a receptive duvet of enquiry, professional conversation and what seemed to be an endless supply of published material relating directly to the subject. Around that period, I had the good fortune to be able to work closely with Sarah Sandow, Viv Hinchcliffe, Jill Porter and others who were steeped in the theory and practice of progressive interventions with those within a distinct community of learners into whom I was gathering more insights. These were memorable times, from which the lessons learned never left me.

And so, it was with immense interest that I have followed the development of Peter Imray's book for this series, which has been jointly written with Mike Sissons and Lila Kossyvaki and involving the inputs from several practitioners from the SLD and PMLD field. In one sense, it presented an opportunity to refresh and update my own thinking on policy and provision for this group of school students.

But I can point to another, more compelling, reason – to which the book's authors themselves refer: the period to which I have already recalled paralleled major changes in the curriculum for all children in the United Kingdom, through the legislation and accompanying statutory requirements regarding the 'National Curriculum'. Whilst being ostensibly based on the laudable principle of equality of access, the new regulations raised major concerns from those within the SLD and PMLD community (Hodkinson, 2009), amongst many others involved in special educational needs. At the heart of this was a real fear that the interventions so necessary for learners with significant needs were being sacrificed on an ideological altar, upon which individualised learning had become a mirage. In fact, Peter and his co-writers refer directly to this concern in the introductory chapter to this volume, stating that 'The long and continuous experiment of England's National Curriculum, from 1988 to date, proves beyond doubt that those with PMLD, CLD and SLD do not and have never, achieved within it'.

But this was not the only worry becoming starkly apparent at that time. The previously dedicated initial teacher education courses, configured for those trainees wishing to work directly with SLD and PMLD learners in schools and in which I'd been so wonderfully immersed, were so abruptly terminated in 1989 (Hodkinson, *op.cit.*). Little in the way of substantive replacement was introduced, leaving this as one of the major acts of educational vandalism of the late 20th century. Critics of the new order maintained that SEN was even more the Cinderella of the teacher education (Thomas, 1993). At a stroke, the opportunity to maintain a well-qualified, appropriately skilled and committed *cadre* of teachers for this specialist sector was extinguished. The deferential nod to 'inclusive education' was precisely that, given the subsequent struggle of specialist settings and mainstream schools themselves to recruit suitably experienced staff to work with those students with the highest level of need. Baby and bathwater spring easily to mind.

Hyperbolic reference to the diminishing opportunities for teachers to obtain SLD-specific knowledge as the 'Bermuda Triangle of Training' (Hinchcliffe, 1996) was a regrettable reality.

Finally, although I have no substantive data to support my own assertion, what also occurred in the subsequent decade was a rear-guard action by a dwindling number of specialist teachers, as knowledge, skills and understanding of the field haemorrhaged. Back in the day, bespoke books, journal articles and monographs on varied aspects of practice in the field of SLD and PMLD were commonplace. Moreover, they were often best-selling volumes, pored over by professionals eager to extend their repertoire of pedagogy and content. As I have intimated, this is impressionistic stuff . . . but it further builds on the trepidation felt because of the negative impact of those inclusive turns that failed to recognise that differing learner needs require adjusted approaches and variations in curriculum.

Nothing much has occurred in policy terms, in the last decade or more, to deflect me from this interpretation. And so, ultimately, it is a privilege to help facilitate a book whose orientation and content takes me back to those heady days. Imray, Sissons and Kossyvaki have assembled a fitting riposte to the vainglorious claim that 'all teachers are teachers of special needs' (DfE, 2014). In the spirit of the statutory requirement, that may well be the case. In terms of the theoretical knowledge, its practical application and the commitment necessary, such assertions are hollow and leave a population of learners disenfranchised.

The authors of this book present us with a bold response to a 21st-century challenge, along with some practical kit to at least begin to redress what still remains as a real risk of imbalance in developing inclusive education systems. Theirs is a voice of reason and experience, calling not for a return to the systemic shortcomings of segregation that many of us recognised in pre- and immediately post-Warnock provision but for re-engagement with those pedagogical approaches which go well beyond the banal and ultimately disrespectful strapline of 'education for all'.

Philip Garner
Series Editor

References

Department for Education. (2014). *SEND Code of Practice: 0–25 Years.* London: DfE. Available from: www.gov.uk/government/publications/send-code-of-practice-0-to-25

Hinchcliffe, V. (1996). A Bermuda Triangle for Training: The Case of Severe Learning Difficulties. In J. Dwyfor Davies and P. Garner (eds.) *At the Crossroads. Special Educational Needs and Teacher Education.* London: David Fulton Publishers.

Hodkinson, A. (2009). Pre-Service Teacher Training and Special Educational Needs in England 1970–2008: Is Government Learning the Lessons of the Past or is It Experiencing a Groundhog Day? *European Journal of Special Needs Education,* 24(3): 277–289. https://doi.org/10.1080/08856250903016847

Lewis, A. and Lewis, L. (1987). The Attitudes of Young Children Towards Peers with Severe Learning Difficulties. *British Journal of Developmental Psychology*, 5(3): 287–292. https://doi.org/10.1111/j.2044-835X.1987.tb01064.x

Nind, M. and Hewett, D. (1988). Interaction as Curriculum. *British Journal of Special Education*, 15: 55–57. https://doi.org/10.1111/j.1467-8578.1988.tb00314.x

Thomas, D. (1993). Gritty, Sensible and Utilitarian – The Only Model? Special Educational Needs, Initial Teacher Training and Professional Development. In A. Dyson and C. Gains (eds.) *Rethinking Special Needs in Mainstream Schools* (pp. 72–98). London: David Fulton.

Introduction

Any sound pedagogy must understand the unique talents and needs of its learners. And, as Ken Robinson has reminded us, if it does not do so, then it will, to that extent, fail them (Robinson and Aronica, 2010). A curriculum which prioritises mathematics, technology and science at the expense of other learning will frustrate and marginalise those pupils whose abilities and passions lie in the field of art or dance or music or literature or practical and physical activity. Their needs will be overlooked; for, in order to get the curriculum right for any group of learners, those learners must be at the centre and not the periphery of our considerations.

This issue of recognising difference is especially acute in the case of pupils who have profound, complex and severe learning disabilities. Despite the high level of diverse needs these pupils experience, they have consistently occupied the wings whilst their mainstream peers have held centre stage. So, instead of asking what works specifically for pupils who have profound, complex and severe learning disabilities, these pupils have been subsumed within versions of mainstream curricula, initiatives, assessment regimes and teaching strategies. There have, of course, been notable exceptions to this simple monolithic approach, and these are discussed in this book. But these have largely taken the form of initiatives in specific areas such as communication, cognition, affect and engagement which – like the needs of the pupils they serve – have then too often been subsumed within the majority, mainstream model.

The present book responds to these issues and proposes solutions. It does so by recognising that learners with different learning needs demand and deserve a different approach to teaching. They, and not the curriculum, must be our starting point. The content of the curriculum is not determined in advance but is derived from a consideration of what has value for them, the learners. Throughout this book, the individual learner appears not as an object – a passive consumer of knowledge – but as a free agent, actively engaged with others in realising their own possibilities. Paying attention to the learner in this way means that, in shaping pedagogy, we must not only answer the question of *what* learning should take place, but crucially, we must also pay the closest attention to the questions of *how* it should happen and, even more importantly, *why* it should happen.

Reference

Robinson, K. and Aronica, L. (2010). *The Element*. London: Penguin.

DOI: 10.4324/9781003369134-1

Part 1

Principles

The book is divided into two parts. The first part establishes a theoretical framework and the second part exemplifies this framework in practice.

These first four chapters represent the pedagogical backbone of the book. They argue the case for a pedagogy which starts by acknowledging the very varied and different needs of learners with profound, complex and severe learning disabilities. Chapters 1 to 3 explore this theme in relation to curriculum, assessment and research design respectively. Chapter 4 introduces and elaborates in detail a principle which permeates all the other chapters; namely, that pedagogy must be grounded in a commitment to the individual's right to flourish in ways that are important to them as the central character of their own education.

DOI: 10.4324/9781003369134-2

1   Defining learning characteristics

Peter Imray, Mike Sissons and Lila Kossyvaki

This book is about children, young people and adults (CYPA) who, consistently and over time, reveal themselves to be working at early and sometimes very early developmental levels. We use the word 'developmental' cautiously, however, because we do not mean to imply that the CYPA who are described as having global learning disabilities[1] are the same but delayed. Learning for those with PMLD, CLD and SLD (all of whom have a global learning disability – GLD) is different, precisely because we cannot base notions of progression on schedules which are founded on the development of a different population; namely, neurotypical, conventionally developing infants and children.

We have used the commonly understood UK descriptors of PMLD (profound and multiple learning disabilities) and SLD (severe learning disabilities), and to these, we have added a new descriptor – CLD (complex learning disabilities). UK readers will note that we have substituted 'disability' for 'difficulty' as a matter of course when we refer to these cohorts. There are a number of reasons for this:

1. We believe that this book has international interest, and the UK is almost alone in not using the term 'disability'.
2. 'Difficult' may well describe some of the individual barriers to learning that CYPA experience, and if they just had that single barrier, the term difficulty may well be sufficient. Put them all together, however, and they will all work with each other and against the individual learner learning effectively, thus rendering the whole a disability.
3. 'Difficulty' can be a relatively mild word and does not adequately describe the enormous consequences to the CYPA affected. We will all experience occasional difficulties in our lifetimes, but we can either (i) work to overcome them, (ii) learn to live with them and/or (iii) arrange our lives so that they don't become insurmountable. It is, however, questionable that these options are viable for those with profound, complex and severe learning disabilities, precisely because the profundity, complexity and severity of the disability militates against the individual succeeding.

DOI: 10.4324/9781003369134-3

Since a National Curriculum (NC) was instituted in the UK in 1988, all 21 authors' teaching experience has come (officially at least) entirely within it. Although all schools and all teachers and TAs within these schools have tried to make the best of the NC[2], all 21 authors reject it as an appropriate model. Irrespective of the level of differentiation, all national curriculums remain academic, upwardly linear in progression and start at levels that confound all but the highest achievers amongst those with global (rather than specific) learning disabilities. Learners must achieve a level of fluent mastery in both literacy and numeracy merely to engage with the other subjects, never mind succeed within them. This is described in the levels achieved by neuro-typical 10/11-year-olds, which seems to be the universally accepted age to move from the primary (generalist) phase to the secondary (specialist) phase of education. In other words, the purpose of any NC is to achieve at least the levels attained by the end of the primary phase, and if this cannot be attained by an individual because of the depth of their learning disability, the curriculum must, axiomatically, be purposeless.

In response to this, Equals, a not-for-profit charity based in England, has, over a 5-year period, between 2016 to 2021, developed a multi-tiered curriculum model relating to PMLD, CLD and SLD. References to these separate but very much related curricula are common throughout the book, and we make no apologies for this; schools cannot be expected to deliver the different curricula this book argues for if there are no different curricula available. We have made no particular effort to go into the considerable detail and depth held within each curriculum (they are all available at www.equals.co.uk and free downloads can also be had of the *Basic Principles* of all of the very detailed schemes of work by application to the lead author)[3], but it should be noted that these are all-age curricula and are certainly not confined to school age alone. The descriptors are fairly obvious, and the arrows relate to any defining characteristics being fuzzier at the edges; it is therefore possible that some learners working at the edges of the definitions noted below may be working within more than one curriculum for some or all of the time.

Severe Learning Disabilities (SLD)

It is difficult to be accurate about the numbers of CYPA with SLD in England because schools are required to register the numbers of their pupils with an EHCP[4] (Education, Health and Care Plan) by indicating what the school regards as their primary (that is, main) additional need. Kennedy (2010, p28) notes that 'one of the consequences of extraordinary advances in care is the growing number of disabled children and young people who have very complex needs' with Pinney (2017) observing that the numbers with complex needs (that is, in her terms, those with PMLD and SLD) continues to rise. In 2020, around 30,000 pupils were identified as having a primary need of SLD (an increase of 17% from 2010) with a further 8,000 having SLD as a secondary need (Public Health England, 2020). This total of nearly 38,000 is, however, likely to be a considerable underestimation, since over 140,000

Pre-Formal Curriculum	Informal Curriculum	**Semi-Formal Curriculum**	National or Common Core Standards Curriculum
PMLD	Complex SLD, SLD/Autism	**SLD, SLD/Autism, MLD**	
Working consistently and over time at the earliest developmental levels	Working consistently and over time at the severest end of the SLD spectrum	Working consistently and over time at or below the earliest reaches of the NC	Working within typical or near typical age related expectations

Figure 1.1 The Semi-Formal Curriculum within Equals Multi-Tiered Curricula Pathway Approach

pupils have autism named as their primary need (DfE, 2019), and many of these are likely to also have SLD. Most research leans towards 70% or so of those with an autism diagnosis having an additional significant learning disability (Fombonne, 2005; Pagnamenta et al., 2011 for example) and, though what constitutes 'significant' is not absolutely clear, it is evident that (i) the existence of a learning disability and, crucially, (ii) the severity of that learning disability will have a significant impact on what we teach. And this is also crucial; the existence of autism will affect *how* we teach; the existence of SLD (with or without additional autism) will affect *what* we teach. In any event, the numbers of those with SLD are still relatively small, perhaps around 100,000 of the whole school population of around 7.5 million (about 1.4%) in England, with just less than half of such pupils being educated in mainstream, predominantly primary, schools.

With the exception of changing their referencing from severe learning difficulties to severe learning disabilities, we take Imray and Colley's (2017) view of an SLD spectrum, covering those pupils and students who are consistently and over time working academically at or below the starting levels of England's National Curriculum and other similar curriculum models such as the Australian National Curriculum or a US Common Core Standards Based Curriculum.

All those with SLD will have, to a greater or lesser degree:

- Communication difficulties.
- Difficulties in concentration and attention.
- Difficulties with understanding abstract concepts.
- Difficulties with both short term and long-term memory.
- Difficulties with sequential memory.
- Difficulties with working memory.

- Inefficient and slow information-processing speed.
- Limited general knowledge.
- Poorly developed strategies for thinking and learning.
- Difficulties with generalisation and problem solving.

(Imray and Colley, 2017, p38)

These are not isolated difficulties but work together and upon each other to make learning both extremely (or severely) problematic and disabling. Further, they are not open to being worked on in isolation but present holistically so that the solution in turn lies in adopting a holistic (rather than compartmentalised) approach to teaching. It may be, for example, that educationalists might consider the difficulties with working memory as soluble, and there have been a number of studies which seem to affirm this (Cowan and Alloway, 2008; Alloway et al. 2009; Klingberg, 2009; Alloway and Alloway, 2015 for example). However, such strategies that have been researched will be enormously problematic for those on the SLD spectrum, since they all rely on a solid base of either language (spoken or written) and/or an understanding of abstract (as opposed to contextualised) instructions in, for example, recalling a series of unrelated and de-contextualised pictures in ever-more-complex patterns. They, further, all note the inter-relationship between difficulties with working memory, short-term, long-term and sequential memory, poor concentration and attention and poorly developed problem-solving skills. It is noticeable that Alloway and Alloway (2015) go into some considerable detail with case studies on specific strategies that might be suitable for particular learning difficulties. SLD does not feature.

Davies (2015) argues that working memory is extremely fragile, has a limited capacity, can lead to memory failure if pressed too hard and is heavily reliant on the ability to maintain concentration and attention to the task on hand. Such overload and/or distraction leads to information being irretrievably lost from the working memory (Gathercole and Alloway, 2008). Further, it has been noted by Swanson and Jerman (2006) that the majority of studies suggest a correlation between memory deficits and difficulties in both maths and reading, since performance depends on speedy and efficient retrieval from the long-term memory, and good temporary storage is crucial when working out both mathematical problems and word de-coding. Swanson and Jerman go on to argue that poor recall of facts from memory increases the cognitive demands of a task, as it then has to be calculated, which in turn puts additional pressure on problem-solving strategies.

The long and continuous experiment of England's National Curriculum from 1988 to date proves beyond doubt that those with PMLD, CLD and SLD do not and have never achieved within it (Ndaji and Tymms, 2009; Imray and Colley, 2017). We have no reason to believe that differentiation works, any more than arguments related to including all learners at the point of curriculum design works (rather than as an afterthought), since there is no evidence relating to the success of Universal Design for Learning (UDL) in the USA or Inclusive Pedagogy in the UK with those with SLD, despite two decades of trying. Nor do we have any reason to believe that any national (or common core standards) curriculum is fundamentally different from all of the others, and indeed, how could they be when they are all concerned with averagely developing, neuro-typical learners?

Apart from the Equals writings noted earlier, there has been very little in-depth discussion into what a curriculum specifically written for those with SLD might look like. Black and Lawson (2017) took a critical look at The Studio, part of the young adult provision of Greenside School in Hertfordshire, England – an all-through (2–19) special school for pupils with severe and profound learning disabilities. Their analysis of educational paths, functions and purposes of learning identified three main purposes of education for all learners; that is, (i) person-becoming, (ii) later life/vocation and (iii) citizenship. In many ways, this echoed earlier writings, such as that of Dee et al. (2006) and their 'being, having, doing' pedagogy. However, both of these only describe post-16 education, with the implied inference being that a generalist academic curriculum is suitable prior to the age of 16. This is, however, surely far too late to start a different curriculum, given the acknowledged need for considerable repetition and over-learning, so that the 'different' curriculum needs to start early in the primary years (Imray and Hinchcliffe, 2014). Zigmond and Kloo (2017) and Travers et al. (2020) concur, both arguing that special and general education are and must be different, with Travers et al. also stating that the 'essential criteria' must involve

> individualized curricula taught with evidence-based practices delivered at sufficiently high intensity, along with relevant behavioral interventions and supports.
>
> (Travers et al., 2020, p173)

Complex Learning Disabilities (CLD)

Complex Learning Disabilities (CLD) is part of the SLD spectrum but sufficiently diverse to merit a separate set of descriptors. Such learners have always existed, but their numbers have increased significantly since the turn of the century (Pinney, 2017) as an unintended consequence, we assume, of the highly significant medical advances pertaining to birth at early gestation. In first-world countries, at least, it is not unusual for babies to be safely born at 26 weeks gestation and, occasionally, even earlier, but the chances of resulting disability, both physical and intellectual, are commensurately high (Johnson et al., 2016). Specialist schools in the UK and, we suspect, many other countries will instantly recognise the learners with CLD described here.

Such learners will have all of the difficulties described in the SLD section earlier, only, as they are at the severe end of severe learning-disabilities, more so. They will have no developed formal communication system, will generally be non-verbal and may be regarded as being non-linguistic communicators.

Pre-Formal Curriculum	**Informal Curriculum**	Semi-Formal Curriculum	National or Common Core Standards Curriculum
PMLD	**Complex SLD, SLD/Autism**	SLD, SLD/Autism, MLD	
Working consistently and over time at the earliest developmental levels	Working consistently and over time at the severest end of the SLD spectrum	Working consistently and over time at or below the earliest reaches of the NC	Working within typical or near typical age related expectations
→	← →	← →	←

Figure 1.2 The Informal Curriculum within Equals Multi-Tiered Curricula Pathway Approach

That is, they will not use language as their main means of communication, even though some may have a number of words, signs and/or perhaps understand and be able to use a limited number of concrete and iconic symbols, but will communicate primarily through expressions of behaviour. Further, such behavioural communications will generally be confined to proto-imperative communications (I want this) and proto-imperative negations (I don't want to do this, I don't want to be here). These negations may be instant, extreme, aggressive and/or violent; that is, they are specifically designed to repel unwanted attentions and usually have a history of being very successful in such aims, especially as learners get older and bigger.

Learners with CLD are markedly different to those with PMLD because they can understand and are able to follow simple instructions, though, significantly, they may not do so or they may choose not to do so. They are, nonetheless, open to being taught simple skills through modelling and demonstration if teachers can ensure engagement, though the secure acquisition of these may well need considerable over-learning and repetition, which is likely to take a number of years of continuous teaching. They are usually ambulant, are likely to have an autism diagnosis and may well have additional sensory processing difficulties, probably suffering from both hyper- and hypo-sensitivities. They may not engage voluntarily with others (peers, staff, family) or may only do so on their own terms and may well be unwilling to give up favoured activities or defer gratification. Crucially, those with CLD are often resistant to engaging with the conventional understanding of education – *I'm here to teach: you're here to learn. I'm in charge: you must follow the rules.*

Profound and Multiple Learning Disabilities (PMLD)

Profound and Multiple Learning Disabilities (PMLD) is a term commonly used throughout the UK to describe people of all ages who have the most severe learning and physical disabilities. First coined by Evans and Ware (1987), it accepts 'profundity' as significantly different from 'severity' as a descriptive term and also recognises that those with PMLD are highly likely to have both external and internal, multiple physical difficulties. They will be unable to follow instructions, and crucially, unlike neuro-typical, conventionally developing children, we cannot expect those with PMLD to be able to use imitation as a means of learning (Imray and Colley, 2017). Goldbart (2023) describes their communicative levels as typically 'characteristic of infants in their first year'. There will be difficulties in developing a complete understanding of object permanence, and further, their understanding of cause and effect is likely to be incomplete or even absent. Though many learners with PMLD might know that something happens when, for example, a switch is pressed (contingency responding), knowing that the same event will follow the same action (contingency awareness), as when, for example, a toy turns a somersault or a bubble machine switches on, may take many years to teach and, for a number, might never be learned (Curriculum for Wales, 2020). It is usual to describe those with PMLD as having high support needs, and this brings in the issue of developing 'relational agency' (Khader, 2008), which is explored in detail in Chapter 4.

Interestingly, Grace (2017) has described people with PMLD as 'sensory beings', who tend to experience life primarily through their senses while

Pre-Formal Curriculum	Informal Curriculum	Semi-Formal Curriculum	National or Common Core Standards Curriculum
PMLD	Complex SLD, SLD/Autism	SLD, SLD/Autism, MLD	
Working consistently and over time at the earliest developmental levels	Working consistently and over time at the severest end of the SLD spectrum	Working consistently and over time at or below the earliest reaches of the NC	Working within typical or near typical age related expectations

Figure 1.3 The Pre-Formal Curriculum within Equals Multi-Tiered Curricula Pathway Approach

focusing on the present moment. This take on the world is, apparently, very different to that of linguistic beings; that is, the vast majority of neurotypical people, who mainly rely on language to experience and get through life. The danger when we, the linguistic beings, interact with sensory beings is that we often assume their understanding of the world is the same or similar to ours. It is likely, therefore, that we 'impose our way of being onto them' (p9), and this is why Grace (2017) suggests that we let sensory beings guide the interaction and teach us how the now can 'be lived and enjoyed' (p10).

Curriculum considerations for teaching learners of all ages with Global Learning Disabilities (GLD); that is, all CYPA with SLD, CLD and PMLD

There has to be a point to the curriculum being offered. We might therefore need to consider what learners might be able to achieve by the time they are 19, irrespective of their current age. Mainstream schools generally operate on shorter time scales so that one curriculum prepares children for the next. In England, this is epitomised by the EYFS (early years foundation stage) curriculum (from the ages of 3 to 6) preparing children for the primary curriculum (from 6 to 11); the primary curriculum then prepares children for the in-depth, compartmentalised curriculum that takes place in secondary schools, which results in the taking of formal qualifications at the end of secondary curriculum (from 11 to 16), then onto higher (A) levels taken at 18, and from there to university, should students achieve at this level. All of these curricula are different; they have to be because of the enormous linear changes that take place in neuro-typical intellectual development between the ages of 3 and 21.

This is, however, not the case for those with PMLD, CLD and SLD, whose linear academic progress will be limited because of the depth of their global learning disabilities. This does not mean that they cannot make progress; just that the progress is much more likely to be lateral rather than linear. Taking a longer-term view, we might look to considering Capabilities (as in the Capabilities Approach described in Chapter 4), so that the consideration revolves around enabling learners to be the best they can be and to do the best they can do, whatever that is and irrespective of disability. This then becomes the ambition.

In order to facilitate such long-term considerations, the long-term process needs to become much more important than the short-term product. The dangers and extraordinary damage done by the institution of short-term (especially SMART) targets, which then become the curriculum (Riddick, 2009; Rochford, 2016), completely reverses the natural order of teaching, which must be driven by pedagogy – the consideration of why one is teaching what one is teaching – leading curriculum – what one is teaching – which, in turn, informs assessment – how one judges whether the teaching has been effective. SMART targets inevitably drive teachers towards next-step teaching above the process of learning. This is especially pernicious for those with PMLD, CLD and SLD because it is not necessary to engage the long-term memory, an essential for learning and understanding (Ofsted, 2019), for an end-of-lesson, short-term target to be 'ticked-off'.

Each individual has to be engaged and at the centre of the educational process, so that a school of 150 or 250 learners should consider having 150 or 250 individualised curriculums. That is, the curriculum has to change to suit the learner; not the learner change to suit the curriculum. There will, of course, be common features that might affect many learners in any school (hence the curriculum pathways), but the learning will not be affected by age or key stage. Progress is ipsative, lateral as well as linear, multi-layered and in the control of the learner. This is where we might challenge the suggestions from Travers et al. (2020) noted on page 9, in that behavioural interventions and supports should not be seen to be separated from what the school is teaching and should therefore not need separate consideration. If learners are engaged and in control of the direction and pace of travel (because they are at the centre of the curriculum) behaviour should be no more of an issue than it might be in any generalised, mainstream setting.

Behaviour becomes an issue when we try to force CYPA into being and becoming that which they are not, and more importantly, express no interest in becoming. In special needs settings, and especially when 'educating' those with autism and global learning disabilities, there has been a strong tendency towards assuming that all CYPA have to fit the existing system and, if they show an unwillingness to do so, must be bent to fit. This directly touches upon the issues of flourishing, freedom, choice and agency discussed in Chapter 4 and has led all the writers in this book to reject a dominant Behaviourist educational methodology found in such schools of thought as ABA (Applied Behaviour Analysis), VBA (Verbal Behaviour Analysis) and TEACCH (the Treatment and Education of Autistic and related Communication handicapped CHildren). All three seem to feature strongly in the USA, and whilst ABA and VBA feature less in the UK and perhaps most of northern Europe, TEACCH is quite commonly used with the CLD and autism populations in specialist UK schools. This is, however, not a book about Behaviourism, so we have left others to argue the points (Dawson, 2004; Zurcher, 2012; for example), preferring instead to concentrate on the educational advantages for the individuals with GLDs held within the various Equals Curriculum Pathways. Nonetheless,

it is really important here to establish that whether it is referred to as Skinner's Behaviourism or Lovaas or ABA or PBS or even TEACCH, all are based upon the principles of behaviour modification. That is, that 'we', those of us who do not need to change our behaviour, those of us who are in charge, those of us who decide on the rules, must modify the behaviour of 'them' to ensure that their behaviours are acceptable to us. Note that there is no requirement for a behaviourist to change in any way other than in manipulating the behaviour of the person being modified. When Pavlov was conditioning his dogs to salivate at the ring of a bell (a conditioned response) he was not concerned with changing his own behaviour, merely that of the dogs.

(Imray, 2018, p26)

We need to think about engagement being a necessary (though not sufficient) pre-condition to learning. Because engagement comes first, we can develop active, rather than passive, learners, who are not working for extrinsic rewards but whose motivation is intrinsic. They work *at* the curriculum because they really enjoy the work *of* the curriculum! This can only come about if the curriculum is meaningful and contextual, where learners learn by doing; again, the exact opposite of so much of any national or common-core-standards curricula, which are by their very nature, theoretical and abstract. There is no doubt that the engagement of each individual must be a central concern and a necessary starting point (Carpenter et al., 2015), but we cannot rest there because we have to stretch the learner and open up the world around them. We have to try and move them on, but we must take each learner with us, so continued engagement must still be present within the new (stretched and opened) learning conditions. The specialist teacher[5] knowledge needed to successfully teach all those with GLD therefore takes the form of deep knowledge of (i) the individual learner, (ii) the nature of learning disability being experienced by the individual learner (PMLD, CLD or SLD) and (iii) the particular curriculum pathway being followed by the individual learner, and of course, where they are on that pathway.

The vital primacy of literacy and numeracy for ALL learners is a false premise. Neither literacy (the process of writing and reading) nor numeracy (the process of exactly measuring) is an innate human capacity, both being cultural artefacts, rule governed, abstract (that is, not necessarily contextualised) and having to be formally taught in strict building-block, linear models. Their complexity is a function of the size of our immensely complex social groupings. Communication, on the other hand, is an innate human capacity, and whilst it is learnt, it is not formally taught for neuro-typical, conventionally developing children. The same might be said of social interaction, independence, self-regulation, self-esteem, physical co-ordination, adroitness, creativity, thinking, problem solving and mental well-being. All of these areas can, however, be incredibly challenging to achieve unconsciously for those with PMLD, CLD and SLD, whatever their age, and therefore must become the vital elements of any functional curriculum.

Those with PMLD and CLD especially will flourish best within a Free Play based curriculum model. This is because:

i.   They are working consistently and over time, at very early developmental levels.
ii.   Engagement has to be at the centre of learning.
iii. Engagement is discovered through the choices and motivations of each individual learner (Carpenter et al., 2015).

iv. Choices and motivations can only be apparent if learners are free to choose or reject and choice can most easily be discerned by, and through, active engagement.

Most learning in the Pre-Formal and Informal Pathways will therefore derive from Free Play, even if the learning is skills-based, as in for example, the manipulation of an object in play may improve the palmar grip, which is so useful when holding a spoon to eat. Because the learners with PMLD are highly likely to have additional and multiple physical disabilities, the Play materials will have to be brought to them, which will not be the case with those with CLD. In either event, however, choice and agency will lie in the acceptance or rejection of the materials/resources offered. It might be best if the Play resources are as pure, simple and undiluted as we can make them when initially offered. We may include pourers such as cups, jugs, colanders, etc., with a large tray of warm water, sand, flour, shaving foam, dry rice, etc., but nothing else. Variations may come later as the learner explores the resources, but these are offered not imposed and can therefore be accepted or rejected by the learner.

Being Free, each individual learner must be free to accept or reject the Play resources offered. Teachers will then have to use their own knowledge of the learner to see how that learner shows interest or lack of interest in the resource. Do they look at it, do they reach out to touch it, do they reach for it when you (very slowly) take it away, do they ignore it, do they turn away from it, do they push it out of the way? Acceptance must be active, though rejection may be passive. Acceptance cannot be passive. Play resources may well be people, and the known and researched methodology of Intensive Interaction (Hutchinson and Bodicoat, 2015, for example) will be tremendously useful here, but they may also take in what (in a generalist curriculum) might be regarded as separate subjects such as music, art, dance, movement and physical exercise such as is taken in a swimming pool, etc. An initial (or even multiple) rejection does not automatically mean that the Play resource should not be tried again; there may, indeed, be very many tries. Teachers may therefore be looking for a graduated, positive response which may encapsulate some or all of (i) rejection, (ii) indifference, (iii) tolerance, (iv) acceptance, (v) pleasure. Once teachers have found out the resource(s) that motivates and engages, they can establish a routine of the learners' Play over an extended period of time and then start to offer stretches and changes which the learner is free to accept or reject. This means that time becomes crucial – that is, teachers must try not to be impatient but look for progress in the longer rather than shorter term and make absolutely sure that these are recorded.

The freedom to accept or reject calls into question any activity where the learner has no choice *as being an educational concept*. It may be described as a care concept, as in, for example, toileting, eating, drinking, dressing, washing, taking prescribed medication, etc., but in order to turn this into an educational concept, the learner has to become an essential part of the process, so that the action is done with, rather than done to, the learner. The potential direct involvement of the learner therefore needs to be considered at the point of planning out such actions, so that they cannot be considered to be complete unless we have directly and consciously enabled the learner to maximise their potential for direct involvement.

Any curriculum written specifically for those with GLD will work on an entirely different time scale to that employed with neuro-typical learners, and though this will be more marked with PMLD than it will with CLD and SLD, it may still take many tens – and quite possibly many hundreds – of opportunities to experience a learning situation before we might consider that it has been established within the long-term memory. That is, more time and, quite possibly, much more time could well be needed according to the profundity, complexity or severity of the learning disability experienced.

We might need to think about what those with PMLD particularly (and perhaps to a lesser degree those with CLD) are likely to know. We might need to consider that what we take for granted may not be known by those with PMLD – what a flower is, the toilet symbol, cheese, a duck, an understanding of time, the connection between raw and cooked pasta, their own feet; the list is not endless, but it may well be an extremely long one. This has serious implications for what we teach and how we teach it, since including unknown and unknowable concepts in, for example, a sensory story now becomes highly problematic if we regard it as a literary event. That is, a sensory story such as *The Bear Hunt*, told regularly (at least weekly) over an extended period of time (perhaps a term and quite possibly longer) may be useful as an exciting visceral event, encouraging anticipation, sequencing, establishing beginnings and ends, and experiencing personal emotional changes. It may not, however, be regarded as a turn-taking, literary, linguistic event (with a number of opportunities to use and learn symbols and/or objects of reference) and should not (we would suggest) be planned out as such.

Those with PMLD and CLD cannot (by definition) be regarded as linguistic communicators. They can, however, be considered to be non-linguistic communicators, and if the logic of placing the learner at the centre of the curriculum is to have any meaning, we should communicate with them by predominantly using their communication system, not ours. We may use language (because it is incredibly difficult not to!), but it must be both limited (generally single word) and contextual when we're working, though more extended conversations can and should happen in more relaxed times throughout the day. If PMLD learners demonstrate a capacity for extended linguistic understanding and use, they don't (by definition) have PMLD. Because those with PMLD and CLD are non-linguistic communicators, the use of VOCAs (voice output communication aids), all of which have linguistic communication at their centre, needs to be extremely carefully considered. Generally speaking, low-tech VOCAs such as a single message 'BIGmac' or jelly switch, which can work as a cause-and-effect tool (as in 'Come and talk to me' or 'A big basin of water please') might be the way to go, as long as you're in the position of providing the person to talk to or the big basin of water, consistently and immediately.

We cannot and must not presume competence but work with our knowledge of the individual learner and be as certain as we can be that the learner is engaged and in control. The gaining of such knowledge is likely to be a constant journey. Presuming competence derives from the knowledge we have of the intellectual and linguistic journeys of neuro-typical, conventionally developing babies and small children and transposing these to all, irrespective of any disability. Presuming competence is especially supported as a model of teaching in literacy, speech and communication (Yoder, 2001; Erickson and Koppenhaver, 2020 for example) but runs the extraordinary risk of consistently teaching to levels of incompetence. Presuming competence says *I don't know, but I'm going to presume you understand (or will eventually understand) at the same level as everybody else and carry on, regardless.* Not presuming competence says *I don't know, but I'm going to look for signs of interest and individual engagement.* If we don't (consistently and over time) see signs of engagement, we should be questioning why we're carrying on. This might well be hope, which could well be a very attractive proposition for all sorts of stakeholders, but it wouldn't be education. Interestingly, Yoder (2001) talks a lot about hope, though one person's continued hope (a positive trait) may well become another person's continued failure.

There can be no prescribed ideas about what constitutes success, since we must take the concept of progress as an ipsative process; that is, any progress (or regress) is measured over time in relation to each individual learner. In this model, there can be no objective (or scientific) agreement about what constitutes poor, good or outstanding progress. We can, however, regard progress as likely to relate to the quality of the teaching (Sissons, 2020). If the teaching is poor, it is likely that the progress will be poor (or the regress will be accelerated); if the teaching is outstanding, it is likely that the progress will also be outstanding (or the regress will be considerably slowed down).

Teaching is best organised by grouping learners in the appropriate pathway and ensuring consistency of staffing across time. There may well, and indeed should, be opportunities for inclusive and collective gatherings of all pupils in the school, whether it is mainstream or specialist, but there is no point in accepting the concept of different if the bulk of teaching and learning is not accommodated in the appropriate pathway. The Equals Curriculum Pathways have been specifically designed for learners of all ages with PMLD, CLD and SLD respectively, and schools would do well to recognise that teachers and TAs will need to come to terms with knowing as much as they can know about PMLD, CLD and SLD respectively. Because there is an awful lot to know, this will take time, and the logical extension of this proposition is that teachers and TAs should be urged to specialise in the same sense that mainstream Secondary Subject Leads specialise.

It may be that a learner will not be able to express a choice, any choice, because of the extraordinary profundity and depth of their learning disability.

Such persons could be regarded as not being able to register on the first milestone of *Routes for Learning*; that is, notice (any) stimuli. Modern Western medical advances have ensured that such learners can live relatively long lives, but it should be noted that this level of profundity is still very, very rare (DCSF, 2009) We must continue to try to engage such learners, but if such attempts are repeatedly and over time consistently unsuccessful, it may be that education becomes an issue of maximising the individual's quality of life.

Conclusion

The defining learning characteristics of those with PMLD, CLD and SLD indicate that they do not pass through the understood intellectual and/or physical developmental levels associated with conventional child development, as described by Piaget (1952), for example. There is, further, no research evidence to suggest that continued working within a national or common-core-standards curriculum, which essentially elevate both literacy and numeracy as subjects of primacy, has anything more than a superficial effect on long-term learning and understanding. Having the ambition of enabling learners to reach the early levels (equivalent to Primary 1 or 2 at age 6 or 7) of a national or common core standards curriculum after 15-plus years of teaching strikes us as being an extraordinarily poor ambition. Our learners deserve far more than this, but they can only achieve their potential if we recognise that they learn differently from neuro-typical, conventionally developing learners. If they learn differently, we ought to be teaching them differently and teaching them different things.

Notes

1 That is, it affects all learning rather than a specific learning difficulty such as dyslexia or dyscalculia, which affects one part of learning.
2 Although the NC originally applied to all four UK countries (England, Scotland, Wales and Northern Ireland) devolution has since enabled all four countries to take control of their own education policies. At the time of writing, they do, however, all still run their own national curriculums, which, in theory, applies to all school age children, irrespective of the level of learning disability.
3 Please email peter.imray@hotmail.co.uk
4 An EHCP indicates to the financing authorities that additional resources are needed for an effective education to take place. Around 4% of all school age children in England have been allocated an EHCP at the time of writing.
5 We use the word 'teacher' as a broad term to describe anyone who is working with the learner in the learner's best interests and not necessarily as a person who has a formal teaching qualification.

References

Alloway, T.P. and Alloway, R.G. (2015). *Understanding Working Memory*. 2nd edition. London: Sage.

Alloway, T.P., Gathercole, S.E., Kirkwood, H.J. et al. (2009). The Cognitive and Behavioural Characteristics of Children with Low Working Memory. *Child Development*, 80: 606–621.

Black, A. and Lawson, H. (2017). Purposes of Education for Young People with Severe Learning Difficulties: Exploring a Vocational Teaching Resource – 'A Stepping Stone to . . .' What?. *Cambridge Journal of Education*, 47(2): 207–226.

Carpenter, B., Egerton, J., Cockbill, B., et al. (2015). *Engaging Learners with Complex Learning Difficulties and Disabilities*. Abingdon: Routledge.

Cowan, N. and Alloway, T.P. (2008). The Development of Working Memory in Childhood. In M. Courgae and N. Cowans (eds.) *Development of Memory in Infancy and Childhood* (pp. 303–342). 2nd edition. Hove: Psychology Press.

Curriculum for Wales. (2020). *Routes for Learning*. Available from: https://hwb.gov. wales/curriculum-for-wales/routes-for-learning. Accessed 29 January 2023.

Davies, G. (2015). *Developing Memory Skills in the Primary Classroom*. Abingdon: Routledge.

Dawson, M. (2004). *The Misbehaviour of Behaviourists: Ethical Challenges to the Autism-ABA industry*. Available from: www.sentex.net. Accessed 17 May 2017.

DCSF. (2009). *Progression Guidance 2009/10. Improving Data to Raise Attainment and Maximise the Progress of Learners with Special Educational Needs, Learning Difficulties and Disabilities*. Nottingham: Department for Children, Schools and Families Publications.

Dee, L., Devecchi, C. and Florian, L. (2006). *Being, Having and Doing: Theories of Learning and Adults With Learning Difficulties. LSRC Research Report*. London: Learning and Skills Network. Available from: https://files.eric.ed.gov/fulltext/ED508507.pdf. Accessed 29 January 2023.

DfE. (2019). Available from: https://assets.publishing.service.gov.uk/government/uploads/system/uploads/attachment_data/file/814244/SEN_2019_Text.docx. pdf. Accessed 15 May 2021.

Erickson, K.A. and Koppenhaver, D.A. (2020). *Comprehensive Literacy for All*. Baltimore: Paul Brookes Publishing.

Evans, P. and Ware, J. (1987). *Special Care Provision: The Education of Children with Profound and Multiple Learning Difficulties*. Windsor: NFER-Nelson.

Fombonne, E. (2005). The Changing Epidemiology of Autism. *Journal of Applied Research in Intellectual Disability*, 18: 281–294.

Gathercole, S.E. and Alloway, T.P. (2008). *Working Memory in the Classroom: A Practical Guide for Teachers*. London: Sage.

Goldbart, J. (2023). Communication as a human right for children with profound intellectual disabilities. *Developmental Medicine & Child Neurology*, 65: 725–726.

Grace, J. (2017). *Sensory-Being for Sensory Beings*. London: Routledge.

Hutchinson, N. and Bodicoat, A. (2015). The Effectiveness of Intensive Interaction, A Systematic Literature Review. *Journal of Applied Research in Intellectual Disabilities*, 28(6): 437–454.

Imray, P. (2018). *Turning the Tables on Challenging Behaviour*. 2nd edition. London: Routledge.

Imray, P. and Colley, A. (2017). *Inclusion is Dead: Long Live Inclusion*. London: Routledge.

Imray, P. and Hinchcliffe, V. (2014). *Curricula for Teaching Children and Young People with Severe or Profound Learning Difficulties*. London: Routledge.

Johnson, S., Strauss, V., Gilmore, C., et al. (2016). Learning Disabilities Among Extremely Preterm Children Without Neurosensory Impairment: Comorbidity, Neuropsychological Profiles and Scholastic Outcomes. *Early Human Development*, 10: 69–75.

Kennedy, I. (2010). *Getting It Right for Children and Young People*. Available from: https://assets.publishing.service.gov.uk/government/uploads/system/uploads/attachment_data/file/216282/dh_119446.pdf. Accessed 2 January 2023.

Khader, S. (2008). *Cognitive Disability, Capabilities, and Justice. Essays in Philosophy*, 9(1): 93–112.

Klingberg, T. (2009). *The Overflowing Brain: Information Overload and the Limits of Working Memory*. Oxford: Oxford University Press.

Ndaji, F. and Tymms, P. (2009). *The P Scales: Assessing the Progress of Children With Special Educational Needs*. London. Wiley-Blackwell.

Ofsted. (2019). *Education Inspection Framework*. Available from: www.gov.uk/government/publications/education-inspection-framework/education-inspection-framework. Accessed 29 January 2023.

Pagnamenta, A.T., Khan, H., Walker, S., et al. (2011). Rare Familial 16q21 Microdeletions Under a Linkage Peak Implicate Cadherin 8 (CDH8) in Susceptibility to Autism and Learning Disability. *Journal of Medical Genetics*, 48: 48–54.

Piaget, J. (1952). *The Origins of Intelligence in Children*. New York: International Press.

Pinney, A. (2017). *Understanding the Needs of Disabled Children With Complex Needs or Life-Limiting Conditions*. London: Council for Disabled Children/True Colours Trust.

Public Health England. (2020). *Chapter 1: Education and Children's Social Care*. Available from: www.gov.uk/government/publications/people-with-learning-disabilities-in-england/chapter-1-education-and-childrens-social-care-updates. Accessed 15 May 2021.

Riddick, B. (2009). P Scales – The Context. In F. Ndaji and P. Tymms (eds.) *The P Scales: Assessing the Progress of Children With Special Educational Needs*. London: Wiley-Blackwell.

Rochford, D. (2016). *The Rochford Review: Final Report. Review of Assessment for Pupils Working Below the Standard of National Curriculum Tests*. Standards and Testing Agency. Available from: www.gov.uk/government/publications/rochford-review-final-report. Accessed 29 January 2023.

Sissons, M. (2020). *Mapping and Assessing Personal Progress (MAPP)*. Newcastle: Equals.

Swanson, H.L. and Jerman, O. (2006). Maths Disabilities: A Selective Meta-Analysis of the Literature. *Review of Educational Research*, 6(2): 249–274.

Travers, J.C., Forbes, H.J., Vickers Johnson, J., et al. (2020). Inclusion and Students With Severe, Sensory and Multiple Impairments. In J.M. Kauffman (ed.) *On Education Inclusion* (pp. 160–175). New York: Routledge.

Yoder, D. (2001). Having My Say. *Augmentative and Alternative Communication*, 17(1): 2–10.

Zigmond, N.P. and Kloo, A. (2017). General and Special Education are (and Should be) Different. In J.M. Kauffman, D.P. Hallahan and P.C. Pullen (eds.) *Handbook of Special Education* (pp. 249–262). 2nd edition. New York: Routledge.

Zurcher, A. (2012). *Tackling That Troublesome Issue of ABA and Ethics*. Available from: www.emmashopebook.com. Accessed 29 January 2023.

2 What works and what matters

Assessing the progress of learners with profound, complex and severe learning disabilities

Mike Sissons

Background

The central theme of this book is 'difference not differentiation', a theme which carries the message that children with profound, complex or severe learning disabilities can properly flourish only within curricula which recognise their unique learning needs and which embody the right kind of content within the right kind of framework. It is perhaps not a surprising thought that such curriculum innovation should bring with it the need to rethink the ways in which we *assess* learning, and it is the aim of the present chapter to illustrate and justify just such a different approach to assessment. To bring this different approach into view, it will be helpful to see how it contrasts with some more traditional models of curriculum and assessment. Taking the National Curriculum for England, in all its various iterations, as paradigmatic, I think we can identify the six features listed below as characteristic of conventional approaches to assessment. Note that, on this model, assessment of progress is straightforward. Since the schedule is linear and hierarchical, progress is simply identified with the number of items which a learner has attained.

1. Curriculum content is identified and divided into subjects – e.g., English, Mathematics, Science, History, Music, etc.
2. The content of each subject is organised into a *linear hierarchy*, from the simplest to the most complex.
3. Learning outcomes are clearly stated and each outcome is supplied with a set of success criteria – e.g., descriptions as to what counts as competent performance.
4. Pupil performance is measured against the assessment criteria and the results inform *summative* assessment – i.e., a measure of how far a pupil has progressed over a fixed period of time.
5. The assessment scores provide a basis for making comparisons between individuals, groups or institutions thereby supporting quality assurance.
6. As a matter of good practice, *formative* assessments of pupil progress are carried out and used to identify improvements to teaching and learning along the way. Formative assessment is a measure of pupil *achievement*

DOI: 10.4324/9781003369134-4

rather than attainment. It is frequent and usually informal, typically consisting of teacher observations of pupil performance which are then evaluated and fed back into the teaching process.

The first three points share features that are central to behaviourist methods (but not unique to them), the core idea being the perfectly general one that, if a skill is too difficult for a learner to perform, it should be broken down into smaller pieces and delivered in chunks.

In fact, these same principles are at work in the P-scales (Department for Education and Standards and Testing Agency, 2017), a set of pre-level-1 National Curriculum descriptors designed as an assessment framework for use with pupils with special educational needs in England. The recognition that the learning of pupils with learning disabilities moves in smaller steps and at a slower pace than those prescribed by the P-scales led to the subsequent production of materials such as PIVATS (Lancashire County Council, 2022) and B squared (B Squared, 2022), which took the P-scale descriptors and National Curriculum content, broke these down into yet smaller steps and thereby effectively inserted more rungs into the ladder whilst adhering to the same model. Organisations such as the Centre for Evaluation and Monitoring at the University of Durham and CASPA (Comparison and Analysis of Special Pupil Attainment) (CASPA, 2022) ran statistical analysis of data supplied by participating schools. These data were assumed to be an accurate representation of pupil progress and, on this basis, were used to draw comparisons between the performance of schools and groups of pupils. Although the P-scales themselves are no longer a statutory instrument in the UK, the assessment materials they have generated are still widely used, and the kind of linear thinking at their core is present in the approaches I shall discuss in the following section.

Firstly, however, we should perhaps acknowledge that this approach is compelling for its simplicity and apparent rigour. It identifies the content to be taught, the order in which that content should be delivered and it adds the further claim that this sequence represents an objective measure of progress. However, this claim to objectivity is only made plausible by the fact that learning which is broken down into simple component parts can be described in terms of strictly defined, observable behaviours which enable reliable (i.e., replicable) judgements to be made by different observers or by the same observers over time. It is difficult to loosen the grip that this apparent rigour of design can exercise on our thinking but, I shall argue, that is what we must do. For, whether or not this model works for mainstream education (that is not my concern here), I am going to argue that it fails completely for the population of learners with profound, complex or severe learning disabilities. It fails because it does not recognise specifically *what* these pupils need to learn, *how* they learn it and *why* they need to learn it. As a direct consequence, the assessment outcomes lack validity in failing to actually measure what they claim to measure. In short, reliability is secured at the cost of validity.

Linear assessment: methodology

A question which all forms of linear assessment must answer is how to arrive at each of the small steps which go to make up the completed hierarchical progression they comprise. In this section, I will briefly survey three approaches to this problem: task analysis, checklists of typical child development and conceptual analysis.

Task analysis

Behavioural task analysis may work well for a very limited class of skills, particularly certain physical skills such as dressing oneself, where the task can be broken down into its smallest component parts, these parts being taught separately and then linked together (or 'chained', in behaviourist terminology) to finally reconstruct the whole task. The problem is that very few tasks admit of being decomposed in this way. Consider the following list (in no particular order): *establishing joint attention, pointing at something to indicate a need, recognising a familiar adult, anticipating an event on the basis of prior experience, moving an obstacle to obtain a desired object, hitting a switch to cause an event, repairing a misunderstanding, sharing space with others, understanding that signs or symbols carry meaning, playing alongside others, sharing toys, turn-taking, adopting appropriate standing distance from others, counting things, exchanging money for goods* and so on and so on. Most of these skills are never explicitly taught to typically developing children and most have been acquired, at least to some degree, before entering school. All have value for most learners – indeed, some play an essential part in the development of cognitive, communication and social skills – but none can be decomposed into 'atomic parts' to be dealt with separately from one another and subsequently recombined to form a meaningful whole. On the contrary, each of these skills has to be taught holistically. It is the *whole* activity, in relation to its *context* together with the *engagement* of the learner which makes the skill meaningful. Learning is richer and more complex than behaviourism allows.

> The [behavioural] approach itself is reductionist in nature. It is difficult to capture the essence of the educational process in some stark behavioural objectives [and] there is . . . the assumption that a child's learning is externally driven and directed.
>
> (Tomlinson, 1989, p20)

Tomlinson argues that behavioural task analysis excludes the pupil's cognitive processes; more broadly, we might say that the pupil's *experience* falls outside its scope. The example of joint attention can be used to illustrate this. Joint attention is (roughly stated) the three-way shared attention between two people and the object with which they are both occupied, and it is a pivotal stage in the early development of communication, cognitive and social skills

(Tomasello, 2019). Though there are some aspects of joint attention which can be separated out and considered in isolation from one another – such as glancing back and forth between the object of attention and one's partner – these behaviours are simply *indicators*; they are not constitutive of the experience itself. As Hobson (2005, p201) observes, experiences need to be shared with others such that,

> an infant joins with another person's subjective state through primary sharing or otherwise coordinating feelings in contexts of primary intersubjectivity.
>
> (p201)

'Sharing' and 'contexts' are key concepts here; they are holistic in that neither can survive separation from the dynamic interactions of shared, involved activity which constitute them, and using sets of behavioural indicators to inform teaching misses this point. Liszkowski (2018) points out that a child who is aware that another is sharing attention with them will likely *not* look at them and will probably only do so in order to check that the other person is directing their attention to the same object of interest. So, although we must understand the concept in question and the kind of behaviours that are associated with it, we cannot specify in advance a closed set of indicators. Instead, we must depend upon sensitive observation and accurate recording of the ways in which an individual child demonstrates shared attention in order to support our judgements. This requirement is obviously even more urgent in the case of learners with physical disabilities and sensory differences. Even in the case of apparently simple motor skills such as hitting a switch or kicking a ball, where component actions such as balance and coordination can be isolated and practised independently from one another, successful performance depends upon being able to bring together all the component actions of the task simultaneously and smoothly in a single unified action (Sloboda, 1986). This is purposeful, goal-directed behaviour, and as such, depends on the active involvement of the learner, but behavioural task analysis fails to see this, placing the learner instead 'in a passive role' (Welsh Assembly Government – WAG, 2006, p8).

Developmental schedules

Behavioural task-analysis, however, is not the only way one might set about constructing a linear assessment schedule. Instead, the sequence of typical child development might be taken as a framework for assessment and, indeed, such a developmental sequence informs the linear and hierarchical P-scales 1(i) to 3(ii). The first question to ask is whether such checklists should be (a) used primarily as a means of alerting us to gaps or delays in typical development whilst leaving open the question of what to teach next, or whether the items on the checklist should be (b) used to plan the sequence and determine the content of learning outcomes. Either way, in the case of learners with learning disabilities, we encounter problems. Suppose we use a developmental checklist in the first way – i.e., to identify gaps in and the rate of progress. The problem here is that the development of pupils with learning disabilities does not map onto typical development. Sensory, physical, medical and neurological differences mean that development is always atypical and permeated with gaps and differences. If, on the other hand, we use developmental scales to plan the sequence and determine the content of learning outcomes, then we encounter a different problem; items which are indicators of typical development may be unsuitable or even completely misleading when it comes to identifying worthwhile learning outcomes.

For example, numerous developmentally based scales – relevant examples in England include 'Development Matters in the Early Years Foundation Stage' (Early Education, 2012) and the 'Downs Syndrome Developmental Journal' (Early Support, 2012) – track language development by identifying the stages at which various grammatical features such as verbs, prepositions, pronouns or passive constructions emerge. But these do not form a good basis for planning teaching activities or learning outcomes. Learners do not encounter language as an abstract, formal, grammatical system; rather, they acquire it as a way of interacting with their world; for example, by making requests, pointing things out, greeting others and expressing feelings – functions which develop within dynamic social contexts which have intrinsic meaning for the learner. (Fuchs, 2016; Liszkowski, 2018). Even the simple act of pointing at an object in order to draw someone's attention to it makes sense only against the background of shared understanding of the context (Tomasello, 2019) and isolating features of language from such contexts reduces them to 'splinter skills'. The meanings of words are too bound up in shared activity to be delivered in separate parcels (Tomasello, 2019).

Added to the problem of splinter skills is the issue of 'spiky profiles'. Pupils with learning disabilities rarely progress evenly across all aspects of their learning (Imray and Hinchcliffe, 2014). For example, a pupil may utter a string of well-formed sentences using a rich vocabulary, but the content may be quite unrelated to their present situation, and they may not understand the need to clarify their utterances for the benefit of the listener. This is not uncommon in the case of autistic pupils with severe learning disabilities. In this instance, the next step would not be to teach more extensive vocabulary and concepts – which a developmental scale might suggest – but to concentrate on much 'earlier' communication skills. Contrastingly, in the case of a pupil who delivers the right information to the right people using only simple two-word utterance, we might focus on creating opportunities for them to practise their existing use of language rather than working on 'higher' skills such as, for example, the use of conjunctions to link sentences.

So, despite the contribution developmental schedules make to our understanding of the sequential appearance of behaviours in the population of neurotypical children, taken *on their own*, they are no guide to planning effective pedagogy or for assessing progress in the case of pupils with learning disabilities. They have (undoubted) value therefore as reference rather than as guide.

Conceptual analysis

There remains a third approach to linear assessment: instead of analysing *tasks* we might analyse *concepts*. So, for example, it would seem reasonable to assume that we should teach children the logical principles which underpin the ability to count before we start teaching them to count. In France, this view became so orthodox that the teaching of counting was practically banned in nursery schools until children had acquired the relevant prerequisite concepts (Butterworth, 1999, p116). Similarly, Gelman and Gallistel (1978) have argued that the concepts which they identify as necessary conditions for counting must be grasped before children can count. More recently, however, Butterworth has argued that children acquire an understanding of the relevant concepts through the act of learning to count things (Butterworth, 2019). In other words, sequences deriving from conceptual analysis (principles *before* counting) do not necessarily map directly onto pedagogy (principles *after* counting). The vital lesson here is that we need to attend to the *way children actually learn*.

In the case of literacy, for example, failure to see this can result in the delivery of instructional programmes which lead pupils through a sequence of activities, perhaps beginning with matching, sorting and identifying objects, then moving on to photographs, then pictures, then iconic symbols, and finally, abstract symbols and letters. But matching, sorting and identifying for their own sake lack any intrinsic meaning – they are mere splinter skills – unless the learner is able to relate them to the end goal. If we attend to such pedagogical issues and not merely to the concepts involved, we will be paying attention to what motivates the learner, what works for them and to the kinds of interactions and settings which best support their developing literacy skills. Indeed, at the end of this process, we may resist the promptings of a linear assessment and conclude that for *this particular learner* her existing communication – say, pointing – serves her better than any form of symbolic representation. And equally, we may recognise that a pupil who does not grasp the communication significance of pointing can nevertheless discriminate symbols and so learn to use them to express a need (though this may not amount to communication in the fuller sense of sharing interests).

Linear assessment: associated issues

The learner at the centre

Crucially, then, and following on from the last point, teaching involves harnessing the motivations of the learner. The challenge is not to take the task apart but to present the right sort of task in the right sort of way – one which demonstrates an understanding not only of the subject matter but of the learner herself. Behaviourism assumes that 'each child will learn the task in the same order' (Tomlinson, 1989, p20), but this licenses exclusive focus on behavioural responses to the task and consequently leaves out the *experience of the learner*.

Routes for Learning (WAG, 2006) notes that the central importance of engagement was emphasised as far back as 1996 in guidance issued by the School Curriculum and Assessment Authority, which stated that, 'as a first principle', 'planning should start from the basis of the needs, interests, aptitudes and achievements of the learners' (WAG, 2006, p10).

Of course, we can and should scaffold learning by simplifying tasks or by emphasising the salient parts of a task, but scaffolding does not involve fragmenting a task by breaking it down into 'atomic' component parts. The focus of the teaching is on *process* and not *product*, and therefore, any worthwhile assessment must be sensitive to that dimension. This, for example, is how 'Attention Autism' creates the right context for developing shared attention to an object (Middletown Centre for Autism, 2022) and how Intensive Interaction works to open up the possibility of interpersonal relationships and communication (Nind and Hewett, 2005). It is through such things as the creation of irresistible activities and the sensitive modulation of the adult's responses to the learner's behaviours that a fertile ground for learning is prepared. By contrast, in focussing attention solely on outcomes (i.e., on measures of product), linear assessment recognises only *what* has been learnt but gives no insight as to *how* learning happens *as* it is happening. Thus, in recording only a series of *whats*, formative assessment ('assessment-for-learning') becomes indistinguishable from merely high-frequency, summative assessment.

SMART targets

Linear assessments comprise descriptions of observable behaviours which can easily be expressed as 'SMART' (Specific, Measurable, Achievable, Relevant and Time-bound) targets. SMART targets specify precise behaviours and the conditions under which they will occur (setting, frequency, success criteria, levels of prompting, etc.). However, as we have noted, such SMART targets are more easily written for certain areas of learning (such as dressing skills) than others (such as communication skills) and insisting that outcomes be expressed in SMART form can therefore have the unintended consequence of narrowing curriculum content; in Tomlinson's words, '*rigid use of objectives can limit the curriculum by encouraging convergence*' (Tomlinson, 1989, p20). They can also, by fixing attention on the target, cause teachers to overlook incidental learning, the different and unexpected ways in which a pupil might demonstrate their learning, and so, fail to notice novel and potentially fruitful directions that learning might take.

One appeal of SMART targets is that they seem to promise greater reliability; that is, increased probability of securing similar judgements across different observers. However, this is likely at the cost of validity, since there is no way, in practice, of establishing whether or not a given behavioural description (e.g., a specific picture exchange) is an adequate indicator of a particular concept (namely, the *communicative* act of making a request). In the present case, if our criterion of success is cashed out in terms of the number of successful exchanges of a symbol for a reward, then this is insufficient to establish that *communication* is taking place; for the exchanges may be due solely to associative learning. If we add further behavioural criteria, such as 'eye contact made during exchange', then we overlook the fact that for some individuals eye contact may not (ever) be part of their repertoire of behaviours and that many individuals may show that they are communicating in ways which we recognise when they happen but could not anticipate. To conclude that a pupil is communicating intentionally, we would want to make many careful observations of the flow of interactions, and this means that recording cannot simply be a tick in a box alongside a SMART target but must be a record of critical and reflective observations. And that means taking into account the *how* of learning as well as the *what*. It follows that reliability cannot be secured by specifying a precise expected outcome in advance, but rather, by means of establishing consensus amongst judgements concerning what has been observed during and after teaching. The demand here is for critical reflection and professional discussion, not the matching of behaviour to descriptor. This shift means that the task of the teacher is not to accumulate data which is to be moderated and matched to standards (a technician's role) but to learn to make acute critical observations and to collaborate with others in subjecting these to scrutiny and reflection (the educator's role).

Abstract thought

In mainstream education, learning is primarily language-based, and this is demanded by the fact that much of the curriculum is concerned with subject matter that is not immediately present in the classroom or is abstract in nature: distant lands, the remote past, morality, numbers, phonemes, graphemes, etc. These are not things with which one can physically interact, and making sense of them places demands not only on language comprehension but also on working memory, both of which are extremely challenging for learners with learning disabilities (Gathercole and Alloway, 2007). Learners also face the further task of relating current learning to their prior learning; so, for example, typical beginning readers can make sense of the task of isolating phonemes and then synthesising them because they already have a prodigious amount of prior learning in place and are able to connect the phonic exercise to the whole enterprise of 'learning to read', to the concept of a word, of text, narrative and the world of books. Without these connections, the phonic exercise remains abstract, isolated from any concrete experiences which might give it meaning – a so-called 'splinter skill'.

The implication of all of this is that any adequate assessment must be responsive to a style of learning which is dependent upon the accumulation of concrete, contextualised and repeated experiences, including social interaction and modelling, since these are the experiences which provide the context for learners who are unable to make the relevant conceptual connections. Learning about money means actually exchanging real money for real goods in real shops; this means having a reason for wanting those goods, and this is linked to what you do with the goods once you have them, and so on. Such learning is holistic in that each part derives its meaning from its connection to all the other parts, and this cannot be captured in a finite set of pre-determined and isolable behaviours.

Lateral progression

The question now arises, how do we recognise the achievement of learners for whom progress is marked by small steps made over long periods of time? Additionally, how are we to recognise progress against learning intentions which are not written in the form SMART targets but which express, in broader, non-specific terms, the outcome of process-based teaching? Consider a pupil who, at a certain time, is using four Makaton signs to communicate her needs and suppose that after a period of, say, 2 years, she is still using the same four signs. On any linear assessment this looks like zero progress. But now, suppose that, over the course of those 2 years, she uses the signs spontaneously, communicates with a wider audience and that she forms the signs more accurately than before. By any measure, this counts as progress. I shall refer to this kind of progress as *lateral* (as opposed to linear). The important point to note, for the present, is that lateral progress focuses attention on *qualitative* aspects of a skill, that such aspects cannot be incorporated into any linear assessment model and that therefore they cannot be formally recognised within such a system.

The lack of such formal recognition brings an additional problem: if, staying with the present example, assessment only sees the acquisition of more signs as indicative of progress, then it follows that there will be pressure to make this a target and teach to it. After all, that is the next item on the linear schedule, and so, only if the learner achieves that target can we demonstrate that teaching is effective. If our pupil fails to learn more signs, then we may feel pressure to aim at some other mode of communication which sits 'higher' on the schedule (maybe a voice output communication aid). But this is a poor basis on which to write a learning outcome, leaving out, as it does, all consideration of what works for the learner.

At this point, it might be objected that linear assessments are more flexible than has been portrayed. Of course, so the objection might go, a hierarchy of steps is identified, but this is not intended to be rigidly prescriptive. We know that learners may take alternate routes from one step to the next. So, for example, Development Matters (Early Education, 2012) emphasises the importance of observing the ways in which the 'unique child' learns. But acknowledging this does not help us assess the progress a child might make with respect to any 'unique' learning intentions we have planned; for these will not appear on the assessment schedule at all. Nor does it answer the problem of lateral progression. And for all the reasons given above ('spiky profiles', limitations on working memory, difficulties with abstract ideas, sensory differences, language difficulties), these are the most pertinent considerations in the case of learners with global learning disabilities.

Non-linear assessment

The rationale behind the foregoing critique of conventional linear perspectives on assessment has been to bring into view the issues which any positive account must address. Here are those issues in summary form.

Planning and assessment must take into account:

- Pupil engagement (the centrality of the learner's motivation, strengths and needs).
- The holistic nature of almost all meaningful learning and its resistance to decomposition.
- The importance of concrete experience.
- Emphasis on the process (the *how*) and purpose (the *why*) of learning, not simply the product (the *what*).
- Experiences in which skills are related to one another and to the rest of the pupil's life in such a way that this interconnectedness is evident to the learner.
- The critically reflective use of resources, including developmental scales and other relevant schedules, to *inform* rather than to unreflectively *dictate* planning.
- The need to secure reliable judgement through critical reflection based on accurate observation (not simply through ticks against SMART targets).
- Recognition of the vital importance of lateral progression.

The remainder of this chapter is devoted to an evaluation of materials which offer positive alternatives to linear, tick-box assessment.

Routes for learning

Routes for Learning (WAG, 2006; Welsh Government, 2020a), which provides detailed guidance on planning and assessment for learners with PMLD, represents one such alternative. It comprises detailed guidance for teachers, a 'Routemap' made up of 43 steps, together with advice on teaching activities and assessment opportunities. Given this focus on early stages of learning, it is not surprising that the framework incorporates concepts which are familiar from typical child development (such as object permanence and causation), six of which (designated 'milestones') occur in a predetermined sequence through which all learners are likely to pass (Welsh Government, 2020b). How, then, if there is a predetermined sequence, does Routes for Learning avoid falling into the trap of imposing a rigid linear pattern on teaching and learning? Firstly, the authors acknowledge that, though there are milestones through which 'every learner is likely to pass', 'learners can take different routes . . . on the Routemap to reach these milestones' (Welsh Government, 2020b, p2). In other words, the pathways through the remaining 37 out of the 43 steps allow scope for individual differences in planning, and the Routes for Learning guidance reminds us that the numbering of steps is for ease of reference only. This shift away from linear thinking is further emphasised by the grouping of steps into 12 themes such that,

> within the themes, Routemap boxes are arranged numerically but learners will not necessarily achieve them in a strict hierarchical sequence. The themes themselves are not discrete routes which we would necessarily expect learners to follow, as they are interlinked in many ways.
>
> (Welsh Government, 2020a, online)

Routes for Learning also incorporates certain other of the key aspects which are bullet-pointed at the head of this section, insisting that it is essential to 'involve learners and follow their lead' as well as 'families and all professionals working within the support team', stressing the importance of recognising that 'the assessment is process-based and looks at the relationship between the learner and his/her environment' and advising that reliability be secured through careful observation and interpersonal judgement supported by reference to the Routes for Learning video exemplars (WAG, 2006, online).

Mapping and Assessing Personal Progress (MAPP)

Routes for Learning focusses exclusively on the needs of learners with Profound and Multiple Learning Disabilities. MAPP Semi-Formal (Sissons, 2018, 2020) provides an alternative to the linear model of assessment whilst addressing the needs of learners with Complex or Severe Learning Disabilities. MAPP is divided into two sections; the first comprises the planning of learning intentions; the second contains a tool for the assessment of progress against learning intentions. The first section is made up of 155 'milestone' statements which, as with the steps in Routes for Learning, are numbered simply for ease of reference and not to indicate that they should be worked through in a linear sequence. To further dispel any temptation towards hierarchical thinking, the milestones, rather than being presented as a single string starting at number 1, are organised into three main areas – *Communication*, *Cognition* and *Personal and Social Development* – each of which is then subdivided into smaller domains (for example, 'communicating needs and wants', 'handling information', 'sensorimotor development', etc.). This division into domains is similar in intent to the thematic organisation of the 43 steps in Routes for Learning. The MAPP milestones identify core skills within domains of learning which serve to inform the process of writing personal learning intentions *when considered alongside* the individual learner's strengths, needs and motivations. They are not to be treated as 'off-the-peg' targets.

Since, for reasons given earlier, 'personal learning intentions' are not written as SMART targets and since, therefore, progress cannot be assessed via a simple tick-box procedure, both Routes for Learning and MAPP advise that evaluation will depend upon skilled observation, careful recording keeping by teachers and triangulation of evidence. This raises a question when it comes to tracking lateral progress for pupils with Complex or Severe Learning Disabilities, since the content of the learning intentions is likely to be wider-ranging than those which are written for pupils with PMLD. As one example, compare 'use a communication book to manage interactions in the context of a practical activity' with 'track a brightly coloured object'; how are we to assess lateral progress with respect to learning intentions which have such rich content? MAPP's response is to provide a framework called the 'Assessment of Lateral Progress' (ALP). The ALP looks at four aspects of skilled performance: independence, fluency, maintenance and generalisation.

- *Independence* refers to the level of prompting or cueing which a learner needs to perform a task.
- *Fluency* refers to the confidence and accuracy with which a task is performed.
- *Maintenance* to the consistency of performance over time.
- *Generalisation* to the ability to transfer a skill to novel contexts, including people, materials and setting.

The thought here, drawing on the work of Dreyfus (2014), is that proficient performance is manifested in the ability to respond flexibly and automatically to the demands made by relevantly similar situations across differing contexts. Each of these four aspects is provided with descriptors to help ensure consistency of judgement between observers, and progress is recorded using a rating scale. ALP aims to fulfil a number of functions: it offers a way of recognising achievement without the need to decompose the task, it charts lateral progression and can do this over extended periods of time and it highlights aspects of learning which otherwise may not be evident (such as a learner having particular difficulty in achieving independence or in generalising their learning). Being content-free, the ALP can be used as a tool for assessing lateral progress with respect to any personal learning intention, including those which are based on areas not contained within MAPP itself (such as physical development) or ones which have been drawn from other resources (such as Routes for Learning).

Ipsative assessment and comparative assessment

Both MAPP and Routes for Learning adopt an approach to personalised planning which renders meaningless any kind of comparative judgements or benchmarking. Such personalised approaches cannot yield the sort of quantitative data which enable the performance of one pupil (or cohort or school) to be compared with another. Instead, we are concerned with *ipsative* assessment; that is, with an individual's progress judged solely in terms of the gains they have made in relation to their own prior learning. This approach, which springs directly from consideration of the pedagogical needs of the population of learners who have profound, complex or severe learning disabilities, leaves us with an apparent problem. If we are unable to compare performance between pupils, then how are we to evaluate the effectiveness of teaching and learning? We cannot point to any externally referenced scores to validate the quality of pupil progress, but neither can this issue be simply passed over as schools have an absolute responsibility to be accountable for their provision. And if the arguments mustered in the first part of this chapter have any traction at all, then the solution cannot be to return to some kind of comparative, quantitative measures of pupil performance based on a set of linear scales.

Precisely this issue of quality-assuring, ipsative assessment is addressed by Recognising and Recording Progress and Achievement – RARPA (Education and Training Foundation, 2015). RARPA is an action research and case-study-based resource which was developed to support those learners with learning difficulties in further education who are not following accredited courses. Five stages are identified in the provision of planning and assessment, which include learner involvement, accurate baselining, identification of appropriate objectives, detailed formative assessment, feedback to learners and summative assessment, including learner self-assessment. This obviously chimes with the spirit of Routes for Learning and MAPP, although adaptations are needed to accommodate the needs of learners with more profound or complex learning disabilities, whose views will necessarily require advocacy. In addition, RARPA stipulates that certain 'organisational systems' must be in place in order to quality assure this five-staged process. These systems include implementation of a quality-improvement cycle, internal moderation, effective performance-management and professional development in relation to the five stages of RARPA and, crucially, external check by peer review. With the probable exception of external review, these processes will already form part of the practice of most schools, but in RARPA, they are formalised and supplemented with guidance and criteria. Formalised in these ways they provide a systematic way of quality assuring ipsative progress based on personal learning intentions.

Conclusion

What are the implications of the foregoing reflections on assessment for schools and other settings? An immediate implication is a shift of emphasis away from the collection and detached analysis of numerical data toward teachers' continuing professional development and collaborative working. This follows from the fact that teaching staff will not be able to operate in isolation, simply drawing down objectives from a checklist. Instead, they need to cultivate the ability to recognise a learner's strengths and motivations and to find ways of building on what engages them. They need to identify realistic, achievable learning intentions and develop skills of observation and reflection in order to assess learners' responses and progress. At an organisational level, this demands collaborative working in order to check out judgements and in order to find ways to unlock learning where this has stalled. All of this needs to be underpinned by specialist knowledge of specific disabilities and the effects that these can have on learning and has to operate within a relevant and appropriately resourced curriculum. These implications for practice are variously explored in Chapters 5–12. They constitute a project of continuing development for both teachers and settings – a project which is demanded by the fact that every individual with profound, complex or severe learning difficulties has unique needs and unique ways of learning. Education for these learners is not about mastering an established body of knowledge such as science or history, and they cannot and should not be pressed into climbing the rungs of a ladder which was not designed for them. What is required is a different curriculum, differently assessed and delivered by highly qualified specialist staff.

References

B Squared. *B Squared* [online]. Available from: www.bsquared.co.uk. Accessed 25 May 2022.

Butterworth, B. (1999). *What Counts*. New York: Simon & Schuster.

Butterworth, B. (2019). *Dyscalculia. From Science to Education*. London: Routledge.

CASPA. (2022). *Comparison and Analysis of Special Pupil Attainment* [online]. Available from: www.caspaonline.co.uk. Accessed 25 May 2022.

Department for Education and Standards and Testing Agency. (2017). *P-Scales: Attainment Targets for Pupils With SEN* [online]. Available from: www.gov.uk/government/publications/p-scales-attainment-targets-for-pupils-with-sen. Accessed 25 May 2022.

Dreyfus, H. (2014). From Socrates to expert systems. In M.A. Wrathall (ed.) *Skillful Coping*. Oxford: Oxford University Press.

Early Education. (2012). *Development Matters in the Early Years Foundation Stage* [online]. Available from: www.foundationyears.org.uk/files/2012/03/Development-Matters-FINAL-PRINT-AMENDED.pdf. Accessed 25 May 2022.

Early Support. (2012). *Downs Syndrome Developmental Journal* [online]. Available from: https://councilfordisabledchildren.org.uk/resources/all-resources/filter/schools-colleges-and-fe/downs-syndrome-development-journal-early. Accessed 25 May 2022.

Education and Training Foundation. (2015). *Guidance on How to Quality Assure RARPA in Provision for Learners With Learning Difficulties* [online]. Available from: www.excellencegateway.org.uk/content/eg6813. Accessed 25 May 2022.

Fuchs, T. (2016). The Embodied Development of Language. In G. Etzelmüller and C. Tewes (eds.) *Embodiment in Evolution and Culture*. Tübingen: Mohr Siebeck.

Gathercole, S.E. and Alloway, T.P. (2007). *Understanding Working Memory: A Classroom Guide* [online]. Available from: www.mrc-cbu.cam.ac.uk/wp-content/uploads/2013/01/WM-classroom-guide.pdf. Accessed 25 May 2022.

Gelman, R. and Gallistel, C.R. (1978). *The Child's Understanding of Number*. Cambridge, MA: Harvard University Press.

Hobson, R.P. (2005). What Puts the Jointness into Joint Attention? In N. Eilan, C. Hoerl, T. McCormack, et al. (eds.) *Joint Attention: Communication and Other Minds* (pp. 185–204). Oxford: Clarendon Press.

Imray, P. and Hinchcliffe, V. (2014). *Curricula for Teaching Children and Young People With Severe or Profound Learning Difficulties*. London: Routledge.

Lancashire County Council. (2022). *PIVATS* [online]. Available from: www.lancashire.gov.uk/pupiltracker/pivats/. Accessed 25 May 2022.

Liszkowski, U. (2018). Origins and Complexities of Infant Communication and Social Cognition. In A. Newen, L. de Bruin and S. Gallagher (eds.) *The Oxford Handbook of 4E Cognition*. Oxford: Oxford University Press.

Middletown Centre for Autism: Best Practice Resource. (2022). *Attention Autism* [online]. Available from: https://best-practice.middletownautism.com/approaches-of-intervention/attention-autism/. Accessed 25 May 2022.

Nind, M. and Hewett, D. (2005). *Access to Communication*. London: David Fulton.

Sissons, M. (2018). MAPP (*Mapping and Assessing Personal Progress*): *Semi-Formal Model*. Newcastle: Equals.

Sissons, M. (2020). MAPP (*Mapping and Assessing Personal Progress*): *Formal Model*. Newcastle: Equals.

Sloboda, J. (1986). What is skill? In A. Gellatly (ed.) *The Skilful Mind*. Maidenhead, Berkshire: Open University Press.

Tomasello, M. (2019). *Becoming Human*. London England: The Belknap Press of Harvard University Press Cambridge Massachusetts.

Tomlinson, P. (1989). The Teaching of Skills: Modern Cognitive Perspectives. In D. Sugden (ed.) *Cognitive Approaches in Special Education* (pp. 28–50). Lewes, East Sussex: The Falmer Press.

WAG. (2006). *Routes for Learning: Additional Guidance*. Cardiff: Welsh Assembly Government.

Welsh Government. (2020a). *Routes for Learning. Assessment Booklet* [online]. Available from: https://hwb.gov.wales/curriculum-for-wales/routes-for-learning. Accessed 25 May 2022.

Welsh Government. (2020b). *Routes for Learning. Explanatory Note* [online]. Available from: https://hwb.gov.wales/curriculum-for-wales/routes-for-learning. Accessed 25 May 2022.

3 The use and abuse of research

Educational research and its importance for learners with SLD, CLD and PMLD

Lila Kossyvaki, Peter Imray and Mike Sissons

In this chapter, we explore the concept of educational research, and based on evidence, we explain why we think that the term has been overly used and sometimes abused in the field of SEND education, particularly when it comes to learners with SLD, CLD and PMLD.

Background

Whilst research can, of course, mean different things to different people, researching a ravioli recipe or the price match for a new laptop is bound to be far less systematic and rigorous than that needed for educational research. Nonetheless, as Grace (2019) has noted, even though the phrase 'research has shown' is commonly and often blithely used, it is difficult to find robust research for the education of learners with SLD and PMLD (Porter, 2015), a state of affairs which has seemed to be the case for quite a long period of time (see Pring, 2004; Porter, 2005; Norwich, 2013; Ware, 2014; Imray and Colley, 2017; Rendoth et al., 2022). Educational research for these cohorts could prove invaluable in (i) producing results which can be directly applied to real world settings and (ii) bridging the gap between academic research and everyday practice at school, home and the community. Before the 2000s, a lot of the educational research in the field of SEND tended to be quantitative (i.e., using numbers, figures and statistics), reflecting the heavy influence of psychiatry and psychology with relatively little qualitative research (Porter and Lacey, 2005). Perhaps as a reaction to this, a number of studies focussing on understanding the social lives and experiences of people with SLD, CLD and PMLD flourished in the following years. Some scholars took it to the other extreme, arguing that educational research cannot be quantitative and rigorous, mimicking the physical sciences, as it deals with human beings (Wellington, 2015). We, as editors of this book, believe that qualitative research can be as important as quantitative, if scientific rigour is applied (Bölte, 2014), but unfortunately, in an attempt to separate themselves from quantitative analysis, some educational researchers have failed to apply sufficient rigour and quality indicators in their work, ending up with studies of dubious quality.

DOI: 10.4324/9781003369134-5

It is relevant to mention here the example of a research approach which has often been overused and sometimes abused by educational practitioners – that of action research. Since the 1990s, there has been an initiative to bridge the gap between research and educational practice, and as a result of this initiative, more teaching staff started being involved in action research (Zeihner, 1993, cited in Shkedi, 1998). A lot of us who are involved in educational research and also work in close collaboration with schools can confirm that there are too many groundless claims made by school staff that they do action research. A closer look at what they do reveals that they keep reflective notes of their practice, which sometimes might drive changes in their setting. This approach does not, however, meet the criteria for being called action research unless certain aspects are in place. According to Porter and Lacey (2005, p23), action research is 'based on reflective enquiry with iterative cycles of planning, action, observation and reflection' often used by practitioners to answer the question 'How can I improve my practice?'. In other words, action research has to entail (i) a cyclical process, where a plan is put in place which after systematic observation and reflection gets revised and put in place again, at least once, (ii) reflexivity and (iii) change (Denscombe, 2017).

As identified by Lacey (2000), education is not well represented in journals which publish research relevant to people with complex needs, and although some progress has been made since Lacey's observation, this is still largely the case over 20 years later. Several UK SEND education journals state in their aims and scope that they publish research of relevance to teaching (e.g., the British Journal of Special Education – BJSE – and the Journal of Research in Special Educational Needs – JORSEN), but they rarely include papers which focus on the PMLD, CLD or SLD populations, which is, perhaps, an indication of the small percentage of people with complex needs within the broader population of people with learning disabilities.

Although there is a growing initiative in the last 20–25 years to involve people with learning disabilities in research (e.g., Abell et al., 2007), the inclusion of people with SLD and CLD is difficult and demands certain adaptations (Murphy and Cameron, 2008). The inclusion of people with PMLD is even more complicated for ethical and practical reasons, and proxies often need to be used (de Haas et al., 2022; Rushton et al., 2023). Therefore, individuals with PMLD appear as the most marginalised group of people in disability research and can end up as voiceless subjects (Mietola et al., 2017). People with SLD and CLD might be at a slighter better place, but their representation in research is also very limited compared to the rest of those with SEND.

Teachers' attitudes towards research

The evidence on teacher attitudes towards research seems to be inconclusive. There are studies which have reported negative teacher attitudes towards research (e.g., Butt and Shams, 2013) while others, although indicating positive teacher attitudes, note that participants appeared reluctant to engage with it (e.g., de Paor and Murphy, 2018). Evidence shows that teachers who abstain from research often have a narrow understanding of what research is and mainly link it with quantitative data and statistical analysis (de Paor and Murphy, 2018), whereas teachers who are willing to use research report that it gives them confidence or helps them in making pedagogical decisions (Sato and Loewen, 2019). Certain teachers definitely perceive research as part of their practice.

> I just feel it [research] makes you more PROFESSIONAL because you've had to go and examine something instead of just thinking of lesson plans and little Freddie in the front row who is being naughty.
> (Furlong and Salisbury, 2005, p56, cited in Porter, 2015)

Teaching is, however, 'a demanding, and at times frustrating profession' (Claxton, 1989, p27, cited in Mills and Earl Rinehart, 2019), and a large proportion of school teachers present high levels of burnout (García-Carmona et al., 2019). This is likely to make engagement with research even more difficult, with limited time and resources appearing as the most prominent barriers (Sato and Loewen, 2019). Additionally, the linguistic, conceptual and physical inaccessibility of rigorous research for school staff is another considerable problem (Marsden and Kasprowicz, 2017). If school professionals do not have free access to good quality studies or they cannot follow the papers because of the jargon included in them, it is very unlikely that they will make the effort, on top of their very busy timetables, to get hold of and read research papers. Educational practitioners from English speaking countries seem to be at a slightly advantageous position, as English is the most widely used language to disseminate research via journal papers and conferences (Sato and Loewen, 2019).

Practitioner or school-based research

Practitioner or school-based research is the research conducted by teaching staff in order to explore their practice in depth (Mills and Earl Rinehart, 2019), a position supported, in England, at least, by the Rochford Review (Rochford, 2016), which urged school staff to engage in research 'to support good practice' (p25).

There are a number of commonly used research design/methodologies in educational research:

- *Case studies*, in which a unit of analysis (i.e., one person, group or event) is selected to conduct detailed contextual analysis on. More than one data collection method, such as observations and interviews, can be employed to validate the data.
- *Surveys* (often synonymous with questionnaires), which are used to collect primarily quantitative data and reach large numbers of respondents on topics such as preferences, opinions or factual information.

- *Ethnography*, which aims to provide a deeper understanding of a phenomenon, often using considerably extensive observations and unstructured interviews.
- *Action research*, which focusses on professional practice and addresses practical problems following a fairly specific cyclical process.
- *Review and Meta-analysis*, which examine the research evidence of previously conducted studies that meet a set of pre-determined inclusion criteria (such as age range, level of intellectual disability).
- *Control group studies*, in which participants are allocated to either an intervention or a control group in randomised control trials (RCTs). For studies like this, pre- and post-intervention data are collected and compared. It is recommended, on ethical grounds, that the control group goes through the intervention after the study is completed so that no participants are placed at a disadvantage.
- *Multiple baseline studies*, which are single case intervention studies where the intervention starts at different time points for each participant (staggered exposure to the intervention) so that the impact of external factors (e.g., school staff absences, timetable changes) on any resulting changes can be minimised. Pre- and post-intervention data are collected and compared here as well.

Practitioner researchers and research consumers need to be aware of the rigour and the strength of the educational studies they conduct or read. For this purpose, there are several lists of quality indicators researchers should put in place when conducting research themselves – or have them in mind when reading studies of other people, so that they can have an idea of their quality and strength. For example, irrespective of the selected methodology, Denscombe (2017) provides a quite detailed list of components needed for robust research to take place in the real world. Such a study has to be situated within the broader relevant literature. Therefore, a detailed review of the literature to identify research gaps should precede any empirical study. The aims and/or research questions should be clearly identified and an explicit account of the methodological details (that is, participants, data collection tools, etc.) should be provided. Both these components are extremely important if one would like to repeat the study.

Intervention studies are very hard to conduct but, nonetheless, much-needed, as interventions are where a lot of the school budget is likely to be spent. Therefore, the following measures are recommended:

- Reports on fidelity (to check the extent to which the delivery of an intervention adheres to its guidelines).
- If observation is one of the data collection tools, inter-observer reliability (the degree of agreement or disagreement between two or more people observing the same event) should be checked so we do not rely on the subjective opinion of one person.
- Carefully and thoroughly considering the ethical position, especially when involving participants with limited capacity to provide or deny consent due to their intellectual impairment.

- Ensuring that any claims made in the study are based on its findings. If, for example, the study is about the impact of an intervention on the engagement levels of the participants, the researchers cannot make claims about its impact on the attention skills of the participants, since engagement is only one component of attention.

Terlektsi et al. (2019) call for:

- Clear and specific objectives and high-quality outcome measures.
- Extended periods of observation.
- Details relating to the intervention, including its theoretical background and rationale for selection. Studies which are conducted in real word settings such as schools and classrooms have strong implications for practice and are preferred.
- Big sample sizes to cater for representation and generalisability of the results, while the limitations of each study should be outlined.
- Research published in peer-reviewed outlets; that is, journals which follow blind assessment of manuscripts by more than one expert in the field to decide whether it is worth publication.

Evidence-based practices

Evidence-based practices (EBPs) is a term that is currently much-used. These are practices with supporting research bases that meet systematic and rigorous criteria like the quality indicators mentioned earlier. There have been demands for EBPs for almost 40 years in the field of SEND (Porter and Lacey, 2005) with directives that all learners, including those with SLD, CLD and PMLD, must be taught both daily living and academic skills using EBPs (No Child Left Behind Act, 2001). Despite this, there are very few EBPs for learners with SLD (NSTTAC, 2013) and, to our knowledge, none for learners with PMLD.

In relation to teaching, evidence-based practices have been defined as:

> clearly specified teaching methods that have been shown in controlled research to be effective in bringing about desired outcomes in a delineated population of learners.
>
> (Mitchel and Sutherland, 2020, p3)

We are not the first to argue there really are insufficient studies to form a purely evidence-based opinion on most aspects related to the education of learners with SLD, CLD or PMLD, yet these learners are, nonetheless, routinely included in such hubristic statements as '*all children can learn to read and write*' (Erickson and Koppenhaver, 2020, p3). We support the notion that teachers should routinely question their practice in the light of research, or at least the reporting of that research, but that research (or the reporting of it) then has an obligation to be accurate. So, does the research enable and facilitate such questioning, or does it obfuscate and confuse?

Imray et al. (2023) warn that, unfortunately, when it comes to establishing what works for those with SLD, CLD and PMLD, obfuscation and confusion are rife. They argue that there are primarily, four reasons for this; namely:

1. There is a strong tendency to quote research that applies to some learners with SEND as though it applies to all learners with SEND.
2. There is insufficient precision in describing the level of learning difficulty being experienced by the learner(s) being researched.
3. There is a common assumption that any academic progress, especially in the areas of literacy and numeracy, should always be the ultimate goal for all learners.
4. There is a conflation between the natural desire for common strategies to be universally applied for all teaching and the need for common curricula content to be universally applied for all teaching. They are not the same things at all.

Returning to the work of Erickson and Koppenhaver (2020), noted above, which is both an extended literature review and an argument for a particular literacy teaching model – namely, comprehensive literacy instruction – we can see difficulties related to the first three of these issues. The title of the book, *Comprehensive Literacy for All: Teaching Students with Significant Disabilities to Read and Write*, expresses the 'all' word loud and clear and will therefore have a significant impact on all school leaders and teachers. Whilst it takes some time for Erickson and Koppenhaver to elaborate on exactly what they mean by reading and writing, they do so very clearly, around half-way into the book, with this statement.

> From a pragmatic stance, comprehensive literacy instruction is based on several assumptions and understandings. First, it is based on the assumption that all children can learn to read and write. . . . Second, it is based on the recognition that we must teach everything about literacy if all students are to succeed as readers. . . . Third, it rests on an understanding that **all students need to learn every aspect of reading from phonemic and phonological awareness to decoding, reading fluency, and comprehension, as well as learning the coherent, cohesive, and strategic application of all these components.**
>
> (Erickson and Koppenhaver, 2020, p92, our emphasis)

The problem with this is that the book, despite referencing 527 works of research, fails to establish that **all** can learn to effectively use the skills noted. There is no doubt that Erickson and Koppenhaver establish that the research can rightly claim that the majority, perhaps even the vast majority, of those with SEND have the potential to be fluent readers, but there is no evidence that this claim stretches to all. Some of the 47 works of research referenced by them which note significant or severe, cognitive or intellectual disabilities or mental retardation (sic) observe that some progress can be made for some learners for some of the time, but none claim that *all* can learn to master 'every aspect of reading from phonemic and phonological awareness to decoding, reading fluency, and comprehension, as well as learning the coherent, cohesive, and strategic application of all these components' (Erickson and Koppenhaver, ibid).

Some, notably Lacey et al. (2007), have taken the view that 'reading' can be more loosely translated so that 'all' can be included in the process of learning to read, but this merely encourages the notion that reading means something other than gaining meaning from text. Moseley (2023), for example, emphasises

> a 'literacy for all' focus, with a wider definition of reading as gaining meaning from some form of stimulus. This means that we look at how our learners are reading interactions, people, situations, objects, events, images.
>
> (p17)

This might be an interesting reflection on Intensive Interaction, but none of these skills require the mastery of phonics and do not constitute any common understanding of reading. In what can be regarded as one of the seminal texts on the process of reading, Rose (2006) is clear, the ability to phonically decode and understand the text being read have to combine. There is no shortcut or alternative route if learners are to achieve the mastery necessary for broader academic attainment, as in, for example, a national or common-core-subject curriculum, and to assume otherwise is in danger of encouraging tokenistic academic inclusion.

With regard to the fourth of Imray et al.'s (2023) observations on research, that the natural desire for common strategies to be universally applied for all teaching is conflated with the need for common curricula content to be universally applied for all teaching, we might turn to Mitchel and Sutherland (2020). In their meta-analysis, titled *What Really Works in Special and Inclusive Education*, Mitchell and Sutherland assert that their aim is to assist teachers to use the 'best available evidence' (p3), and whilst they are insistent that one size does not fit all, they argue that certain common elements of effective teaching are universal. Quoting Siraj-Blatchford et al. (2011), they note that teachers who are effective in teaching disadvantaged learners routinely demonstrate skills in a bundle of strategies, such as having excellent organisational skills, establishing a positive classroom environment, personalising their teaching, using evaluative feedback and making regular use of plenary sessions in class. Such generalist teaching strategies form the 'teacher craft knowledge' noted within *Inclusive Pedagogy* (Florian and Black-Hawkins, 2013, p815) and mark out what the 'good teacher' does routinely, with all pupils. This point is re-enforced by Mitchel and Sutherland in their claim that

> with some exceptions, there are no disability-specific teaching strategies. Most of the strategies (presented) in the book are relevant to all learners with additional education needs – indeed, to all learners.
>
> (Mitchel and Sutherland, 2020, p8)

Note, once again the use of the word 'all'. The problem here is that Mitchel and Sutherland are exploring *how* one teaches, not *what* one teaches. If the what of teaching is irrelevant, unmotivating, unconcerned with individual learners' engagement, only admitting of specific, linear and academic outcomes, it will naturally exclude those with PMLD, CLD and SLD. This population is the 1% or 2% of the school population (Pinney, 2017) who repeatedly fail to achieve in national curricula or common-core-standards curriculum models across the globe (Imray and Colley, 2017).

Interestingly, Mitchel and Sutherland's (2020) claim for there being 'no disability-specific teaching strategies' is, in turn, based on their referencing of Lewis and Norwich's (2005) *Special Teaching for Special Children?* This latter work can be seen as a landmark work in relation to alternative and different pedagogy for those with SEND because it appears to indicate that there is no justification for assuming that pedagogic difference is in any way significant for any particular group of learners. That is, it adopts a 'unique differences' position which accepts that individual learners may well have differences that are unique to them as individuals (a reflection on all children being different) but rejects the notion that particular definable groups of learners display differences which could engage with different pedagogic notions. Their argument is that all children broadly learn the same way, even though that may be on a continuum.

Lewis and Norwich assembled a band of experts in the various elements of SEND, who all agreed that (i) what research there is seems to indicate that a different pedagogical stance is not justified for different learning difficulties and disabilities and (ii) that their individual and expert opinions are that a unique position is largely acceptable. There were clear areas of uncertainty with several chapters indicating

> that curriculum commonality could only be at the broadest level of common principles, as otherwise the diversity of educational needs would call for specialization.
>
> (Lewis and Norwich, 2005, p209)

Crucially however, Lewis and Norwich were asking their experts to judge on the need for a different 'how', not a different 'what'.

> In asking whether pupils with special educational needs require distinct kinds of pedagogic strategies, we are not asking whether pupils with

special educational needs require distinct curriculum objectives. **We are asking whether they need distinct kinds of teaching to learn the same content as others without special educational needs**.

(Norwich and Lewis, 2005, p7, our emphasis)

The emphasis, for Lewis and Norwich, is on learning the same content, and as this is so, it is a notion with which it is extremely difficult to argue. The authors of this chapter, and indeed the writers published in this book, are not, however, asking whether those with PMLD, CLD and SLD need distinct kinds of teaching to learn the *same* content as others without special educational needs because we accept that learning the *same* content is, and always has been, impossible for all of these learners, irrespective of their chronological age. The 10-year longitudinal experiment conducted by Durham University, expounded by Ndaji and Tymms (2009) and supported by the Rochford Review (Rochford, 2016), is very clear. The profundity of their learning disabilities ensures that those with PMLD will not progress even into the beginnings of England's National Curriculum, and the severity of the learning disabilities experienced by those with SLD will limit their involvement to the earliest stages of the National Curriculum, perhaps at the very best, the equivalent to that attained by averagely developing children at age 7 (Standards and Testing Agency, 2020).

However, the emphasis on making progress within the *same* curriculum allows Mitchel and Sutherland (2020) to reference Lewis and Norwich in their assertion that

there is little evidence to support the notion of disability-specific teaching strategies, but rather that all learners benefit from a common set of strategies, even if they have to be adapted to take account of varying cognitive, emotional and social capabilities.

(Mitchel and Sutherland, 2020, p7)

This view is consistent with earlier iterations when, for example, Davis and Florian (2004) described discussions on real pedagogical differences for different groups of learners as being *'unhelpful'*. This, however, merely emphasises the grip of the notion of a *national* curriculum, even if that national curriculum is a common-core-standard one, as in the USA, for example, in that the single solution to all difficulties and the 'right' of all children to access this single solution has been firmly suppressing any opportunity to think otherwise. The moral correctness of an inclusionist doctrine has effectively throttled experiment, and it is difficult to contemplate how research can be contemplated when no alternatives to the established are allowed. The teachers who have written the eight chapters in Part 2 of this book have experimented despite the system, not because of it. This cannot be a healthy state of affairs, and we are therefore calling for a new initiative in educational research which celebrates classroom evidence-informed practices.

Finally, again, as noted by Imray et al. (2023) and as a classic case of a 'research informed' piece of writing, it would be remiss of us to not reflect on the extraordinary abuse of research in the 2022 iteration of England's 'government policy' on literacy in schools; namely, *The reading framework: Teaching the foundations of literacy* (DfE, 2022). This boldly claims to

> concentrate on good practice for those with moderate to severe SEND and complex needs, most (but not all) of whom will be in specialist provision.
>
> (DfE, 2022, p55)

and that

> consensus is growing among academics and teachers that the best reading instruction for children with SEND is SSP (systematic synthetic phonics), taught by direct instruction. They can learn to read and write and can make progress towards or attain functional literacy.
>
> (ibid, p55)

To support this claim, the DfE quoted 'evidence' from five separate studies, which Imray et al. then went back to in order to conduct an analysis. Unfortunately, the simple process of reading through the original research revealed that not a single one of the five works stated what the DfE suggested they stated. This was not the fault of the original researchers; the problem lies with the false interpretation put on the research. Imray and Sissons (2021) make the point: there is absolutely no research evidence to suggest that those with SLD, CLD and PMLD can be taught to *master* SSP. Note, we are not inferring that those with SLD cannot achieve some sort of *functional* literacy, but there is no research evidence (including the five studies quoted) which can lead us to believe that the teaching of SSP is fundamental to this process. The phonics model is essential teaching if children are to become *fluent* readers, but not everyone is able to become a fluent reader, and a different model to phonics therefore needs to be applied (Imray and Sissons, 2021). And this makes no difference whether it is taught in mainstream or special/specialist settings; it does not matter whether such schools and/or teachers are good or outstanding; it makes no difference which SSP schema is used. There simply is no evidence that SSP works for *all* learners.

Whilst the arguments noted here may appear to be entirely negative – concentrating, as they do, on what pupils cannot do – it seems to us that this is an essential first step. Once we clear our minds of trying to teach what cannot be taught, we can concentrate on what pupils can do. Those with SLD, CLD and PMLD can achieve highly meaningful and important progress, especially in the areas of Communication, Independence, Social Relationships, Self-Regulation, Thinking and Problem Solving and Creativity, all areas of learning (with capital letters) focussed on within the Equals Multi-Tiered Curriculum

Approach (Equals, 2020), but their chances of achieving in such areas will be seriously impaired if we continue wasting most of their precious time in education on pointless academic (literacy and numeracy) goals.

Evidence-informed practice

We are not proposing that evidence-informed practices (EIPs) replace EBPs, but they can represent highly valuable evidence whilst a bank of EBPs is properly established. EIPs are an integration of research evidence, personal expertise and the voice and the needs of the individuals (Guldberg, 2020). However, conducting practitioner or school-based research aiming for at least EIPs, although very much needed, is only one side of the coin. Teaching staff also need to become more 'discernible readers' (Porter, 2015, p407) of research by others so that they can 'benefit from work that other people have done before and learn from their successes and mistakes' (Kossyvaki, 2019, p19). The use of the internet and open access publications (i.e., academic institutions pay a fee to provide free access to their employees' publications) are likely to make research more accessible to school staff (Porter, 2015). It has to be highlighted, however, that, usually, only affluent academic institutions from developed countries can afford this high fee and as a result only certain papers make it with no associated fee to the wider public.

Disseminating practitioner or school-based research findings is an issue of significant importance, since, as we have already seen, school-based research is not commonplace. Although the need for the results of school-based research to be published and communicated is strongly highlighted (Clarke and Erickson, 2006, cited in Mills and Earl Rinehart, 2019; Kossyvaki, 2019), practitioner researchers do not often disseminate their findings. This might be because of lack of time and resources, because school staff do not believe their findings are of any use beyond their setting or they do not feel confident enough with the process of getting themselves out in journal papers and conferences (Collins, 2012, cited in Porter, 2015). On that note, Kossyvaki (2019) questions whether it is ethical to keep knowledge within the boundaries of one setting, when, by sharing it, the lives of learners, practitioners and families have the potential to improve.

Conclusion

Clearly, the ideal of evidenced-based research informing educational practice is a sound one, and this chapter seeks to explain how teaching staff might be able to contribute to the (at present) limited knowledge of how best to teach those of all ages with SLD, CLD and PMLD. There is a particular opportunity to use evidence-based or at least evidence-informed practice as long as potential researchers concentrate on real learning, as opposed to partial, rote or temporal learning. Sissons (2020) argues strongly that real learning is both longitudinal and lateral for all those with SLD, CLD and PMLD, who will and do all struggle to show long term linear progress in academic subjects such as Mathematics and English. Unfortunately, to date, at least, the limited number of research studies for this population seem to have concentrated on academic achievement alone, automatically and perhaps without question, assuming this to be the 'gold standard'. Also, these studies often do not make clear reference to the level of the learning disabilities of their participants. Therefore, readers cannot ensure that those with global and complex learning disabilities were represented and generalising the foregoing findings to these cohorts can be in many cases – a risky enterprise.

We urge practitioners in the field of SLD, CLD and PMLD to (i) be critical consumers of research, (ii) use research to improve their practice, (iii) evaluate interventions and strategies which appear to work in practice and (iv) disseminate their findings. We very much support the view that research in schools

> should not be seen as an individual activity but one that is best carried out as a collaborative venture.
>
> (Porter, 2015, p407)

And finally, a plea for education and educational research to continue beyond the years of formal schooling. At present, to our knowledge in most parts of the world, education seems to fade away when people with learning disabilities leave school, but education in different forms and shapes should go far beyond the school years and, ideally, last for the entirety of the life of this population.

> People with learning disabilities find learning difficult but that does not mean that they should not do it! In fact, it is because they find it difficult that more should be provided and for longer.
>
> (Lacey, 2000, p100)

References

Abell, S., Ashmore, J., Beart, S., et al. (2007). Including Everyone in Research: The Burton Street Research Group. *British Journal of Learning Disabilities*, 35(2): 121–124.

Bölte, S. (2014). The Power of Words: Is Qualitative Research as Important as Quantitative Research in the Study of Autism? *Autism*, 18(2): 67–68.

Butt, I.H. and Shams, J.A. (2013). Master in Education Student Attitudes Towards Research: A Comparison Between Two Public Sector Universities in Punjab. *South Asian Studies*, 28(1): 97–105.

Davis, P. and Florian, L. (2004). *Teaching Strategies and Approaches for Pupils with Special Educational Needs: A Scoping Study*. Nottingham: DfES Publications.

de Haas, C., Grace, J., Hope, J., et al. (2022). Doing Research Inclusively: Understanding What It Means to Do Research with and Alongside People with Profound Intellectual Disabilities. *Social Sciences*, 11(4): 159.

Denscombe, M. (2017). *The Good Research Guide: For Small-Scale Social Research Projects*. London: McGraw-Hill Education.

de Paor, C. and Murphy, T.R. (2018). Teachers' Views on Research as a Model of CPD: Implications for Policy. *European Journal of Teacher Education*, 41(2): 169–186.

DfE. (2022). *The Reading Framework. Teaching the Foundations of Literacy*. Available from: https://assets.publishing.service.gov.uk/government/uploads/system/uploads/attachment_data/file/1050849/Reading_framework_Teaching_the_foundations_of_literacy_-_July_2021_Jan_22_update.pdf. Accessed 1 March 2022.

Equals. (2020). *The Equals Multi-Tiered Curriculum Model*. Newcastle: Equals. Available from: www.equals.co.uk.

Erickson, K.A. and Koppenhaver, D.A. (2020). *Comprehensive Literacy for All*. Baltimore: Paul Brookes Publishing.

Florian, L. and Black-Hawkins, K. (2013). Exploring Inclusive Pedagogy. *British Educational Research Journal*, 37(5): 813–828.

García-Carmona, M., Marín, M.D. and Aguayo, R. (2019). Burnout Syndrome in Secondary School Teachers: A Systematic Review and Meta-Analysis. *Social Psychology of Education: An International Journal*, 22(1): 189–208.

Grace, J. (2019). *Multiple Multisensory Rooms: Myth Busting the Magic*. London: Routledge.

Guldberg, K. (2020). *Developing Excellence in Autism Practice: Making a Difference in Education*. London: Routledge.

Imray, P. and Colley, A. (2017). *Inclusion is Dead: Long Live Inclusion*. London: Routledge.

Imray, P., Kossyvaki, L. and Sissons, M. (2023). Evidence-Based Practice: The Use and Abuse of Research. *Support for Learning*, 38(1): 51–66.

Imray, P. and Sissons, M. (2021). A Different View of Literacy. *Support for Learning*, 36(2): 222–237.

Kossyvaki, L. (2019). Why is Research Important? Reflections for Professionals and Parents. *PMLD Link*, 31(2): 19–20.

Lacey, P. (2000). Don't Forget Education!. *Journal of Learning Disabilities*, 4(2): 99–103.

Lacey, P., Layton, L., Miller, C., et al. (2007). What is Literacy for Students With Severe Learning Difficulties? Exploring Conventional and Inclusive Literacy. *Journal of Research in Special Educational Needs*, 7(3): 149–160.

Lewis, A. and Norwich, B. (eds.). (2005). *Special Teaching for Special Children?* Maidenhead: Open University Press.

Marsden, E. and Kasprowicz, R. (2017). Foreign Language Educators' Exposure to Research: Reported Experiences, Exposure Via Citations, and a Proposal for Action. *The Modern Language Journal*, 101(4): 613–642.

Mietola, R., Miettinen, S. and Vehmas, S. (2017). Voiceless Subjects? Research Ethics and Persons With Profound Intellectual Disabilities. *International Journal of Social Research Methodology*, 20(3): 263–274.

Mills, J. and Earl Rinehart, K. (2019). Teachers as Researchers. *Teachers and Curriculum*, 19(1): 1–5.

Mitchel, D. and Sutherland, D. (2020). *What Really Works in Special and Inclusive Education: Using Evidence Based Teaching Strategies*. London: Routledge.

Moseley, S. (2023). *Teaching Reading to All Learners Including Those with Complex Needs*. Abingdon: Routledge.

Murphy, K. and Cameron, L. (2008). The Effectiveness of Talking Mats With People With Intellectual Disability. *British Journal of Learning Disabilities*, 36: 232–41.

Ndaji, F. and Tymms, P. (2009). *The P Scales: Assessing the Progress of Children With Special Educational Needs.* London: Wiley-Blackwell.

No Child Left Behind Act. (2001). Pub. L. No. 107–110, 115 Stat. 1425 (2002).

Norwich, B. (2013). *Addressing Tensions and Dilemmas in Inclusive Education.* London: Routledge.

Norwich, B. and Lewis, A. (2005). How Specialized is Teaching Pupils With Disabilities and Difficulties? In A. Lewis and B. Norwich (eds.) *Special Teaching for Special Children?* Maidenhead: Open University Press.

NSTTAC. (2013). National Secondary Transition Technical Assistance Center. *Evidence-Based Practices and Predictors in Secondary Transition: What We Know and What We Still Need to Know.* Charlotte, NC: NSTTAC.

Pinney, A. (2017). *Understanding the Needs of Disabled Children With Complex Needs or Life-Limiting Conditions.* London: Council for Disabled Children/True Colours Trust.

Porter, J. (2005). Severe Learning Difficulties. In A. Lewis and B. Norwich (eds.) *Special Teaching for Special Children? Pedagogies for Inclusion* (pp. 53–66). Maidenhead: Open University Press.

Porter, J. (2015). Engaging with Research. In P. Lacey, R. Ashdown, P. Jones, et al. (eds.) *The Routledge Companion to Severe, Profound and Multiple Learning Difficulties* (pp. 399–410). London: Routledge.

Porter, J. and Lacey, P. (2005). *Researching Learning Difficulties: A Guide for Practitioners.* London: Sage.

Pring, T. (2004). Ask a Silly Question: Two Decades of Troublesome Trials. *International Journal of Language and Communication Disorders*, 39(3): 285–302.

Rendoth, T., Duncan, J. and Fogett, J. (2022). Inclusive Curricula for Students With Severe Intellectual Disabilities or Profound and Multiple Learning Difficulties: A Scoping Review. *Journal of Research in Special Educational Needs*, 22(1): 76–88.

Rochford, D. (2016). *The Rochford Review: Final Report. Review of Assessment for Pupils Working Below the Standard of National Curriculum Tests.* Standards and Testing Agency. Available from: www.gov.uk/government/publications/rochford-review-final-report.

Rose, J. (2006). *Independent Review of the Teaching of Early Reading.* Nottingham: DfES.

Rushton, R., Kossyvaki, L. and Terlektsi, E. (2023). Musical Preferences of People With Profound Intellectual and Multiple Disabilities: A Participatory Design With Proxies. *British Journal of Learning Disabilities*, 1–10.

Sato, M. and Loewen, S. (2019). Do Teachers Care About Research? The Research – Pedagogy Dialogue. *ELT Journal*, 73(1): 1–10.

Shkedi, A. (1998). Teachers' Attitudes Towards Research: A Challenge for Qualitative Researchers. *International Journal of Qualitative Studies in Education*, 11(4): 559–577.

Siraj-Blatchford, I., Shepherd, D.L., Melhuish, E., et al. (2011). *Effective Primary Pedagogical Strategies in English and Mathematics in Key Stage 2: A Study of Year 5 Classroom Practice Drawn From EPPSE 3016 Longitudinal Study* (DfE – RB129). London: Department for Education.

Sissons, M. (2020). *MAPP (Mapping and Assessing Personal Progress): Semi-Formal Model.* Newcastle: Equals.

Standards and Testing Agency. (2020). *National Curriculum Assessments: Pre-key Stage 2: Pupils Working Below the National Curriculum Assessment Standard. Teacher Assessment Framework.* Available from: https://assets.publishing.service.gov.uk/

government/uploads/system/uploads/attachment_data/file/903553/2021_Pre-key_stage_2_-_pupils_working_below_the_national_curriculum_assessment_stand-ard_PDFA.pdf. Accessed 24 August 2022.

Terlektsi, E., Wootten, A., Douglas, G., et al. (2019). *A Rapid Evidence Assessment of the Effectiveness of Educational Interventions to Support Children and Young People With Hearing Impairment* (GSR Report Number 40/2019). Cardiff: Welsh Government.

Ware, J. (2014). Curriculum Considerations in Meeting the Educational Needs of Learners With Severe Intellectual Disabilities. In L. Florian (ed.) *The Sage Handbook of Special Education* (pp. 491–503). 2nd edition. London: Sage.

Wellington, J. (2015). *Educational Research: Contemporary Issues and Practical Approaches*. London: Bloomsbury Publishing.

4 A pedagogical argument for adopting a capabilities approach in the teaching of those with PMLD, CLD and SLD

Mike Sissons, Julia Barnes, Peter Imray and Andrew Colley

In England, as in many countries around the world, there has been a notable absence of any overarching theory relating to how educators might tackle the education of children, young people and adults with profound, complex and severe learning disabilities. This vacuum has been filled mainly by an inclusionist philosophy that has suffered by (i) being uncertain of its defining terms (Norwich, 2013 for example), (ii) assuming moral superiority to a point of rejecting alternative views and closing down debate[1] and (iii) being largely unsuccessful in practice, even after over 20 years of endeavour.[2] Further, espousing the rhetoric of inclusion has directly led to the teaching of a national or common-core-standards curriculum model to all learners in all educational settings; that is, a dominant and dominating view that a common curriculum is best for all. We do not wish to state that nothing of worth has come out of the inclusionist agenda, but the natural wish for none to be excluded from the process of education has, in most countries, been interpreted as *all* must be included in the *same* education, without consideration as to whether this is appropriate for the individual or not. In England, as in the UK as a whole, schools working with learners of all ages with PMLD, CLD and SLD are doing their best for these learners, despite the system, not because of it.

The long established Quality of Life (QoL) arguments, particularly in the work of Lyons and Cassebohm (2011, 2012), are obviously closely related to a necessary concentration on well-being, happiness and lives lived well. Johnson and Walmsley (2010), Colley (2013), and Colley and Tilbury (2022) all offer important contributions to the debate, but all concentrate primarily on the education and lives of those with PMLD, whereas we are seeking to extend the discussion so that we can place all those with CLD and SLD, as well as those with PMLD, truly at the heart of the curriculum.

In order to do this, we wish to guide educationalists towards the adoption of a Capabilities Approach (CA). Norwich (2014) feels that a CA may have the potential to replace the language of needs and rights with that of capabilities which enables individual choice. On a similar note, Terzi (2010) suggests

DOI: 10.4324/9781003369134-6

that placing the well-being of learners with disabilities and special educational needs at the centre of their education as well as expanding their capabilities will enable a shift from academic educational goals to social, relational and participatory elements. To this direction, Robeyns (2006) proposes that, as a Capabilities Approach is multi-dimensional, it enables the intrinsic and non-academic roles that education plays for learners of all abilities, and we explore these points in more detail towards the end of the chapter. It may indeed be the case that there is ample justification for Education as a whole, irrespective of ability or disability, to adopt a CA, but that comes outside of the remit of this book!

The concept of Capabilities derives originally from the works of Amartya Sen (1985,2005), since adapted from the original economic model to a broader political philosophy by Martha Nussbaum (1999, 2007, 2011) as the basis of a theory of political justice. Nussbaum has addressed the issue of physical and learning disability, but the works of Kittay (2003) and particularly Khader (2008) specifically highlight issues of personhood in posing the question of what it is that makes a human human and bring to the fore the issues of dependence and independence, flourishing and choice. Such considerations have led to the notion of Relational Agency (Khader, 2008).

Relational agency

Kittay, whose daughter has severe physical and intellectual disabilities, argues that our recognition of the value of the lives of other persons flows from our ability to understand them also as 'some mother's child' (Kittay, 1999, p32).

> This means that recognizing the value of persons is related to recognizing their constitution through a care relationships (sic) and their participation in a web of affective ties. Since they proceed from intuitive conceptions of what we want to protect life for, these conceptions of the person are justified differently from Nussbaum and Sen's. The conception of the person as an agent-in-relation does not arise out of a particular conception of a species norm. Instead, it posits agency and relationship as general desiderata that acquire different sorts of meanings in different types of flourishing lives.
>
> (Khader, 2008, pp106–107)

The emphasis here is that dependence is, to a degree, the norm for us all, and in childhood, in sickness, and perhaps, in old age, it is particularly obvious. For some, especially those with life-long, global learning disabilities (and their families) permanent dependence and independence can encompass perplexing and seemingly contradictory boundaries, but adopting a CA can simplify the dilemmas thrown up by concentrating specifically on issues of flourishing, freedom, choice and agency.

Relational agency enabling flourishing, freedom and choice and agency

These four concepts are so central to a CA that it will be good to get some settled idea as to what each of them means. A common and workable definition of flourishing is 'the ability to be and to do', and this is fine as far as it goes. However, as many things that people can be or do are either trivial or undesirable, we need to fill out the idea of flourishing with a little more detail. One way to do this is to see how it is used in one of the most developed versions of a CA – that of Martha Nussbaum. In Nussbaum's CA, the concept of flourishing is intimately bound up with the core idea of 'central capabilities', of which she lists ten in all; namely, life, bodily health, bodily integrity, senses, imagination and thought, emotions, practical reason, affiliation (living in harmony with other species), play and control over one's environment (Nussbaum, 2007, 2011). These ten central capabilities give us a broad outline of the considerations necessary to ensure that all human beings are able to lead lives worthy of human dignity (Nussbaum, 2011). They are not derived from a concept of human nature but represent a set of values formed from a

> conception of the human being as in need of a rich plurality of life activities, to be shaped by both practical reason and affiliation.
>
> (Nussbaum, 2003, p124)

In other words, the central capabilities are not concerned with what people *happen to be like* but with what they might *aim to become*, and as such, are fundamentally ethical and normative; they answer the question 'what can this person be or do?' by setting out those activities that 'seem definitive of a life that is truly human' (Nussbaum, 1999, p39). Following Nussbaum, to flourish means to develop the capacity to realise all ten capabilities at least up to a minimal level or 'threshold' (which is left unspecified), and to do this is to live a life worthy of human dignity.

This account of what it means to flourish gives us the following way into understanding the concepts of freedom and choice. Flourishing entails two things: in the first place, an individual must have the requisite *abilities* to realise a capability (Nussbaum calls these 'internal capabilities') and secondly, they must also have the *opportunity* to so act (Nussbaum calls these 'combined capabilities'). It is of limited use, for example, teaching someone how to prepare a snack (an internal capability) if they then have no access to any kitchen equipment, ingredients, the ability to decide what to eat, to work with other people and so on (combined capabilities). So, within a CA, *freedom* means more than just 'negative freedom' – it is not enough to develop an individual's abilities and to grant them the *right* to practice abilities; real freedom also demands provision of access to means (resources, support, opportunities, etc.) and the removal of barriers in order to realise capabilities. This concept of freedom applies across the board to all ten capabilities. Furthermore, freedom operates between capabilities; that is, it must be left to each person to *choose* whether or not they wish to make use of the internal and combined capabilities which are open to them (Nussbaum refers to realising a capability as a 'functioning') so that, if we ask whether or not it is permissible to pressure an individual into realising a capability, the answer must be 'no'. In this respect, Nussbaum, echoing Aristotle, argues that a satisfaction achieved without choice is unworthy of the dignity of human beings (Nussbaum, 2011, p125) and, quoting Sen, she writes

> capability is thus a kind of freedom: the substantive freedom to achieve alternative functioning combinations.
>
> (Nussbaum, 2011, p20)

These considerations give us a way of making concrete the otherwise vague notions of flourishing, freedom and choice and puts some flesh on the ideas, so that:

- *Flourishing* is the ability to achieve ends which are worthy of a life which is fully human.
- *Freedom* is the ability to practise internal and combined capabilities.
- *Choice* is the ability to decide to exercise or not to exercise any given capability.

Agency

An agent is someone who performs an action, as opposed to having an action happen to them or in them or done for them (Blackburn, 2008), and as such, the concept of agency is closely linked to the concepts of choice and freedom.

Khader (2008) makes use of the concept of agency in responding to what she sees as a serious problem for individuals with PMLD or SLD in Nussbaum's 'central capabilities'. Recall that, for Nussbaum, a minimum level of functioning must be possible *in all ten* capabilities to satisfy the demand for a truly human life such that, if even *one* of the capabilities is closed off to a person, then their life is, to that extent, less than fully human (Nussbaum, 2000). Now Khader sees a difficulty arising from the central capability of 'Practical Reason' which Nussbaum defines as

> being able to form a conception of the good and to engage in **critical reflection** about the planning of one's life.
>
> (Nussbaum, 2011, p34, our emphasis)

This demands a level of cognitive ability which lies beyond the capabilities of many – perhaps all – individuals with SLD – and certainly all with

PMLD – even if the threshold of practical reason is set very low indeed. The issue is made even more urgent by the fact that Nussbaum insists that practical reason organises and pervades all the other capabilities, since it is nothing less than the capacity to consider alternative capabilities and to decide between functionings (Nussbaum, 2011). Khader asks, if this is so, how can Nussbaum escape the conclusion that the lives of people with SLD and PMLD are, to some degree, less than 'truly human'?

Khader's solution is to propose a less stringent concept of reason than that which Nussbaum proposes. Drawing on Kittay (2003), she offers the concept of agency as the ability to shape one's world and the world of others; to have one's way of flourishing be recognisable by others as an 'imaginative possibility'. So, the agency we desire for all persons is tied to the potential for affecting one's world and being in relation with other persons. Understanding agency in this context makes room for the agency of those who cannot fully exercise practical reason through critical reflection (Khader, 2008).

This latter sentence retains a place for practical reason as a central capability for those who are able exercise it, but to be fully human it is not necessary to be an entirely autonomous, independent and self-directed individual.

Such a notion of independent flourishing is unavailable to many people with SLD and PMLD and, in acknowledging the dependency of people with SLD and PMLD on others (a way of being for everyone in different phases of their lives), Khader proposes that we conceive of agency as sustained by relationality.

> The capability to be with others who recognise us as human ranks along-side agency among the most important capabilities. In the case of persons who live in lifelong dependency relationships because of severe cognitive disabilities, ranking relationality with agency indicates that relationality is necessary for the sustenance of agency (and vice-versa).
>
> (Khader, 2008, p108)

Whether we follow Nussbaum in conceptualising agency in terms of the individual's exercise of practical reason or locate it, instead, as Khader does, within the relationships which exist between individuals, it is clear that people with SLD and PMLD will be able to secure political rights only through some form of guardianship. Critical reflection and action on such matters will necessarily be carried out by others on their behalf. But the emphasis changes. In Nussbaum's CA, guardians act as surrogates, and real agency is lost. By contrast, in Khader's CA, practical reason is not where the sense of agency is located. It is located in the relationships between individuals and at this level agency is preserved.

It is easy to envisage that the notion of Relational Agency applies merely to an individual, or perhaps, a small number of individuals who know the person with PMLD or SLD really well. Such a concept is extraordinarily well conceived in Crombie et al.'s (2014) reflection on why Pear Tree School (a specialist PMLD/SLD school in Lancashire, England) was granted an 'outstanding'

Ofsted rating. In answering this, Richard Crombie, Lesley Sullivan, Kate Walker and Rebecca Warnock, all either directly teaching at or profession-ally associated with the school, identified that the unconscious and largely unnoticed professional practice of the staff team and their ability to attune to and empathise with learners led them to anticipate the needs and intentions of their learners. Attunement may therefore be a key to Relational Agency with the communication partner 'reading' a person's emotional, psychological, cognitive and physiological signals and sensitively responding in ways that are meaningful and convey understanding (Calveley, 2018). Watson and Corke (2015) highlight that attunement is a two-way process involving both partners 'letting go' and trusting each other, and their approach to the issue of Play can be seen to be reflective of the huge influence Intensive Interaction has had upon curriculum development for those with profound, complex and severe learning disabilities. Based on human infant-caregiver interactions, Intensive Interaction (Nind and Hewett, 1988; Hewett and Nind, 1998) is an approach to teaching the fundamentals of communication and social interaction to peo-ple who are at an early stage of communicative development and is explored more fully in Chapter 6. The principles of Intensive Interaction create agency by placing the person with learning disabilities at the centre of the learning process through acknowledging the importance of phatic or declarative com-munications (that is, communications that have a social function), rather than merely concentrating on imperative communications relating to needs and wants (Hewett, 2012). This can, however, only come about over time with a deep understanding of the nature of the learning difficulties experienced, *com-bined with* a deep understanding of the individual experiencing those learning difficulties (Colley and Tilbury, 2022). Owning one without the other is only half of the relationship.

Further, we might also take a wider political view of what adopting a CA can achieve, in moving beyond the concept of an individual relationship to that of the state's relationship with individuals. Newark and Rees (2022) mark out England's education system's slippage into becoming the state's primary means of promoting a meritocracy that naturally (and coldly) promotes the educationally successful, without thought or consideration for those who (by chance) do not succeed. This is not a matter of inclusion or exclusion; it is, frighteningly, a matter of almost complete unconcern.

> [Accepting] the limits of merit is an important correction to the arro-gance of contemporary entitlement and an opportunity to reassert the importance of luck, or grace, in our political thinking. The more we are able to accept our achievements are largely out of our control, the easier it becomes to understand that our failures, and those of others, are too. And that in turn should increase our humility and the respect with which we treat our fellow citizens. Ultimately, as the writer David Roberts put

it: 'Building a more compassionate society means reminding ourselves of luck, and of the gratitude and obligations it entails'.

(Freedman, 2022, cited in Newark and Rees, 2022)

This building of a compassionate society might therefore begin with the state acting upon its obligation of Relational Agency to enable those with PMLD, CLD and SLD to live the lives that *they* want to live, not the lives that the state allocates to them.

Applying these notions to those with profound, complex and severe learning disabilities

The central arguments of this book congregate around the idea that those with profound, complex and severe learning disabilities will have enormous difficulty exercising the capacity (or capability) of flourishing, freedom, choice and agency within a conventional curriculum designed for neuro-typical learners – even one that has been heavily differentiated. Those who flourish within a national or common-core-standards curriculum will do so whilst receiving their education *as well as* after it has finished. It is, indeed, highly likely that such an education will merely constitute a stepping stone towards greater flourishing, freedom and choice. This will not, however, be the experience of all – and especially not the lived experience of those who may well continue to need education well beyond the time allocated to the neuro-typical population. The time scales worked on (at least in first world economies) move seamlessly through a graduated series of preparations, with early years (2 to 5) and a concentration on developing skills through play preparing for the concentrations on literacy and numeracy at primary (6 to 10), which, in turn, prepares for in depth subject study at secondary (11 to 16) and then to a greater degree of specialisation (17 to 18). The individual should, providing they achieve the requisite academic success, be prepared for university (19 to 21) and an even higher degree of concentrated study. Whether they move on to university or not, the education received should (in theory at least) prepare children for adulthood and some prospect of making one's own way in the world. So, do these time scales and concentrations work for everyone in our increasingly inclusion conscious countries? Unfortunately, no.

What we have yet to tackle is that flourishing, freedom, choice and agency may only apply to those who are successful in the education system that is offered to all, in part because the state has failed to consider that different learners need different curricula, different timescales and different support; otherwise, the issue of education for some might become a bit pointless. That is, we have been so concerned with the issue of education for all that we have forgotten to ask the question *'education for what?'*.

Putting the individual at the centre

The huge strengths of adopting a CA for exploring and reframing fulfilling lives for those with profound, complex and severe learning disabilities are that it is pragmatic and normative, focussing as it does on actual functioning in terms of being and doing (Nussbaum, 2007) as well as on realistic opportunity. It calls for a society in which all persons are treated as worthy of regard and in which each has been put in a position to live human lives of dignity (Nussbaum, 2000). Placing the well-being of students with disabilities and special educational needs at the centre of the educational process in this way suggests a shift from narrowly defined educational outcomes in terms of academic achievement only to broader aims, including social, relational, participatory and communicative elements (Terzi, 2010) with an emphasis on exploring the 'voice' of the learner and finding innovative ways of listening and understanding (Nussbaum, 2007).

Such innovation is at the heart of all of the Equals Curricula (Equals, 2020 for example), in that each places the learner at the very centre of the educational process. The beginning of this process is engagement.

> Sustainable learning can occur only when there is meaningful engagement. The process of engagement is a journey which connects a child and their environment (including people, ideas, materials and concepts) to enable learning and achievement.
>
> (Carpenter et al., 2015, p22)

Carpenter et al. go on to point out that neuro-typical, conventionally developing learners can and do self-generate motivation on the basis that they have the ability to understand the nature of education and its demand that learning goals are fulfilled. This, however, becomes hugely problematic for those with profound, complex and severe learning disabilities when we know that abstraction, compartmentalised learning and generalisation are so very, very problematic (Lacey, 2010; Imray and Colley, 2017). Further, Lacey's (2009) acute observation that, whilst we must work with the learner where they are, we must not leave them there, reminds us that engagement is only half of the conundrum; for, if learning is truly to take place, stretch and challenge must also be tackled.

Moljord (2021) suggests that the main purposes for learning for young people with severe learning disabilities can be encapsulated in the four concepts of becoming, citizenship, later life and vocation. She goes on to suggest that the most important educational experiences for these young people are to live their own lives and to encounter the world.

> [A] school for all must aim for the equal distribution of capabilities – capability equality – providing all learners with the best possible educational experiences, enabling them with the competence to live the lives

they have reason to value and expanding their opportunities for the various life paths they might take. Thus, enhancing schools' capabilities to meet learners with ID (intellectual disability) correlates with a basic educational responsibility: enhancing pupils' capabilities to encounter the world.

(Moljord, 2021, p1151)

Equally importantly, we need to go beyond the concept of education having a pre-defined time limit which might get add-ons in the further education experienced at post-18 level. For some – especially those whose profound and complex learning disabilities who may confound the prospect of employment – education beyond the age of 18 must not be considered as *further* education, since the time scales for learning will be totally different; and the more profound, complex and severe the learning disabilities are, the more different the time scales will be. In England, at least – and we suspect that we are not the only nation to experience this – the notion of work and of finding meaning and self-fulfilment in employment is not open to any with SLD, except for an extremely small percentage of the most academically able. This was not always so but has become this way since the 1980's Thatcher governments and seems now, reprehensibly, to be an accepted situation. For these learners, neither specialist nor mainstream schools are able to plan for the expectation of guaranteed, long-term employment, precisely because there is a need for a continuation of education and/or Relational Agency beyond school, which no-one (state or employers) seems willing or able to fund. Once again, we discover that the notion of different not differentiated is not merely rhetoric. These are real issues that have to be addressed.

Conclusion

In advocating the constant need for professional reflection, Viv Hinchcliffe issues a warning that is salutary for those who decide upon education policy.

For [those] who have not spent time in classrooms with children with SLD and PMLD, it may be difficult to appreciate how unpredictable teaching is and how impenetrable and unfathomable working with these children can be.

(Hinchcliffe, 2022, p505)

That is, teaching children, young people and adults with these levels of learning disabilities requires specialist understanding of what it is to have PMLD and/or CLD and/or SLD. This book argues that this will require a particular relationship with both the individual learner and the specialist curriculum, which can enable flourishing, freedom, choice and agency within the concept of a clear understanding of an individual learner's right to exercise or not exercise a specific capability. We – those who advocate – those who can directly affect Relational Agency – have to be very clear that our main purpose is to find out what does and what does not exercise the person. We therefore need to be constantly striving to understand what the individual wants to do and wants to be, and we should be hell-bent on enabling them to be the very best at being and doing what *they* want to be and do.

The overwhelming advantages of adopting a Capabilities Approach for exploring and reframing fulfilling lives for those with PMLD, CLD and SLD is that it guides the institution of education away from a model that is seen to be an end in itself. The didactic, teacher- and systems-driven model that leads to the accumulation of qualifications which then leads to employment opportunities (or lack of them!) *may be* appropriate for neuro-typical, conventionally developing learners but cannot be seen to be relevant to those who are unable to access the literacy and numeracy fluency necessary for the gaining of these qualifications. For many of those with PMLD, CLD and SLD, education and Relational Agency with both individuals and the state may need to be a lifelong option.

Notes

1 Robinson and Goodey (2018), specifically citing severe and profound learning disability, suggest that *'resistance to inclusion is not rational, and that it amounts to a thought disorder, in the psychiatric sense'* (p426).
2 There are, for example, 152 separately functioning education authorities in England; not one claims to be fully inclusive.

References

Blackburn, S. (2008). *The Oxford Dictionary of Philosophy*. Oxford University Press.
Calveley, J. (2018). Intensive Interaction and Complex Health Needs: Tuning-in, the Cornerstone of Effective Practice. *PMLD Link*, 30(2): 38–41.
Carpenter, B., Egerton, J., Cockbill, B., et al. (2015). *Engaging Learners With Complex Learning Difficulties and Disabilities*. Abingdon: Routledge.
Colley, A. (2013). *Personalised Learning for Young People With Profound and Multiple Learning Difficulties*. London: Jessica Kingsley.
Colley, A. and Tilbury, J. (2022). *Enhancing Wellbeing and Independence for Young People with Profound and Multiple Learning Difficulties: Lives Lived Well*. 1st edition. Abingdon, Oxon: Routledge.
Crombie, R., Sullivan, L., Walker, A., et al. (2014). Unconscious and Unnoticed Professional Practice Within an Outstanding Special School for Children and Young People with Complex Learning Disabilities. *Support for Learning*, 29(1): 9–23.
Equals. (2020). *The Equals Multi-Tiered Curriculum Approach*. Newcastle: Equals.
Freedman, S. (2022). *The Big Idea: Do We Want to Live in a Meritocracy?* Available from: www.theguardian.com/books/2022/jan/10/do-we-want-to-live-in-a-meritocracy
Hewett, D. (2012). Blind Frogs, the Nature of Human Communication and Intensive Interaction. In D. Hewett (ed.) *Intensive Interaction: Theoretical Perspectives*. London: Sage.
Hewett, D. and Nind, M. (1998). Introduction: Recent Developments in Interactive Approaches. In D. Hewett and M. Nind (eds.) *Interaction in Action: Reflections on the Use of Intensive Interaction* (pp. 1–23). London: David Fulton Publishers.
Hinchcliffe, V. (2022). Developing Thinking Teachers: Reflective Practice in Schools for Children with Severe Learning Disabilities and Profound and Multiple Learning Disabilities. *Support for Learning*, 37(4): 502–519.

Imray, P. and Colley, A. (2017). *Inclusion is Dead: Long Live Inclusion*. Oxon: Routledge.

Johnson, K. and Walmsley, J. (2010). *People with Intellectual Disabilities: Towards a Good Life?* Bristol: The Policy Press.

Khader, S. (2008). Cognitive Disability, Capabilities, and Justice. *Essays in Philosophy*, 9(1): 93–112.

Kittay, E.F. (1999). *Love's Labor: Essays on Women, Equality, and Dependency*. New York: Routledge.

Kittay, E.F. (2003). When Caring is Justice and Justice is Caring: Justice and Mental Retardation. In E.F. Kittay and E.K. Feder (eds.) *The Subject of Care* (pp. 257–277). New York: Rowman and Littlefield.

Lacey, P. (2009). Developing the Thinking of Learners with PMLD. *PMLD Link*, 21(63): 15–19.

Lacey, P. (2010). Smart and Scruffy Targets. *The SLD Experience*, 57(1): 16–21.

Lyons, G. and Cassebohm, M. (2011). Curriculum Development for Students With Profound Intellectual and Multiple Disabilities: How About a Quality of Life Focus? *Special Education Perspectives*, 12(2): 24–39.

Lyons, G. and Cassebohm, M. (2012). The Education of Australian School Students With the Most Severe Intellectual Disabilities: Where Have We Been and Where Could We Go? A Discussion Primer. *Australasian Journal of Special Education*, 36(1): 79–95.

Moljord, G. (2021). Aiming for (What) Capabilities? An Inquiry into School Policy for Pupils With Intellectual Disabilities. *Scandinavian Journal of Educational Research*, 65(6): 1141–1155.

Newark, B. and Rees, T. (2022). *A Good Life: Towards Greater Dignity for People With Learning Disability*. Confederation of School Trusts. Available from: https://icm. cstuk.org.uk/assets/CST-Publications/CST_AmbitionInstitute_Whitepaper_AGoodLife.pdf.

Nind, M. and Hewett, D. (1988). Interaction as Curriculum. *British Journal of Special Education*, 15(2): 55–57.

Norwich, B. (2013). *Addressing Tensions and Dilemmas in Inclusive Education.* London: Routledge.

Norwich, B. (2014). How Does the Capability Approach Address Current Issues in Special Educational Needs, Disability and Inclusive Education Field? *Journal of Research in Special Educational Needs*, 14(1): 16–21.

Nussbaum, M. (1999). *Sex and Social Justice*. New York: Oxford University Press.

Nussbaum, M. (2000). Women's Capabilities and Social Justice. *Journal of Human Development*, 1(2): 219–247.

Nussbaum, M.C. (2003). The Future of Feminist Liberalism. In E.F. Kittay and E.K. Feder (eds.) *The Subject of Care. Feminist Perspectives on Dependency*. New York: Rowman and Littlefield.

Nussbaum, M.C. (2007). *Frontiers of Justice – Disability, Nationality, Species Membership*. Cambridge, MA: Harvard University Press.

Nussbaum, M.C. (2011). *Creating Capabilities: The Human Development Approach*. Cambridge, MA: Belknap Press.

Robeyns, I. (2006). Three Models of Education: Rights, Capabilities and Human Capital. *Theory and Research in Education*, 4(1): 69–84.

Robinson, D. and Goodey, C. (2018). Agency in the Darkness: 'Fear of the Unknown', Learning Disability and Teacher Education for Inclusion. *International Journal of Inclusive Education*, 22(4): 426–440.

Sen, A. (1985). *Commodities and Capabilities*. New Delhi, India: Oxford University Press.

Sen, A. (2005). Human Rights and Capabilities. *Journal of Human Development*, 6(2): 151–166.

Terzi, L. (ed.). (2010). Afterword: Difference, Equality and the Ideal of Inclusion in Education. In *Special Educational Needs: A New Look* (pp. 143–164). 2nd edition. London: Continuum.

Watson, D. and Corke, M. (2015). Supporting Playfulness in Learners with SLD/ PMLD. In P. Lacey, R. Ashdown, P. Jones, et al. (eds.) *The Routledge Companion to Severe, Profound and Multiple Learning Difficulties* (pp. 365–374). Oxon: Routledge.

Part 2

Practice

The book is divided into two parts. The first part establishes a theoretical framework and the second part exemplifies this framework in practice.

In Chapters 5 to 12, we hear the voices of a number of highly experienced practitioners who describe the ways in which they have developed and implemented the principles described in the opening chapters within their own settings. All of these chapters are rooted in practice and, taken together, present us with a series of case studies which offer models of ways in which change can be – and is being – effected. They describe a different rethinking of educational provision for learners of all ages with profound, complex and severe learning disabilities, consonant with the ideas outlined in Part 1. In so doing, they provide evidence of the impact of their various innovations on learners, parents, carers and staff.

DOI: 10.4324/9781003369134-7

5 Learning to be, learning to do

Informal, empowering and with infinite possibilities

Gillian Carver and Timmy Holdsworth

As of January 2023, St Ann's School has a roll of 110 students, aged 11 to 19 years, all of whom live in the London Borough of Ealing or have recently moved to or been rehoused in neighbouring boroughs.

Ealing is London's fourth most populous borough with approximately 350,000 residents, 26% of whom are aged under 19 years, a higher proportion than the England and London average. Ealing is also the third most ethnically diverse local population in the UK with 85% of pupils being of minority ethnic origin, compared to 33% nationally. Over 170 languages are spoken across the borough, and in schools, the proportion of children and young people who speak English as an additional language is around 60%, compared to the national average of 19% (Ealing JSNA, 2021).

The Ealing SEND Local Offer lists St Ann's as being a special secondary school for children and young people with severe to profound and multiple learning disabilities and autism. As with all of England's special schools, the complexity of student need has significantly increased during the last two decades (Pinney, 2017), and whilst the school designation shorthand might be SLD/PMLD/ASD, the reality is that students with complex learning disabilities (CLD) often functioning at very early developmental levels, have become the fastest growing cohort and are those to whom we attribute credit for demonstrating the need to develop a very different Informal Curriculum.

The early beginnings: moving towards an Informal Curriculum

During the academic year 2014/2015 and within a short period of time, we had a number of students in different classes who all fell within the defining learning characteristics of CLD noted in Chapter 1, who were all routinely in crisis and presenting with very challenging behaviour; that is, violent incidents were a daily event. They were at real risk of exclusion, but given St Ann's strong ethos of inclusivity and staff expertise, we challenged ourselves to come up with something different and started by analysing our current practice.

All of these students routinely in crisis had at least 1:1 experienced staffing in their designated mixed SLD/ASD class group and were following a heavily differentiated National Curriculum timetable. Positive handling techniques

DOI: 10.4324/9781003369134-8

were well-established throughout the school, and staff were skilled in de-escalation, including taking students out of class for movement breaks to help reduce rising levels of anxiety. However, over time, most of these students were spending more time out of class than in class, and in spite of everyone's best efforts, they were routinely experiencing crisis episodes of extreme, challenging behaviour. This necessitated senior staff responding to the ensuing alarms and generating more anxiety and upset for the individual student, their peers and all the staff involved.

These reactive situations being played out for different students in different locations around the school were clearly not sustainable. Learning opportunities for these students were seriously compromised, and such unpredictable interruptions to classroom routines significantly impacted on the learning and wellbeing of their peers. In addition, staff felt deskilled and worried that they were failing not only the individual student in crisis but all of the students in each of the affected classes.

Part of the solution was evident – that we needed to be much better at listening to behaviours (Imray and Hewett, 2015). That is, each of these students in their individual ways were consistently trying to communicate to us that they could not cope with the demands of the classroom and that they needed a very different curriculum, delivered in a very different way, if their well-being and consequent access to learning was going to be improved. Unfortunately, because these communications were delivered to us in highly negative ways (staff perception) but highly effective ways (student perception) we concentrated too much on the behaviour, over and above the communication. The listening therefore became key, but crucially, we had to give agency to the voice. The beginnings of a proactive, highly personalised, process-driven teaching and learning methodology with a strong emphasis on play were established.

The evolution of Telstar provision

After considerable internal discussion and many debates over time, we decided to be radical and place eight students, all with ASD/CLD and extreme challenging behaviour, together in one class group (Telstar Class), opting for a student-led, play-based, no-demand learning approach.

- Student-led because we needed them to know that they had control over their day and that their voices would be listened to.
- Play-based because they were all working at early developmental levels which militated against an academic curriculum.
- No-demand because the demands were about *our* need to establish routine and order, which often directly conflicted with *their* need to be listened to.

We were confident about the skills of the highly experienced teacher and the carefully chosen ten teaching assistants. We were confident about the appropriateness of a student-led, play-based, no-demand learning approach. We were less confident about how eight highly anxious, challenging young people who were returning to school after the long summer break were going to cope with each other and the staff team in one unfamiliar learning space. The group of students included the unknown quantity of one new 11-year-old student who had previously been educated at another school, separately, and with 2:1 staffing. Our risk assessment in terms of the well-being and life chances of these students was that there was a clearly identified and much greater risk in doing nothing. By placing them altogether in customised accommodation but with personalised learning pathways determined by each individual student, any potentially high risk was mitigated by the chance of greater – and possibly life-changing – returns.

The lack of timetable, structure, routine and demand neither resulted in aggressive behaviour nor passivity. Almost immediately, students were more relaxed and they appeared happier. They were free to engage in a range of carefully positioned, multi-sensory play resources if they chose to do so, but equally, they were free not to engage, should that be their preference. For staff, the guiding principle was 'less is more'. Minimal linguistic communication with simple sentence structures, space and extended time were recognised as being prerequisites to promote student engagement. Staff quietly modelled possible play activities, with no expectation that a student would join them but ready to build on any fleeting learning inroads if the opportunity arose. Snack-making sessions, outdoor play, visits to other areas of the school, minibus trips and walks into the local community also punctuated the day. The rhythm of engagement was unique for each individual and varied over time, but the common denominator was how gradually (but consistently) each student was able to move towards agency, having a voice and making choices that were listened to and acted upon. The presence of other potentially anxious students had not materialised as a confounding factor, and peace and calm had broken out!

Possibly for the first time in their lives, Telstar students were beginning to realise their right to empowerment and were 'learning to be' and 'learning to belong' in a positive way and on their own terms.

The Local Authority were also on board with the Telstar initiative and provided the school with repurposed but much appreciated, additional portacabin accommodation. The extra space and the opportunity to customise the interior further enhanced the delivery of an Informal, student-led, no-demand curriculum. Students were housed in a standard double portacabin with two large rooms which could be subdivided by sliding doors into four smaller spaces if required, two plasma screens, a light sound system, bespoke padding to the walls and CCTV. Telstar also had a small, central showering/bathing/toileting area and a tiny utility room. The three exit doors led to Telstar's own outdoor space with a trio of robust swings and a sizeable learning pod/garden shed. Telstar students retained easy access to the rest of the school field and play equipment and to the main buildings. They were free to come and go as they pleased but always accompanied by their allocated member of staff.

Staff were timetabled to individual students on an hourly rota basis to share knowledge, promote collective responsibility and provide each student with a diverse range of potential learning experiences. Staff no longer felt isolated and sometimes overwhelmed by the intensity of interaction, as they might have done when supporting an individual student throughout the day in a discrete room in the main school. The Telstar team spirit was evident, staff were energised, solutions focussed and supportive of each other. Working lunches, which included the analysis of CCTV footage and the sharing of ideas and strategies for working with particular students, were held on a fortnightly basis and, together with regular morning briefings, a cohesive team spirit emerged where everyone felt listened to and valued.

Telstar staff quickly became aware as to how the portacabin provision supported students to better self-regulate when they were beginning to feel anxious and enabled staff to offer better co-regulation opportunities when students were in crisis, potentially for extended periods of time. The shower and bath facilities were in constant use, the swings and large bucket swing were never unoccupied and proved an essential part of the toolkit to address dysregulation, meet sensory processing needs and provide reassurance and pleasure.

The Telstar Curriculum Pathway 'Learning to Be and Learning to Do' became established, focussing on four key learning areas whilst simultaneously developing self-regulation skills. These areas were and still remain:

- Communication and Play.
- Cognition and Play.
- Physical and Sensory Development.
- Independence and Community Learning.

All Telstar students, in common with all students throughout the school, had five MAPP (Mapping and Assessing Personal Progress, Sissons, 2018) learning intentions set by the class team with input from the multidisciplinary team, which reflected their priority needs in the learning areas noted earlier. These were assessed in every session, and staff were required to become increasingly adept at observing a student, knowing them well and almost imperceptibly providing extension learning opportunities during any of the student's chosen activities, so that the flow of engagement wasn't interrupted.

In addition, Telstar students were assessed every hour by their allocated 1:1 member of staff to determine how well each individual student had managed their anxiety and self-regulation during that hour and recorded a RAG (red, amber, green) rating. Staff always give the most anxious rating that has been noticed during that period, so that, if a student was red for 10 minutes of an hour, the whole period is recorded as a red. This has been very challenging for the staff, as we are such a positive school and always focussing on what students are doing well and achieving. Over time, the staff have come to an understanding that we are seeing RAG data as a positive tool that supports us to analyse and reduce anxiety rather than seeing reds as denoting a failure.

In an 18-week cycle in 2015, just prior to the institution of Telstar Class, all eight students were behaviourally assessed, with a simple clicker device recording one click for every 'red' incident. It was a crude assessment but one which produced some interesting results. Pathman (pseudonym), a 12-year-old student who displayed persistent low level negative behaviours, was recorded to exhibit a daily average of 62 violent or aggressive 'incidents' such as pinching, nail-digging, biting, spitting and occasionally throwing objects, with a low point of 18 and a high point of 122 per day. Staff could not come within one metre of Pathman (three metres for peers!) without the possibility of injury, usually in the form of pinching and/or nail-digging. Authority figures, such as the class teachers, were particularly vulnerable. Pathman presented as 'extremely anxious', with most of his behaviours being either 'leave me alone' or 'get away from me' communications or were so habitual that he appeared not to be particularly aware that they were happening.

One term after the institution of Telstar, all eight students (including Pathman) were RAG rated. The results for the group are nothing short of astonishing.

Apart from the exceptional decrease in overt challenging behaviours (16 for all eight students over a 7-week period, when Pathman alone displayed more than that on his very best day), it is of considerable interest to note that 'amber' indications did not generally spill into 'red'. The inference from this is that the fact that the control students were given to self-regulate, obviated the need to communicate extreme dissatisfaction through exhibiting challenging behaviours. In all, staff and parents noted considerable improvements in

- The number of positive communicative initiations, especially through the use of signing.
- The ability to work collaboratively with staff.
- The ability to be with and work alongside peers.
- Concentration and attention.
- Self-regulation.
- A willingness to engage positively with siblings.
- Calmness and happiness at home.
- A willingness to come into school.

Table 5.1 Individually assessed, 45-minute-long sessions taken over one continuous 7-week period in the 2015/16 academic year. This covered all eight students, one term after the institution of Telstar Class with levels of challenging behaviour (CB) explained

Colour code	Definition	Number of sessions	% of total
Green	No issues	1,919	93.7
Amber	Some indications of stress leading to an expectation of CB occurring	113	5.52
Red	Individually defined CB displayed	16	0.78
Total		**2,048**	**100**

Telstar reimagined in design build accommodation

During the academic year 2018/2019, the Local Authority recognised the success of and future need for Telstar's highly specialist provision by agreeing to purpose build a new Telstar at a cost of £1.6m for 15 students onsite.

St Ann's brief to the architects was to provide light, space, fluidity of movement and clear lines of vision between each zone, elevated vantage points and a continuity between indoor and nature-rich, outdoor areas. In addition, essential requirements were a wet classroom, a large central teaching and learning hall, a kitchen, a utilities area, personal hygiene facilities, a multisensory room, plasma screens, retreat areas, a soft-play zone, a cinema corner and easily washable floors and walls. The build had to meet a robust, medium-secure specification incorporating some elements of 'access control' technology and secure storage facilities. The outside areas had to include swings, a sunken trampoline, a covered sand pit and spaces to run about in or just chill out. The 'free to roam' philosophy remained an integral part of the Telstar set-up, but the opportunity to have an access control facility to some parts of the building enhanced our ability to maintain everyone's safety on those rare occasions when a student may present in a state of extreme anxiety.

Over the last 8 years since its early beginnings in 2015, there is no doubt that the impact of Telstar has been transformational for individual students, their families and for the whole school. The approach has ensured that, through building unconditional trusting relationships with staff, students truly have agency. They have a voice and they make choices, and through 'Learning to Be', are no longer passengers in their own lives. In addition, over time, they are also 'Learning to Do' because they want to 'do', because it feels better and because it affords them more control. Their previous sole strategy of communicating 'something is wrong' through negative behaviour is now extremely rare and is replaced by enhanced communication and self-regulation skills. Some Telstar students have successfully transitioned into the main school, and families and respite providers have reported that students now seem calmer, happier, more able to engage and use their functional skills in everyday activities.

The wider application of the informal curriculum across school

As a result of the Telstar project, a further legacy has been the wider application of the Informal Curriculum across the whole school for the growing number of students (currently five classes) with complex learning disabilities. These students are primarily non-linguistic communicators who have a wide variety of complex sensory processing needs, difficulties tolerating change and transitions and a short attention span. Many are highly active and impulsive, and the majority have significant personal care needs around continence and eating and drinking. The difficulties experienced in making sense of the world and communicating their needs can also manifest as high levels of anxiety, which can, in turn, lead to episodes of very challenging behaviour. Although the impact of their behavioural needs on themselves, others and their environment is less intense than for Telstar students, many have the potential to require Telstar provision in the near future had we not provided a different curriculum. If we fail to listen to their behaviours and acknowledge their learning needs, we should not be surprised about the consequences.

The guiding principle remains the Capabilities Approach (see Chapter 4); that is, enabling all learners to have voice and agency. Our task is to provide and facilitate a nurturing environment, fostering trusting, respectful relationships, with a succession of highly motivating activities and, when required, slow, gentle, non-intrusive teaching. The relentless aim of our Informal, student-led curriculum is to foster students actively 'doing' (playing and participating in daily living tasks) and – crucially – enjoying their achievements and wanting to do more, as success breeds success.

Reflections of an experienced, informal-curriculum class teacher

The environment of an Informal classroom is crucial to facilitate effective learning and the progression of our students. The classroom organisation needs to be well-thought-out and mindful of the importance of play, interaction and sensory stimulation and most significantly the importance of encouraging student-led learning. Therefore, at St. Ann's, practitioners are focussed on creating a motivating, stimulating and accessible multi-sensory environment for students working on the Informal Curriculum.

Typically, the classroom will be set up in different zones. Unlike mainstream classes, where students are assessed in discrete subjects which follow rigid timetables, the Informal class will have activities and experiences set up where students can be assessed in all areas of the curriculum simultaneously. The aim is for a number of activities or play areas to provide the opportunity for students to communicate, explore, interact and focus on their personal sensory and physical needs. In creating this type of learning environment, staff are able to observe students making small steps of progress towards a number of their learning intentions at the same time. For example, one messy play activity using flour and water can encourage a student to explore two very different textures or choose one over the other, thus communicating a preference. The learner also has the opportunity to request 'more' or 'less'; mix the two stimuli together for 'cause and effect'; use their fine motor skills to knead the dough; sit alongside their peers for 'parallel play' or even 'sharing', 'turn-taking' and possibly even 'co-operative play'. Staff can extend this simple activity by providing small pots and spoons or even adding a third texture such as dry pasta for the students to explore. They may decide to start filling and emptying the small pots or even wear them! There are countless possibilities when we use play activities as a vehicle to assess our students.

We have found that setting up the classroom in a 'cosy', 'homely' manner has encouraged students to want to stay within the classroom and join the group on a more regular basis. To achieve this, a focal point is created around the whiteboard using low, comfortable chairs, sofas and a soft rug and cushions for those students who prefer to sit on the floor. This small area at the front of the classroom is as inviting as the family room in a family home, and this is where most teacher-led stories and activities take place. Students and staff will congregate here in the mornings to greet each other and fulfil their morning routine and will return to this area at different intervals throughout the day (some may not even leave!). Consistency is extremely important, and having this aesthetically pleasing, constant zone that does not change will help students feel more comfortable and secure in their classroom.

The rest of the classroom is set up like a carousel with a selection of three or four zones that could consist of, for example, a soft play area, messy play table, sensory area (lights, smells, touchy feely stimuli, sounds), switch toy area (cause and effect toys), a table with activities for fine motor skills (puzzles, Lego), a music area, crafts area, etc. The premise being that students can make choices and explore different areas in their own way and at their own pace. There are many ideas that practitioners can draw upon and the appeal of the Informal Curriculum is that teachers are not constrained but are encouraged to use their creativity to create unique learning experiences for their students which provide ample opportunities for ongoing assessment to take place. Teachers will tend to recreate very similar activities for students because repetition is key for Informal students to be able to practise their skills with increasing confidence. When the same activity or experience is repeated for the learners, staff are able to see and record the small steps of progress much more clearly as time passes. It is, however, important to note that the learning spaces need to be as separate and clutter-free as possible (do not mix unrelated objects and stimuli in one space). It can be easy to unintentionally create a confusing mess which overwhelms the students. Easy access to outdoor spaces is also essential. Our many swings and sunken trampolines have proved to be some of our best tools to support students to self-regulate when they feel the need.

We have found that folding group tables on wheels are especially practical in the classroom because, aside from the fact that they are space-saving, they can be placed close to students who are less inclined to join in. This way they are able to observe the activities and interact in their own time and space. The ease of moving these tables in and out of the classroom makes the space more versatile, especially for those smaller learning spaces.

An important aspect which must be considered carefully when organising an informal classroom environment is to ensure all students have the means and motivation to communicate and to promote as much independence as possible. With regards to communication, the class staff need to observe, research and learn how their students prefer to interact. At St Ann's, we are advocates of a 'Total Communication Method'. This means that our students communicate in their own way, and it is our responsibility to interpret their wants and needs. We do not elevate one communication method over another. Encouraging students to communicate in their own preferred way will increase their confidence, thus motivating responses, interaction and choice-making.

The classroom should have accessible communication aids such as symbols. If symbols are too complex, then photographs of different choices and objects of reference which relate to different activities or daily routines can be used. Some students have the cognitive ability to benefit from a personalised communication book; others may have a communication bag with objects of reference. In any case, all means of communication should be reachable and at the students' level around the classroom. Each class will have a different selection of communication aids which will differ in type and in size depending on the mix of students and the range of their abilities. Displaying communication aids in an accessible manner and setting up the classroom with an array of activities in a clear and approachable fashion all contribute to the learner becoming increasingly independent in their familiar, stimulating and friendly classroom environment. The design of the classroom in this way is totally dedicated to our student-led approach and learning through Play. Open shelves with labelled boxes filled with safe resources are also conducive to encouraging independence in our students. Practitioners can either create symbol- or photo-labelled boxes with similar resources in them that students can access themselves or even create individualised boxes with students' photos which will contain their favourite resources. Having personalised boxes not only promotes independence but encourages learning self-occupation and learning to self-regulate during moments of over-stimulation and high arousal. Teachers need to keep this in mind when creating their classroom zones, as having an area for self-regulation, such as a dark tent or soft furnishing quiet area away from distractions, or indeed, access to a space outside of the classroom, will be highly supportive of those students who need some time out.

Naturally, the size of the classroom will dictate how many different zones one can have. In an ideal world, the classroom would be large enough to accommodate as much variety as possible without becoming too busy. However, the reality is that one can only have two or three activities happening at once, with the other fixed zones, such as the self-regulation area and the focal-group area, at the front of the class. Teachers will have to use their professional judgement to decide how to set up their classroom to best suit the needs of their particular learners.

On the whole, we have found that the formula for creating the perfect Informal classroom environment is to make it feel like a home-away-from-home for both students and staff. If students feel comfortable in their surroundings, the staff will feed off this positive energy and vice versa. We want learners to feel confident and safe enough to take ownership of their learning, and in order to do this, we have to provide them with a rich learning environment where they can showcase their skills and knowledge. There are no limits to the activities and experiences that we can provide for our students, particularly when the Informal Curriculum staff routinely share their ideas, their successes, their many consumable resources and their irrepressible enthusiasm to motivate and engage their learners to play, enjoy and achieve.

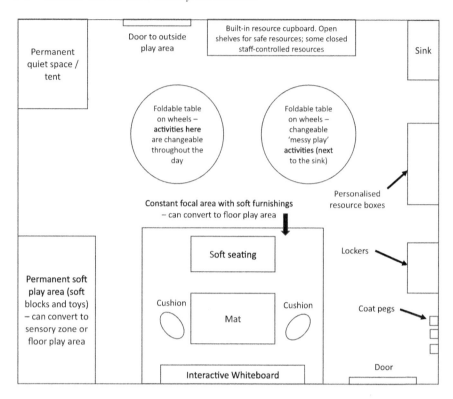

Figure 5.1 Room set-up plan

There have undoubtedly been challenges; these are some of them!

- Communicating clearly with parents/carers the benefits of the Informal Curriculum for their young person and working with them to discover small steps of progress along the way.
- Maintaining the high staffing-levels required by secondary aged students with CLD within the context of shrinking budgets.
- Maintaining high levels of staff training around the theory, practice and value of Play throughout each student's secondary career and into adult life.
- Supporting and encouraging a minority of staff to relinquish control (being 'the adult in charge') and instead allowing students to lead.
- Facilitating regular opportunities for staff to meet, discuss the progress of individual students and further personalise the offer of motivating learning activities.
- Capitalising on every single learning moment, however fleeting, so that staff are adept at 'teaching through stealth' and are always looking to introduce additional challenge.

- Convincing other multidisciplinary professionals that this is a valid way to work with students with CLD, even though it doesn't conform with their training or previous practice.
- Room constraints, such as having no adjoining door to an outside space, or toilets not in close proximity.
- Ensuring systems are in place for cost-effective purchase and the constant availability and the sharing between staff of fresh, consumable, messy play ingredients.
- Sourcing and retaining sympathetic, effective cleaners who understand the benefits of messy play!

Conclusion

We are under no illusions that there is still a long way to go on our Informal Curriculum journey. However, our collective experience and our growing evidence base is that, for students with CLD, this approach works. This *different* curriculum promotes *different* outcomes that enhance the young person's life rather than narrowing their opportunities to become more autonomous. Process-based methodology, Play and listening to behaviours underpin the daily practice of skilled practitioners and the students' lived experience of the Informal Curriculum. Consequently, the need for students to communicate through crisis behaviour becomes increasingly redundant, and with much lower levels of anxiety, they are able to enjoy far more capacity to focus on the rewards of learning.

Informal Curriculum students across school are, over time, making measurable and sustained small steps of progress, and three ex-Telstar students have, in the last 2 years, successfully transitioned into the main school, having benefited from the 'Learning to Be, Learning to Do' curriculum. Parents/carers are reporting that students seem calmer and happier at home and are more able to cope with the inherent challenge of everyday activities, such as going into a supermarket, sitting with the family in a restaurant or even visiting the barber's – all routinely practised in school hours by having daily access to our very supportive local community.

It is evident that Post-19 students with CLD require a similar curricular offer if they are to continue to thrive. Our recent experience is that Post-19 provisions are yet to adopt this very different curriculum and unfamiliar way of working, so that, on leaving school, students can be left without a placement or be placed in a provision at high risk of quickly breaking down. We are committed to working with a broad range of FE-sector and social-care colleagues so that the promise of education to age 25 (as perceived by parents/carers) becomes a reality for this potentially marginalised group of young people.

As SEND practitioners, we are in a trusted and privileged position to make decisions and take calculated risks. Our students with complex, life-long disabilities are not, and we owe it to them and their families to reject the status quo and not perpetuate approaches that patently haven't worked for this cohort of learners. The prize of a better future can be won if we dare to be different and enable the personalities, interests, talents and 'joie de vivre' of our amazing young people to emerge!

References

Ealing JSNA. (2021). *London Borough of Ealing Joint Strategic Needs Assessment (JSNA): 'Focus on' Children and Young People.* Available from: https://data.ealing.gov.uk/wp-content/uploads/EALING-JSNA-Focus-On-CYP-2021_FINAL.pdf. Accessed 14 February 2023.

Imray, P. and Hewett, D. (2015). Challenging Behaviour and the Curriculum. In P. Lacey, R. Ashdown, P. Jones, et al. (eds.) *The Routledge Companion to Severe, Profound and Multiple Learning Difficulties* (pp. 192–200). London: Routledge.

Pinney, A. (2017). *Understanding the Needs of Disabled Children With Complex Needs or Life-Limiting Conditions.* London. Council for Disabled Children/True Colours Trust.

Sissons, M. (2018). *Mapping and Assessing Personal Progress (MAPP).* Newcastle: Equals.

6 Learning to learn through interaction and motivation

The impact of two teachers' reflections on their interactions with students with PMLD

Lana Bond and Diego Gazquez Navarro

Introduction

When teaching children, young people and adults with profound and multiple learning disabilities (PMLD), one of the most evident barriers to their learning is the communication difficulties they face, in both expressive and receptive communication (Goldbart and Ware, 2015). Although most people with PMLD do not communicate using formal communication like speech, symbols or signs (*ibid.*), this, as anybody who has spent some time teaching them can confirm, does not mean that they cannot communicate. We all communicate in many different ways, and it has to be ensured that everyone's way of communication is valued. However, the communication needs of the population described earlier will not be met if those supporting them do not understand how to build the foundations for their communication development. Empowering people to make choices and decisions, supporting them to connect with others and providing environments that create and support coherence can be great strategies to develop ownership of learning and quality of life for children, young people and adults with PMLD. The development of communication skills should be seen, therefore, as a major focus for those teaching these students.

It is interesting to see here that the need for a real connection is supported in special schools for people with PMLD and what impact this can have on feelings of well-being. As Larsen and Prizmic (2008, p259) state

> emotional well-being can be thought of as a composite of positive affect and negative affect that ebbs and flows and has a momentary character reflecting a person's emotional status at any given time.

More precisely, Larsen and Prizmic (*ibid.*) discuss how these individual momentary incidents of positive and negative affect accumulate over time to generate a 'running average' of emotion. This definition recognises the

DOI: 10.4324/9781003369134-9

difference between long-term and short-term happiness and explains over time how they both impact on one another. In a similar vein, Lacey (1996, p63) writes

> to attend to the emotional well-being of people with profound and multiple learning disabilities is to assert their very humanness and their right to quality of life.

In this chapter, we are exploring two avenues that emphasise the development of communication to reach the same implicit end: a sense of agency (versus helplessness) and happiness (versus frustration, distress, depression, etc.). These two paths are Intensive Interaction and the Diagnostic Intervention Model (DIM).

Intensive interaction

Intensive Interaction is a way of making a connection with someone (Nind and Hewett, 2001), a way of creating a safe space to explore social interactivity and communication (Hewett et al., 2015). It is a time to be with a student without a predetermined activity or target planned (Hewett, 2012). The sessions over time can become dynamic and fun, filled with exchanges of behaviour (Hewett et al., 2015). The technique and style of the practitioner is essential. The principles of Intensive Interaction (Hewett, 2018) include 'tuning in' to the student, allowing them to control the content and speed of the interaction, joining in and embracing the natural pauses that occur. Intensive Interaction is a process-central approach emphasising the importance of practitioners' skill to enable the student to explore, practice and rehearse the Fundamentals of Communication (FoC) (Nind and Hewett, 1994). FoC are the essential components upon which all other learning is built (Hewett, 2020). FoC 1 include sharing space with another person, eye contact and sharing exchanges of behaviour, while FoC 2 identify the emotional learning that is explored and can be learned over time as one participates in the Intensive Interaction sessions. These include feelings of security, safety, self-esteem and enjoyment. Without knowledge and understanding of the FoC, all other learning can be disrupted (Smith, 2022). Intensive Interaction enables students and practitioners to connect and feel together, to engage in repetitive cycles of motivating activities directed by the student. It is a safe time to explore the communication in a personally motivating way, such as through exploring faces, sounds, touch or turn taking games (Hewett et al., 2015).

There have been many studies into the effectiveness of Intensive Interaction (Kellett, 2005; Samuel et al., 2008; Mouriere and Scott-Roberts, 2017 for example). Some of them have explored the impact on child behaviour when using Intensive Interaction as a positive behaviour support strategy (Tee and

Reed, 2017; McKim and Samuel, 2021). Other studies have shown an increase in understanding and use of communication relating to the FoC (Harries and Wolverson, 2014; Calveley, 2017). In recent years, there has been an increase in studies relating to intensive interaction and emotional well-being (Weedle, 2016; Stagg, 2022).

The Diagnostic Intervention Model (DIM)

The theoretical background of the Diagnostic Intervention Model (DIM) is rooted in Janssen's et al. work (2002, 2006, 2010, 2012 for example) who argue that (i) deafblind students need a planned intervention to become successful communicators, (ii) educators are responsible for creating and maintaining 'harmonious interactions' and (iii) communication will only develop if students are empowered to take an active part in these interactions. The purpose of DIM is to nurture harmonious interactions by skilling the educators in terms of recognising the signals of the students, attuning to them and adapting the context to encourage predetermined objectives. Successful interventions have to be personalised to the specific students and educators in terms of explicit aims for both interactive partners.

The intervention protocol is explicit and consists of the following five steps:

1. *Determining the question.* Highlighting an issue in regards to a student's interaction.
2. *Clarifying the question.* Specific interaction coaching needs are determined, including the type of coaching (individual, group or a mixture of both).
3. *Interaction analysis.* Video recordings of interactions are analysed and the intervention aims are devised based on eight categories of interaction behaviours: (i) initiatives, (ii) confirmations, (iii) answers, (iv) turns, (v) attention, (vi) regulation of intensity, (vii) affective involvement and (viii) acting independently.
4. *Implementation of the intervention.* The coaching sessions. These may include video analysis of interactions, hands-on coaching, etc.
5. *Evaluation.* A final video analysis is compared to the first one to evaluate the impact of the intervention.

Although DIM's focus is on deafblind students, its principles can also be used with people with PMLD.

The remainder of this chapter presents two small research projects examining the impact of child-led interventions (i.e., Intensive Interaction and DIM) on students with PMLD. The focus on both studies is on improvements in communication skills and emotional well-being, while the second study also explores the staff experience. Both studies have been conducted and written up by class teachers. Their projects will be presented one after the other but there are some concluding comments from both studies at the end.

Study one: Intensive Interaction

Participants, setting and aims of the study

Three secondary-aged students from one class who had reached a plateau in their learning and it seemed overall that they did not enjoy their time at school took part in the study. The students were all non-linguistic communicators. They did not use any formal-language-based communication system and had no known symbolic understanding. For the purposes of this study, the students will be referred to as Bonnie, Anthony and Matilda. It was decided by the whole class team that these pupils would benefit from sessions dedicated to increasing feelings of well-being and the connection between the students and members of staff. It was also believed that this way the students would increase their participation in and engagement with classroom activities and routines.

Methodology

The research took place over an 8-month period during which the students engaged in three timetabled Intensive Interaction sessions per week. Some video baseline assessments of the students involved in class activity and solo play were taken before starting the Intensive Interaction sessions, but the learning outcomes for each student were defined as the study progressed. Further video records were made weekly. Weekly review meetings were held with the classroom team to review footage, discuss practice and identify the students' emergent learning outcomes. Reviewing the recorded sessions included using freeze-frame and slow-motion to ensure all minute details of the sessions could be seen. Some eye contact may be fleeting or a momentary softening of facial features; these tiny details can be seen to full effect.

The classroom team consisted of three teaching assistants who volunteered to be involved in the study. Each member had attended Intensive Interaction courses and had previous experience of conducting sessions. Three session videos were chosen for data analysis: the first recorded session in September (session 1), one in January (session 2) and the last recorded session in April (session 3). The videos were reviewed retrospectively (after the emerging learning outcomes were identified for each student) to evaluate the number of instances the students had displayed these emergent outcomes and comparisons were made.

During the three weekly timetabled sessions but also throughout the school day (as the pupils could initiate intensive interaction sessions any time they wished beyond the timetabled sessions), classroom staff made themselves available to the students with open body language and waited with a smile so that the student could start the session. The session length varied greatly as the length of time of the session was determined by the students.

Results

Data based on video-observations from the timetabled and also non-timetabled pupil-initiated sessions (three time points – beginning of the study, half way through and at the end) as well as interviews with the students' parents at the end of the study are presented here.

Video data

Anthony

Anthony did not smile at all in the first session. Halfway through the study, the number of smiles dramatically increased and Anthony was smiling on average for nearly 3 seconds, which was a marked difference. At the coded session from the end of the study, Anthony only smiled six times; however, each smile was nearly a minute long. In that session, the member of staff and Anthony engaged in lively turn-taking play filled with constant smiling and giggles. Anthony also greatly increased his initiations as the study progressed. He seemed to relish being in control of the activity. The session with the greatest average smile time is the same session as the one with the greatest number of initiations.

BONNIE

The videos were analysed with a focus on eye contact, smiling, smiling with eye contact and duration of eye contact. The results are shown in the following table.

The instances of eye contact, smiling and smiling together with eye contact increased as the study progressed and Bonnie was exposed to intensive interaction. Closer analysis of the data revealed that the average smile time duration for sessions 1 and 2 lasted for 5.5 and 30.3 seconds, respectively, illustrating a significant increase. A drop at time three (still well above time one) can be attributed to the fact that the number of instances of smiling had increased and so had the initiations. This is likely to mean that the interactions had become more complex with more being expected by the child from the adult. The duration of engagement also increased for Bonnie the longer she was exposed to intensive interaction. Table 6.2 also illustrates the number of initiated sequences and the average time engaged in activity for each session.

Table 6.1 Number of incidents of smiling and initiations (including average smile duration) for each of the three times

	Time 1	Time 2	Time 3
Smiling	0	44	6
Initiations	7	57	74
Average smile duration (in secs)	0	2.8	54.6

Table 6.2 Number of incidents of eye contact, smiling and smiling with eye contact (including average smile duration) for each of the three times

	Time 1	Time 2	Time 3
Eye contact	2	10	25
Smiling	6	7	20
Smiling and eye contact	1	2	17
Initiations	8	8	60
Average smile duration (in secs)	5.5	30.3	17.8
Average engagement duration (in secs)	22.25	169.25	183.86

Table 6.3 Number of incidents of smile, eye gaze and vocalisations (including average smile duration) for each of the three times

	Time 1	Time 2	Time 3
Smile	0	72	59
Eye gaze	2	32	33
Vocalisations	0	33	81
Average smile duration (in secs)	0	3.27	5.47

MATILDA

Matilda's smiles increased over time. Her initiations were split into eye gaze and vocalisations, which both increased too. Especially her vocalisations increased in frequency and sound complexity.

Parent interview data

An interview was held at the end of the data-collection period with the students' parents to inquire as to whether they had noticed any changes in behaviour at home. All parents saw certain changes. Anthony's parents reported a sense of him being more content. Bonnie's mother appeared very excited about the progress her daughter was making at home. She actually commented about her daughter: 'she's blossoming!'. She also reported that Bonnie had become much more sociable with other members of the family, which seemed to have had a very positive impact on the functionality of the family. Finally, Matilda's parents reported that they felt there was more intentionality behind her communication. More specifically, her mother said 'I have noticed I give her more choices because I know she has an opinion and she can visually look to make that decision'.

Reflections on the study

Overall, increased incidents of smiling, eye contact, vocalisations and initiations were recorded at the end of the study. Also, the parents of the three students reported positive changes in their offspring's life at home. This study suggests that the participants experienced increased engagement and feelings of happiness as the intervention progressed. As specific learning targets were not set prior to the study, each student's learning outcomes gradually emerged over time (Watson and Fisher, 1997). In a sense, it was the students who chose the path of their own learning, not the adult. Learning about communication in the early stages of development is very complicated for students with PMLD (Ware, 2003), with much information related to body language, facial expression and language needing to be digested and understood. Intensive Interaction is a method for making this complicated information more accessible and meaningful to the student. The repetitive cycles of activities allowed the students to rehearse FoC (Zeedyk et al., 2009), leading to a deeper understanding and use of them. By addressing the humanness of the students and giving them the opportunity to take the lead, by going at their pace and responding in the moment, they all started to develop skills which are necessary for effective communication while fostering feelings of emotional well-being.

Study two: the Diagnostic Intervention Model (Dim)

Participants, setting and aims of the study

Two primary school aged students with PMLD and multisensory impairments (deafblind) and two Teaching Assistants (TAs) took part in this study. For the students, the pseudonyms Anna and Charlie are used, whereas the TAs are called Claire and Kate. Anna and Charlie were non-linguistic communicators and generally interacted with the physical world through reflexive (i.e., involuntary) responses. The aim of the study was to improve the quality of the interactions between the students and teaching staff. More precisely, we wanted to find out whether the support we were providing in class to develop the students' interactional skills was appropriate or it needed some changes as well as to explore how we could measure, fairly objectively, the quality of those interactions.

Methodology

Aspects of DIM were put in place to explore certain teaching strategies used to support the development of communication skills of the students. For this reason, staff coaching and training was employed.

Some of the defining elements of the intervention model were changed or omitted during the study. Firstly, instead of having specific and limiting objectives for staff and for students, a process-based approach was used: providing room for reflection and observing the impact of that reflection in our

Table 6.4 Glossary of interactive turns from DIM

	A	B	C	D	E	F
Glossary of interactive turns	student initiates	student responds	student acts independently/no response to the adult (NR)	adult initiates	adult responds	adult acts independently/no response to the student (NR)

interaction with the students. This was a more inclusive approach when coaching the two TAs because it did not focus on negative elements of incompetency but on potential, reflection and improvement. Secondly, the eight core categories of interactive behaviours, listed in the literature review above, were not used in this study but the more accessible interactive turns (see Table 6.4) to analyse the interactions.

Two sets of video data were analysed: Time 1 (at the beginning of the study, April) and Time 2 (at the end of the study, July). The length of each video recording of interactions to be coded was 5 minutes. The data gathering method used was the interactive turn element of an observation tool developed by Janssen et al. (2003, cited in Axelrod, 2004) for the Diagnosis Intervention Model. The students were observed during unstructured activities. When using the interactive turn elements, in harmonious interactions, the optimum scenario is that in which students are mostly initiating interactions (A) and adults are responding to students (E). Non-harmonious interactions would present adults dominating the interaction (D, F) and students responding (B) or not responding (C).

After the TAs were video-recorded interacting with the two students, the videos were watched, and the TAs were asked to comment in order to find aspects of their practice they would like to change. Once these were identified, weekly training topics were scheduled for our coaching/training meetings in class where different strategies were presented to support interaction, and then, discussions followed. The TAs had the opportunity to reflect and give feedback on their practice. Some of the topics discussed were intensive interaction, building security, developing intentionality, turn taking, etc. The notion of 'interaction' was introduced using an Interpersonal Communication (Baumeister and Leary, 1995) perspective, the process by which two individuals mutually influence each other's actions. This way, 'Interaction' differs from 'communication' in the sense that it does not imply passing any information. At the end of the study, the video data on students was presented to the TAs who were again asked to comment.

Results

At the beginning of the study, the TAs watched their interactions with the students and commented on them.

Kate's comments on her interactions with Charlie

Kate consistently initiated the interactions and Charlie merely responded to the stimuli used. Kate mentioned that she believed that she was expected to keep the students 'busy' all the time instead of waiting for responses. She also reflected on the need to pass the control of the interaction to the students.

Claire's comments on her interactions with Anna

Claire was satisfied with her interactions with Anna in an unstructured situation. Although Anna was unresponsive most of the time, Claire initiated and responded to Anna sensibly. Claire had a different reaction when she saw the video of the structured activity. She commented that things had to be done in a different way and 'Anna was probably scared during that session'.

The coaching process

The use of the video and the analysis of the interactions proved to be an effective way of stimulating reflection and encouraging changes in practice as a class. For example, Kate started to wait for Charlie to be more active in his interactions, and both TAs were introducing changes in the group sessions to better support all of the students in class beyond the participants in this study. During this period, Claire and Kate had continued introducing changes in their practice (i.e., looking more at student faces to see their reactions and not rushing when moving the students from one place to another).

Pre-Post-coaching data

Anna's interactions reflected that the emphasis of the interaction had moved from being adult initiated (mostly Ds and Bs) pre-coaching to being a dialogue of responses (mostly Es and Bs) post-coaching. Surprisingly to the class team, there were even two initiations from Anna post-coaching.

Charlie's interactions also showed a progression from being dominated by Kate pre-coaching to a completely different scenario post-coaching when Kate initiated only twice out of 28 interactive turns and Charlie initiated five times (again to our surprise). Kate also allowed Charlie to explore sounds in class without interfering (and that was reflected in the 13 times that Charlie appeared 'disconnected').

In informal interviews with the TAs which followed, both of them said they were pleased with the results and expressed the intention to continue using this coaching approach to reflect on their practice after the end of the study.

Reflections on the study

This study emphasises the difficulties that educational professionals working with students with PMLD with additional multisensory impairments experience when trying to interact meaningfully with them. It highlights the need

Table 6.5 Anna's interactions pre- and post-coaching

Total of interactive turns	Total As student initiates	Total Bs student responds	Total Cs student acts independently/NR	Total Ds adult initiates	Total Es adult responds	Total Fs adult acts independently/NR
Pre-coaching data						
23	0	7	4	7	4	1
Post-coaching data						
65	2	22	6	12	23	0

Table 6.6 Charlie's interactions pre- and post-coaching

Total of interactive turns	Total As student initiates	Total Bs student responds	Total Cs student acts independently/NR	Total Ds adult initiates	Total Es adult responds	Total Fs Adult acts independently/NR
Pre-coaching data (April)						
101	0	34	9	48	6	4
Post-coaching data (July)						
28	5	0	13	2	8	0

for staff to reflect on current practice in order to improve it. Otherwise, the risk of children and educators taking part in disharmonious interactions is very high in busy school environments.

There were some principles of DIM that were found to have been beneficial for the classroom practice; in particular, the video analysis of interactions, the notion of 'interactive turns' and the individual and group reflection on how to improve the interactions with the students.

The team found the participation in the study rewarding and inspiring. They were particularly impressed by the impact this process had on the deafblind children with PMLD who participated. The study also empowered Claire and Kate with confidence in their work to an extent they had not seen before and they had been working together for years.

Concluding comments

The foregoing two studies show examples of teachers thinking outside the box for the education of students with PMLD. The authors presented innovative ways to teach students with very particular and complex needs and provided some encouraging results about their effectiveness. As we have seen already, all humans need meaningful connections in order to thrive in life. For those people with PMLD, the connections must be felt within familiar settings, including school, in order to be able to show their true selves, their true potential and engage with learning. More precisely, the two small studies presented in this chapter show an increase in the participants' ability to communicate feelings of emotional well-being. Some students showed increased incidents of smiling, eye contact and a willingness to participate in class activities. All of them developed their sense of agency and spontaneity in their interaction with others. Especially in study 1, it was the students who chose the path of their own learning (i.e., emergent learning outcomes). Educational staff supporting the students also felt more confident in their role.

The results presented earlier suggest that approaches such as Intensive Interaction and DIM can help to meet the learning needs of students with PMLD, including those with sensory impairments, which is in line with previous studies in the field (Kellett, 2000; Kellett, 2005; Samuel et al., 2008). Traditionally, educational settings favour sequencing learning for building on knowledge. The two small studies of this chapter question whether this linear view of learning is limiting for students with PMLD and propose to consider basing communication goals on values rather than just on learning. This way, the starting point would be 'What sort of persons do we want to emerge from our schools?'. And that would involve consideration of all sorts of questions such as 'What knowledge does each student need in order to engage critically and meaningfully with the world, and not just focusing on skills?' or 'What sort of skills does each student need to develop?'.

Education is about growth and development. Learning about communication in the early stages of development is very complicated for students with

PMLD, with much information needing to be digested and understood (i.e., body language and facial expression, cultural rules about what constitutes socially accepted interaction, etc.). Strategies that allow students with PMLD to lead interactions and learn at their own pace can make this process more manageable and meaningful to them. The smiles, happy and confident vocalisations as well as the initiations of the students in these studies are the best proof of what appropriate teaching can achieve to prepare our students for lives worth living today.

References

Axelrod, C. (2004). Supporting High Quality Interactions with Students Who are Deafblind. Part Two: Research to Practice. *SEE/HEAR*, 10(1): 15–30.

Baumeister, R.F. and Leary, M.R. (1995). The Need to Belong: Desire for Interpersonal Attachments as a Fundamental Human Motivation. *Psychological Bulletin*, 117(3): 497–529.

Caveley, J. (2017). Gaining the Power of Initiation Through Intensive Interaction. *Learning Disability Practice*, 20(1): 19–23.

Goldbart, J. and Ware, J. (2015). Communication. In P. Lacey, R. Ashdown, P. Jones, et al. (eds.) *The Routledge Companion to Severe, Profound and Multiple Learning Difficulties* (pp. 258–270). London: Routledge.

Harries, C. and Wolverson, E. (2014). Intensive Interaction: To Build Fulfilling Relationships. *The Journal of Dementia Care*, 22(6): 27–30.

Hewett, D. (2012). What is Intensive Interaction? Curriculum, Process and Approach. In D. Hewett (ed.) *Intensive Interaction: Theoretical Perspectives* (pp. 137–154). London: Sage Publications.

Hewett, D. (2018). *The Intensive Interaction Handbook*. London: Sage publications.

Hewett, D. (2020). The Story of Intensive Interaction. In A. Mouriere and P. Smith (eds.) *The Intensive Interaction Classroom Guide* (pp. 4–14). Oxon: Routledge.

Hewett, D., Firth, G., Bond, L., and Jackson, R. (2015). Intensive Interaction: Developing Fundamental and Early Communication Abilities. In P. Lacey, R. Ashdown, P. Jones, et al. (eds.) *The Routledge Companion to Severe, Profound and Multiple Learning Difficulties* (pp 271–280). London: Routledge.

Janssen, M.J., Riksen-Walraven, J.M. and van Dijk, J.P.M. (2002). Enhancing the Quality of Interaction Between Deafblind Children and Their Educators. *Journal of Developmental and Physical Disabilities*, 14(1): 87–109.

Janssen, M.J., Riksen-Walraven, J.M. and van Dijk, J.P.M. (2003). Toward a Diagnostic Intervention Model for Fostering Harmonious Interactions Between Deaf-Blind Children and Their Educators. *Journal of Visual Impairment & Blindness*, 97(4): 197–214.

Janssen, M.J., Riksen-Walraven, J.M. and van Dijk, J.P.M. (2006). Applying the Diagnostic Intervention Model for Fostering Harmonious Interactions Between Deaf-Blind Children and Their Educators: A Case Study. *Journal of Visual Impairment & Blindness*, 100(2): 91–105.

Janssen, M.J., Riksen-Walraven, J.M., van Dijk, J.P.M., et al. (2010). Interaction Coaching With Mothers of Children With Congenital Deaf-Blindness at Home: Applying the Diagnostic Intervention Model. *Journal of Visual Impairment & Blindness*, 104(1): 15–29.

Janssen, M.J., Riksen-Walraven, J.M., van Dijk, J.P.M., et al. (2012). Enhancing Sustained Interaction Between Children With Congenital Deaf-Blindness and Their Educators. *Journal of Visual Impairment and Blindness*, 106(3): 177–183.

Kellett, M. (2000). Sam's Story: Evaluating Intensive Interaction in Terms of Its Effect on Social and Communicative Ability of a Young Child With Severe Learning Difficulties. *Support for Learning*, 15(4): 165–171.

Kellett, M. (2005). Catherine's Legacy: Social Communication Development for Individuals With Profound Learning Difficulties and Fragile Life Expectancies. *British Journal of Special Education*, 32(3): 116–121.

Lacey. P. (1996). The Inner Life of Children With Profound and Multiple Learning Disabilities. In V. Varma (ed.) *The Inner Life of Children With Special Needs* (pp. 63–80). London: Whurr.

Larsen, R.J. and Prizmic, Z. (2008). Regulation of Emotional Well-Being. In M. Eid and R.J. Larsen (eds.) *The Science of Subjective Well-Being*. New York: Guildford Press.

McKim, J. and Samuel, J. (2021). The Use of Intensive Interaction Within a Positive Behavioural Support Framework. *The British Journal of Learning disabilities*, 49(2): 129–137.

Mouriere, A. and Scott-Roberts, S. (2017). Measuring the Impact of Intensive Interaction on Joint Attention and Intentional Communication; Using FOCAL Wheels. *Good Autism Practice*, 18(1): 34–45.

Nind, M. and Hewett, D. (1994). *Access to Communication: Developing the Basics of Communication With People With Severe Learning Difficulties Through Intensive Interaction*. London: David Fulton.

Nind, M. and Hewett, D. (2001). *A Practical Guide to Intensive Interaction*. Kidderminster: British Institute of Learning Disabilities.

Samuel, J., Nind. M., Volans, A., et al. (2008). An Evaluation of Intensive Interaction in Community Settings for Adults With Profound Intellectual Disabilities. *Journal of Intellectual Disabilities*, 12: 111–126.

Smith, P. (2022). What Do Students With Autism and Learning Difficulties Need to Learn? In A. Mouriere and P. Smith (eds.) *The Intensive Interaction Classroom Guide* (pp. 15–28). Oxon: Routledge.

Stagg, D. (2022). Developing a Whole School Approach to Using Intensive Interaction to Promote Social Communication and Well-Being. In A. Mouriere and P. Smith (eds.) *The Intensive Interaction Classroom guide* (pp. 52–62). Oxon: Routledge.

Tee, A. and Reed, P. (2017). Controlled Study of the Impact on Child Behaviour Problems of Intensive Interaction for Children With ASD. *Journal of research in Special Educational Needs*, 17(3): 179–186.

Ware, J. (2003). *Creating a Responsive Environment for People With Profound and Multiple Learning Difficulties*. 2nd edition. London: David Fulton Publishers.

Watson, J. and Fisher, A. (1997). Evaluating the Effectiveness of Intensive Interactive Teaching With Pupils With Profound and Complex Learning Difficulties. *British Journal of Special Education*, 24(2): 80–87.

Weedle, S. (2016). The Use of Intensive Interaction With People With Severe Profound Intellectual Disability. *Learning Disability Practice*, 19(9): 27–34.

Zeedyk, S., Caldwell, P. and Davies, C. (2009). How Rapidly Does Intensive Interaction Promote Social Engagement for Adults With Profound Learning Disabilities. *European Journal of Special Education Needs*, 24(2): 119–137.

7 The power of play

An approach to developing creativity and tolerating uncertainty

James Waller

Sunningdale School is a specialist school for children with severe, profound and multiple learning disabilities including those with autism, aged between 2 and 11 years old. It is in Sunderland, Tyne and Wear, in the northeast of England. The school has 136 pupils, grouped into 17 classes that are arranged across four theoretical pedagogical pathways. These begin on transition from the Early Years Foundation Stage and run through Key Stages 1 and 2 until the pupils' transition to relevant secondary provisions at the end of year 6. The pathways are the Pre-Formal Pathway, the Semi-Formal Explore Pathway, the Semi-Formal Play Pathway and the Formal Pathway. Since 2020, the school has had no pupils on roll for which the Formal Pathway (akin to a National Curriculum pathway) was a developmentally appropriate approach.

Prior to 2020, the school was arranged into age-based class groups, each consisting of 12 pupils with a range of learning characteristics, communication needs and widely varying developmental levels. Whilst personalised planning supported by an understanding of engagement motivators ensured pupils consistently worked towards appropriate outcomes, the very wide range of pupil developmental levels was operationally difficult to manage and inevitably led to a lack of engagement and progress for some pupils. In between 2018 and 2020, a significant analysis was undertaken to define groups of homogenous learner characteristics based on those of individual pupils in terms of their (i) ability to engage, (ii) communication methods and complexity and (iii) social play stage and developmental levels. This led to the adoption and development of the foregoing four curriculum pathways. These represented a more targeted use and refinement of pre-existing approaches used within the school as well as enabling the development of ideas and approaches to compliment them. Each curriculum pathway is designed to have a defined approach in terms of its provision that extends to the curriculum areas taught, numbers of pupils in a class, staff to pupil ratios, underlying pedagogy and recommended developmental frameworks. This chapter is concerned with the pedagogical approaches used to underpin the Semi-Formal Explore and Semi-Formal Play Pathways.

DOI: 10.4324/9781003369134-10

The Semi-Formal Explore Pathway at Sunningdale School has been designed to effectively meet the needs of pupils with Complex Learning Disabilities (CLD), the definition of which is set out in Chapter 1. These pupils will have very complex communication and interaction needs coinciding with their severe cognition and learning disabilities. The pupils within this pathway will not engage and explore their environment well and will have difficulties with flexibility in thinking, leading to an inability to cross-contextualise skills and a lack of ability to tolerate uncertainty. The Semi-Formal Explore Pathway's approach is analogous to Equals' Informal Curriculum. Classes in this pathway constitute between five and eight pupils, a teacher and support staff. The staff to pupil ratio is 1:2. For clarity, I will refer to this curriculum pathway as the Informal Pathway throughout this chapter.

The Semi-Formal Play Pathway at Sunningdale School has been designed to meet the needs of pupils with Severe Learning Disabilities (SLD) who are autonomous across a range of contexts, have a more developed ability to engage with their environment effectively but are still continuing to develop their 'realisation' through the Engagement Model (Standards and Testing Agency, 2020a), as well as their ability to apply their learning to varying contexts and functional situations. The pupils in this pathway will have a more developed 'theory of mind' (that is, an understanding that someone else thinks differently to themselves) than those in the Semi-formal Explore Pathway. It utilises subject areas that are similar but not the same as those outlined in the Equals Semi-Formal Curriculum: Communication, Language and Literacy; Thinking, Problem Solving and Maths; Play and Leisure; Physical Development; Expressive Arts; Independence; The World Around Me; Relationships and Health Education; Outdoor Learning and Religious Education. For clarity, I will refer to this curriculum pathway as the Semi-Formal Pathway throughout this chapter.

Be more . . .

Within the context of an underlying approach, all pupils are planned for and taught at Sunningdale School in a highly personalised way, by using developmental Personalised Learning Plans facilitated through an environmental context established by individual engagement profiles. The pedagogy used across the school's Semi-Formal and Informal Pathways is based on Play.

The starting point, however, for the school's present curriculum and pedagogical arrangement was the development of its current vision and ethos. The school's vision is encapsulated in the phrase 'Be More . . .'. That is, we want every child to be more in whatever way is important to them. They might want to be more communicative; they may want to be more active; they could want to be more creative, be more engaged, be happier, be more comfortable, be more flexible, be more resilient, be more sociable or any and all of the above at the same time. This will be different for every child. Believing not only that every child can 'Be More . . .' but that they can 'Be More . . .' in whatever way is important to them, means that we:

- Never underestimate a child's potential.
- Acknowledge every child's potential will be different and individual to them.
- Recognise that the aspirations for every child will be different and individual to them.

As a result, the school strives to ensure that

- Every child's targets, curriculum, assessment and outcomes are different and individual to them.

This ethos was arrived at through engagement with a range of stakeholders, including parents, carers, governors, teachers, teaching assistants, multi-agency professionals and, of course, the pupils themselves. During this process, individuals were asked what skills or qualities they wished the children to possess or develop by the time they left Sunningdale School. What was striking about the responses was that not a single pupil, parent, teacher, teaching assistant, governor or professional identified anything to do with what we often think of as 'Subject Specific' learning – learning that resembles the areas set out in the English National Curriculum or defined by the Standards and Testing Agency's (2020b) Pre-Key Stage Standards. The skills and qualities that they did identify were numerous but either centred around or were directly identified as resilience, problem solving, independence, the ability to communicate their needs, to be happy, to be friendly, to have friends, to be safe, to be healthy, to be emotionally regulated, to be creative, to be sociable and to be able to navigate the world beyond the classroom or the safety of their bedroom.

The issue, as we saw it, was that the approach to develop these qualities has often been to create an environment or approach that is structured, secure, predictable and almost algorithmic. However, the world beyond the classroom, school or bedroom is unpredictable, unreliable, unfair and full of other people (who are also unpredictable, unreliable, unfair, and for the most part, inconsistent). In fact, more often than not, those so-called safe, secure and predictable environments (the classroom, school and bedroom) are also unpredictable, unreliable, unfair. So, how did we decide to go about meeting the aspirations of our pupils, parents and other stakeholders to prepare our pupils with CLD and SLD with the skills required to navigate this ever-changing environment?

'Knowing what to do when you don't know what to do'

The foregoing description of Intelligence has been attributed to Jean Piaget (Lucas and Spencer, 2022). This is what we want for our pupils at Sunningdale

School. We want them to be able to develop a wide range of skills, knowledge and understanding, of course, but our main goal is that our pupils leave the school able to apply that skill, knowledge and understanding to the world beyond the classroom; to use it functionally in order to make sense of and interact with the world around them. We want to help pupils to become creative thinkers who can explore, investigate, make connections, collaborate and tolerate uncertainty. If they also learn to read as part of that process – well, that is awesome.

Sunningdale School has utilised an Early-Years-influenced Play-Based learning-approach to support teaching and learning across all Key Stages since 2012. Play is one of the most important ways in which young children gain essential knowledge and skills. Children play to make sense of the world around them and to find meaning in an experience by connecting it to something already known. Through Play, children express and expand their understanding of their experiences (Unicef, 2018). At this point, 'the value of play in human development and experience is beyond dispute' (Moylett, 2022, p44). It provides the underlying pedagogy for both of the pathways outlined earlier. The way it is adapted and applied across the two, however, is quite different.

In the school's Informal Pathway, we are keen to develop independence and agency.

> Allowing children to choose their activities and providing opportunities for self-direction may be especially important in promoting the development of independence for children with disabilities and social interaction among children with disabilities and their peers.
>
> (Reszka et al., 2012, p53)

Structured teaching has been advocated for some time as an effective way for teaching those with autistic spectrum conditions. The predominant claims usually reference a reduction in anxiety and challenging behaviours (Mesibov and Shea, 2010, for example). However, the artificial imposition of strict structure suggested by systems such as the TEACCH (Treatment and Education of Autistic and Related Communication Handicapped Children) methodology (Schopler and Reichler, 1971) with its extrinsically motivated, strictly timetabled, low-stimulation approach, lacks a reflection of real-world application and there have been questions raised regarding its effectiveness (Virues-Ortega et al., 2013). Tolerating Uncertainty is defined by Lucas et al. (2013) as a sub-disposition of Creative Thinking. It is key to dealing with unstructured real-world situations and is developed through working in an unstructured way (Lucas and Spencer, 2022). It becomes most important when goals, actions and environments are not fully set out and predictable. It is the phrase we use at Sunningdale School to describe the idea that we want our most complex pupils to be able to remain regulated, to problem solve and effectively apply their knowledge and skills in unfamiliar and less predictable situations. Tolerating uncertainty (along with tolerating others) is one of the key attributes we want our pupils with Complex Learning Disabilities, those accessing the Informal Pathway, to develop.

'Agency' refers to an individual's capacity to make sense of what they observe and experience, and as such, their ability to act intentionally on the world around them (Porpora, 2015, cited in Moylett, 2022). Play is a key approach in developing agency, enabling children to take on an active role and ownership of their experiences as well as helping them to be capable, autonomous and have ownership of their own learning. If we are aiming to develop agency, we need to put the child in an exploratory environment. An over-adherence to structure, routines and regulation in the pursuance of compliance and conformity can lead to and reinforce an inflexibility of thought. It has been suggested (Souza et al., 2022) that individuals with autism and particularly those with a co-morbid intellectual disability do not assimilate new information into (and therefore modify) schema as readily as typically developing peers. A lack of central coherence in 'seeing how the pieces of the puzzle fit together' has been described (Frith, 1991), and it has been well reported (Baron-Cohen, 2011, for example) that those on the autistic spectrum find it very hard to acquire Theory of Mind. At Sunningdale School, we made the decision that we wanted pupils to be active agents, as opposed to passive recipients, in their learning and development. We want them to be active explorers and be able to apply their thinking.

So, how do we go about this exploratory Play? The starting point for this is an understanding of what each child's ability to engage with their environment looks like. Qualitative recordings of pupils' engagement in the areas of Initiation, Persistence, Anticipation, Exploration and Realisation (The Engagement Model, 2020) are made regularly and used to build up a picture of how developed each of these are for all pupils in the school. This is an important baseline in establishing how developed each child's ability to engage with their environment is.

Alongside this, we also record pupils' motivators in terms of *Activities, Resources, Environments, Levels of Support* and *Times of the Day*. This information is used to create overall teaching environments and develop approaches that create the maximum potential for learning for individual pupils. We believe that, without engagement, there is no deep learning, meaningful outcome, real attainment or quality progress and effective teaching therefore becomes impossible (Hargreaves, 2006; Carpenter, 2010).

This information is recorded in as much depth as is possible. For example, the specific motivating 'activity' for the pupil may be recorded initially but, over time, as this becomes better understood, deeper information about the nature of the activity or resource will be recorded so that this can be duplicated across other activities, resources or environments. If we understand at a schematic-, process- or sensory-level a pupil's most motivating activity, resource, environment, level of support and time of day, then we can combine that information to create the optimum conditions for encouraging initiation, facilitating exploration, developing persistence and ultimately scaffolding the child's realisation and cross contextualisation.

A highly personalised approach

Using our understanding of how to engage the child in their environment is a powerful tool for not only developing the specific areas of engagement in and of themselves but it is also key in securing independent initiation. This is vital for our pupils with Complex Learning Disabilities if they are going to establish agency over and independence within their environment as well as make broader developmental progress. As such, pupils are planned for and taught at Sunningdale School in a highly personalised way, using Personalised Learning Plans that cross reference and interact with a variety of educational, therapeutic and curriculum documentation and approaches. This includes Occupational Therapy, Physiotherapy and Speech and Language Therapy plans. Pupils' Personalised Learning Plans directly link back to their Education, Health and Care plan (EHCP), demonstrating the golden thread that runs through each individual pupil's education right back to their own aspirations.

At the stage where we start to develop an understanding of the child's engagement motivators, there is a shift in approach from 'child-led learning' towards what is really 'adult-facilitated-child-led learning'. This is because the environments, activities and scenarios that will be presented in the classroom will be based on an in-depth, pre-existing knowledge of the child: their prior learning, developmental levels, sensory regulation needs as well as their engagement motivators and presentation.

Whilst this is adult-facilitated through the careful design of the environmental elements of the provision set out, pupils have agency to engage (or not) with the environment in their preferred way. This is based on the premise that children are most relaxed when following their own agenda and not an adult's (Carpenter et al., 2015). This is our starting point for what is sometimes termed a 'low demand' approach, as described in the Equals Informal Curriculum (Equals, 2021). Underpinned by our simple yet precise understanding of pupils' engagement and their developmental levels, skills and knowledge, pupils are presented with appropriate environments (in the complete sense) that can be accessed on their own agenda, under their own agency. Pupils are 'offered' their opportunities to engage. The goal is that pupils with CLD remain well-regulated emotionally and, as such, better able to actively engage with the environment. Their engagement is on their terms, thereby ensuring that they are relaxed and regulated.

Autonomy and ownership

As described earlier, the aim is to provide the opportunity for the pupil to take on an active role and ownership in their learning. Ephgrave (2018) maintains that children are most deeply engaged when they have autonomy and suggests this is no less true for a child on the autism spectrum or a child with additional needs. Balancing this, however, is vital in working towards meaningful outcomes. There comes a point where the interactions of classroom staff become profoundly important in supporting and extending the pupil's learning. How, why and when these take place in order to be purposeful and effective is key to the approach in this pathway.

The primary role of the classroom staff in this Play-Based, low-demand approach is their role in the social development of pupils' play and interaction skills. The school utilises the social stages of play originally defined by Parten (1932) to describe pupil's social organisation of their play. These are: Onlooker, Solitary, Parallel, Associative and Cooperative (see Table 7.1). Learners do not necessarily progress through these in order (Smith, 1978), but they have been useful as succinct descriptions of social play-based behaviours, particularly for identifying where pupils may take part in common activity without being truly cooperative toward a common goal (the difference between *Associative* and *Cooperative* play).

The initial aim is to engage the child as an *onlooker* – that is, an individual that watches others play without participating – and then to become a cooperative player who can co-ordinate their play with others, eventually within the context of rules and demands placed on them by others.

The very first step for a number of our learners with CLD is simply being interested. We have built an environment based around their motivators, but the initial role of the staff is to model that they can engage with the environment however they like. It is important to remember they may have never had this opportunity before. At Sunningdale School, classroom *staff* in the Informal Pathway are encouraged to play in their classrooms. By themselves! This will be at the cognitive level of play relevant to the pupils in their class, be that functional play, constructive play, pretend play or even rule-based games. I have observed a teaching assistant in an Informal Pathway class playing solitarily at an activity for 25 minutes before being joined by a pupil in parallel play that quickly developed into associative play. This was a major 'wow-moment' for this pupil. What we have anecdotally discovered at Sunningdale School is that, for learners with CLD, the tiny socio-developmental steps from, firstly,

Table 7.1 Social stages of play*

Social play type	Description
Onlooker	Watching others play without participating oneself.
Solitary	Playing alone and independently, with no attempt to get close to other children.
Parallel	Playing alongside other children and with similar materials but with no real interaction or cooperation.
Associative	Playing with other children in some common activity but without division of labour or subordination to some overall group goal.
Cooperative	Playing in a group that is organised for the purpose of carrying out activity or attaining some goal, with coordination of individual members' behaviour in pursuit of the common goal.

* Based on information from Parten (1932, cited in Vasta et al., 1999)

just tolerating being in the room to being an active onlooker and, secondly, from being an onlooker to taking part in self-initiated solitary play is a huge step in unlocking self-initiated learning and the beginning of an ability to tolerate uncertainty.

Once a pupil is initiating their own engagement with the activities and resources in the environment and will persist long enough that there is opportunity for extension, the expectation is that staff will engage in parallel and eventually associative and cooperative play with the pupil. We have anecdotally found this to have an impact on our learners with CLD's general tolerance of others in close proximity as well as in tolerating others using the same resource(s). This also provides classroom staff with opportunities to model use of resources closely linked to the child's developmental levels or even to demonstrate new learning without overtly placing an instructional demand on the pupil. In relation to the child's levels of regulation, this approach supports attunement and begins to underpin secure attachment and well-being. It is well reported that repeated moments of both attunement and mis-attunement shape a child's emotional well-being (Goleman, 1995). The greater the instance of negative response the child experiences, the less reliable they see others as and they are forced to cope with an unhealthy level of uncertainty (Schofield and Beck, 2006). By taking time to develop the relationship between classroom staff and the individual pupils, we are making a deliberate effort to help the child move beyond their insular level of actual development and access what Vygotsky famously referred to as the 'zone of proximal development' (1987), to be supported to make progress and access their actual potential.

Physical space

In terms of the physical spaces and resources that are used in the Informal Pathway classes at Sunningdale School, this can be anything and everything. Every classroom space is made up of a large open space with washable vinyl flooring; shelving units containing baskets, buckets and tubs of resources; tables of varying heights, shapes and sizes; tough trays (both raised and on the floor); water trays; rugs, beanbags and carpeted areas; and durable interactive touch screens. The specific resources are based on the pupil's motivators and developmental levels. They include everything from cups, bowls, colanders, sieves, cornflour and a whole host of edible 'goop', right through to white boards, pens, tablet devices and books as well as everything in between. Every classroom has its own outdoor classroom space that facilitates immediate access to outdoor learning opportunities. This is always accessible. All of the classrooms have their own bathroom and every two classrooms share a 'Sensory Den'. This is a small break-out room that is used according to the needs of the class. They are all equipped with specialist lighting and soft surfaces.

The Informal Pathway classes at Sunningdale School also have access to the 'Explore Area', a suite of indoor and outdoor spaces that flow into one another including an integrated sensory room, gymnastic rings, bucket swings, scramble nets, climbing wall and wet room. This area can be accessed by any pupil at any time.

A range of well-known strategies are also used to engage pupils within the context of the approach and where they align with the child's engagement, social or developmental needs. These include approaches such as *Intensive Interaction* (Nind and Hewitt, 1994) and even, sometimes temporarily, more structured approaches such as Gina Davies' *Attention Autism* (Robinson et al., 2018). Where they are used, they are integrated into the approach within a class rather than as a 'tag-on'. Relevant communication strategies are also adopted, including individualised use of Augmentative and Alternative Communication (AAC), where relevant.

So, what difference does it really make?

The impact of the approach described earlier on the progress of pupils with CLD at Sunningdale School has been widespread. In its infancy, there was a noticeable change in emotional regulation. This was, at first, anecdotal, with staff around school commenting on how calm the Informal Pathway classrooms were and how well-regulated these classes appeared compared to how the individual pupils had presented previously. As data takes time to gather, other metrics became clearer later.

By the third term of adopting an Informal low demand approach, the school had seen a significant reduction in instances of physical intervention, even with the most complex pupils. By the sixth term, there were none.

Every term, pupils at Sunningdale School are ipsatively assessed, based on a range of factors unique to them. Evidence for this assessment is varied and heavily moderated. Deep-dive pupil progress meetings are used to undertake detailed, personalised judgements on how well pupils are progressing towards their goals. Teachers prepare carefully for this termly process by ensuring that judgements of progress are evidenced by cross-referenced sources, with next steps and targets negotiated and recorded.

Sources include developmental assessment frameworks, engagement profiles, understanding of engagement motivators, recorded observations (video, photographs, written), deep-dive pupil progress meetings and professional opinion. The developmental assessments that form part of this process are also matched to the needs of the individual pupil and the overarching aims of the curriculum pathway that they are currently accessing. There is no set school-wide developmental assessment that underpins the tracking of developmental progress for individual pupils. Classroom staff have access to a range of commercially and publicly available developmental assessment frameworks to support their outcome setting and assessment. Each aspect of this is heavily moderated across the curriculum pathway, between curriculum pathways and externally, with other schools that also utilise the specific assessment frameworks. This involves external moderation with a range of different school groups to ensure each framework that teachers may refer to is clearly understood, robustly moderated and that individual judgements are accurate. External moderation also focusses on the accuracy of descriptions in engagement profiles and motivators. Internal monitoring and moderation also take place to consider the depth and use of engagement motivators in classroom set-ups, accurate matching of activities in classrooms to Personalised Learning Plan (PLP) outcomes, quality of PLP outcomes, observed levels of regulation and engagement, quality of recorded evidence, evidence of subject coverage and a range of focussed teaching and learning observations.

Judgements are made in each area of a pupil's development across their Cognition and Learning, Communication and Interaction, Sensory and/or Physical Development, and Social, Emotional and Mental Health. Specific outcomes are set in each of these areas. These may relate to specific developmental skills, curriculum knowledge, behaviours or characteristics of learning, such as engagement. There is no set number of sub-targets or outcomes identified within each of these areas, as this is highly individualised and based on the specific needs of the pupil. In each area of a pupil's development, progress and attainment is judged to be:

- Little Progress: requiring a case study and intervention.
- Good Progress and/or
- Excellent Progress.

These judgements are made termly as part of a deep-dive pupil progress meeting between a classroom teacher and senior leaders. This can last for up to 3 hours for one pupil and explores every aspect of a pupil's provision and development. As outlined earlier, these judgements are qualitative and highly personalised. There is no specific 'cut-off' between each category. There is no quantitative measure on any assessment framework that dictates the difference between the judgements, but all are based on the range of factors outlined earlier and involve a deep understanding of the pupil, combined with a deep understanding of both complex learning disabilities and the curriculum they're working on.

In order for progress with a specific outcome or area to be defined as 'Excellent Progress', the pupil's engagement motivators must be well-understood and -defined. It must be evident that these have been utilised in the classroom environment to secure intrinsic engagement with learning: there must be evidence that the pupil is engaged in meaningful learning. The outcome(s) being judged must be relevant to the pupil's longer-term aspirations and/or development. There is an expectation that the pupil will have made developmental progress, even if that is laterally via increased *maintenance, fluency, independence* or *generalisation* (as defined in Mapping and Assessing Personal Progress, Sissons, 2018). Quantitative progress against outcomes or identified assessment frameworks is considered in making the judgement for the individual pupil, but its influence on the judgement is qualitative, based on the individual circumstances, disability and the general learning characteristics of the individual.

For a pupil to be considered to be making 'Good Progress', they will usually be making developmental progress, at least laterally, but the other cross-referenced and heavily moderated sources of evidence may suggest that this could be better. Usually, this will occur where a child's engagement motivators are not well-understood or classroom staff feel that they do not fully understand an aspect of the child's development such as their expressive communication or self-regulation.

Where a child is making no demonstrable progress or their presentation of engagement and engagement motivators are not well-understood, they would be considered to be making 'Little Progress'. In these cases, prolonged discussion and observation of the pupil will take place in the identified area(s) of development and classroom staff will be supported by middle and senior leaders (as well as identified multi-professionals) to better understand how to engage the pupil in learning and support their progress.

After the first full academic year of implementation (September 2021-June 2022) of the approaches, ipsative assessments of pupils that accessed the Informal and Semi Formal curricula following the previous non-pathway-based approach included 22 pupils in the Informal Pathway and 45 pupils in the Semi-Formal curriculum pathway.

The following table shows the overall data.

The largest impact was in the area of Communication and Interaction.

Communication and interaction

21 pupils (96%) in the Informal Pathway were assessed to be making Excellent Progress in Communication and Interaction, an increase of 22.5% from 16 (73%) at the end of the previous academic year.

Table 7.2 Number of students following the Informal and Semi-Formal Pathways showing Excellent Progress

Informal Pathway		Semi-Formal Pathway	
Communication and Interaction			
2020–2021	2021–2022	2020–2021	2021–2022
16/22	21/22	36/45	39/45
Social, Emotional and Mental Health			
2020–2021	2021–2022	2020–2021	2021–2022
14/22	16/22	34/45	29/45

Those in the Semi-Formal Pathway assessed to be making Excellent Progress in Communication and Interaction increased from 36 (80%) the previous year to 39 (87%) the following June.

Social, emotional and mental health

Sixteen (73%) of the pupils accessing the Informal Pathway were assessed to be making Excellent Progress, which was a two-pupil (9%) increase on the 14 pupils (64%) the previous year. Deep-dive pupil progress discussion revealed that these assessments were supported by developments for these pupils in emotional regulation and the development of an ability to tolerate demands and less predictable circumstances as well as joint attention. This was evidenced predominantly through associative Play.

Twenty-nine (64%) of pupils in the Semi-Formal Pathway were assessed as having made Excellent Progress, a decrease from 34 (76%) the previous year. However, no pupils in either Pathway were assessed as making less than good progress. Deep-dive pupil progress discussion revealed highly individualised reasons for the five pupils who were no longer judged to be making Excellent Progress, which included better insight into their ability (or lack thereof) to self-regulate in uncertain situations; that is, when goals, actions and environments were not fully set out and predictable. This had not been easily identifiable previously and became (as at 2022) an area of focus for these pupils.

Tolerating uncertainty

Tolerating uncertainty is a difficult disposition to measure but is possibly best evidenced by increased absence of instances of dysregulation in circumstances where complex pupils are faced with unplanned events, unusual environments and unfamiliar visitors. Deep-dive discussions with teachers suggest that this is the single biggest area of impact across the Informal Pathway. Individually (as well as in a group), this very complex pupil group have seen huge changes in their ability to remain self-regulated and communicate effectively in these circumstances. This has opened up wider curriculum opportunities available to them that further support cognitive development and academic progress. They are able to take part in wider community activities and develop their independence in the community more effectively. Some pupils are accessing numeracy and reading strategies more effectively.

Conclusion

Possibly, the best anecdotal evidence of the progress the CLD pupil group has made at the school is the fact that visitors, including parents, governors and other educational professionals cannot always identify the classes that constitute this pathway. 'I thought your pupils would be more complex' is now a regular comment of those visiting the school (followed as a close second by the question, 'How do you get them to do that?').

The answer is simple. We never underestimate a child's potential but recognise that the aspirations for every child will be different and individual to them. As a result, we offer a different curriculum: we do not differentiate a curriculum that was designed to teach something completely different to what our pupils need to learn. We strive to ensure that every child's targets, curriculum, assessment and outcomes are different and individual to them. Ken Robinson (Robinson and Aronica, 2015) famously wrote:

> Many schools are organised as they are because they always have been, not because they must be.
>
> (p. 191)

Ours isn't.

References

Baron-Cohen, S. (2011). *Zero Degrees of Empathy.* London: Allen Lane.

Carpenter, B. (2010). *A Vision for the 21st Century Special School* (Complex Needs Series 1). London: SSAT.

Carpenter, B., Egerton, J., Cockbill, B., Bloom, T., Fotheringham, J., Rawson, H. and Thistlethwaite, J. (2015). *Engaging Learners With Complex Learning Difficulties and Disabilities.* Abingdon: Routledge.

Ephgrave, A. (2018). *Planning in the Moment With Young Children: A Practical Guide for Early Years Practitioners and Parents.* London: Routledge.

Equals. (2021). *Informal Curriculum.* Available from: https://equals.co.uk/.

Frith, U. (1991). *Autism and Asperger Syndrome.* Cambridge: Cambridge University Press.

Goleman, D. (1995). *Emotional Intelligence.* New York: Bantam Books.

Hargreaves, D. (2006). *Personalising Learning 6: The Final Gateway: School Design and Organisation.* London: SSAT.

Lucas, B., Claxton, G. and Spencer, E. (2013). *Expansive Education: Teaching Learners for the Real World.* Maidenhead: Open University Press.

Lucas, B. and Spencer, E. (2022). *Teaching Creative Thinking: Developing Learners Who Generate Ideas and Can Think Critically.* Carmarthan: Crown House Publishing.

Mesibov, G.B. and Shea, V. (2010). The TEACCH Programme in the Era of Evidence-Based Practice. *Journal of Autism and Developmental Disorders,* 40: 570–579.

Moylett, H. (2022). *Characteristics of Effective Early Learning: Helping Young Children Become Learners for Life.* London: Open University Press.

Nind, M. and Hewitt, D. (1994). *Access to Communication: Developing the Basics of Communication With People With Severe Learning Difficulties Through Intensive Interaction.* London: David Fulton.

Parten, M.B. (1932). Social Participation Among Preschool Children. *Journal of Abnormal and Social Psychology,* 27: 243–269.

Reszka, S.S., Odom, S.L. and Hume, K.A. (2012). Ecological Features of Preschools and the Social Engagement of Children With Autism. *Journal of Early Intervention*, 34(1): 40–56.

Robinson, K. and Aronica, L. (2015). *Creative Schools: The Grassroots Revolution That's Transforming Education*. New York: Viking.

Robinson, L., Bond, C. and Oldfield, J. (2018). A UK and Ireland Survey of Educational Psychologists' Intervention Practices for Students With Autism Spectrum Disorder. *Educational Psychology in Practice*, 34(1): 58–72.

Schofield, G. and Beck, M. (2006). *Attachment Handbook for Foster Care and Adoption*. London: BAAF.

Schopler, E. and Reichler, R. (1971). Parents as Co-Therapists in the Treatment of Psychotic Children. *Journal of Autism and Childhood Schizophrenia*, 1(1): 87–102.

Sissons, M. (2018). *Mapping and Assessing Personal Progress (Semi-Formal)*. Newcastle: Equals.

Smith, P.K. (1978). A Longitudinal Study of Social Participation in Preschool Children: Solitary and Parallel Play Reexamined. *Developmental Psychology*, 14: 517–523.

Souza, C., Garrido, M.V., Horchak, O.V., et al. (2022). The Distinctive Pattern of Declarative Memories in Autism Spectrum Disorder: Further Evidence of Episodic Memory Constraints. *Journal of Autism and Developmental Disorders*, 1–11.

Standards and Testing Agency. (2020a). *The Engagement Model*. Available from: www.gov.uk/government/publications/the-engagement-model.

Standards and Testing Agency (2020b). *Pre-key Stage 2: pupils Working Below the National Curriculum Assessment Standard. Teacher Assessment Framework*. Available from: https://assets.publishing.service.gov.uk/government/uploads/system/uploads/attachment_data/file/1109305/2021_Pre-key_stage_2_-_pupils_working_below_the_national_curriculum_assessment_standard.pdf.

UNICEF. (2018). *Learning Through Play: Strengthening Learning Through Play in Early Childhood Education Programmes*. New York: UNICEF.

Vasta, R., Haith, M.M. and Miller, S.A. (1999). *Child Psychology*. 3rd edition. New York: Wiley.

Virues-Ortega, J., Julio, F.M. and Pastor-Barriuso, R. (2013). The TEACCH Programme for Children and Adults With Autism: A Meta-Analysis of Intervention Studies. *Clinical Psychology Review*, 33(8): 940–963.

Vygotsky, L.S. (1987). *Mind in Society*. Cambridge, MA: Harvard University Press.

8 Letting the learners lead

The value of meaningful, personalised learning experiences

Jo Williams

Dee Banks School is an all-age (3 to 19) specialist school in Chester, England which caters for learners with severe, complex and profound and multiple learning disabilities, many of whom also have a diagnosis of autism. There are currently 118 pupils on roll who are grouped into 16 classes, ranging in size from five to 11 learners. As Deputy Headteacher, my leadership responsibilities include curriculum and assessment development, two things I have always been passionate about improving since I began working in the field of special education many years ago. Sadly, the much-needed innovation longed for by teachers like myself has been impacted by the high-stakes testing and accountability approach to education improvement (Smith and Smith, 2020). I feel very fortunate to have been afforded the opportunity in my current role to make significant changes in my own school with the support of an open-minded team of leaders and staff.

At Dee Banks, like many other schools, we have always maintained that the individual needs of our pupils are at the centre of our work. Many moments of joy, wonder and success have been celebrated with subsequent efforts to recreate this engagement and unlock learning potential. Those working closely with individual pupils develop a nuanced understanding of their responses and interactions and build positive, lasting relationships. This tacit knowledge the staff hold of each and every pupil is invaluable to our work and must be used in the most effective way. Throughout this chapter, I hope to illustrate the changes we have made in striving towards a truly pupil-led approach, the meaningful impact this is having on our learners and their families and the valuable lessons learnt along the way.

Recognising the need for change

Our reasons for seeking change were crucial in driving us towards significant curriculum development. Making changes to fall in line with England's DfE guidance or further break down existing National Curriculum schemas had been commonplace, but there were many reasons (outlined below) which called for an entirely different approach.

DOI: 10.4324/9781003369134-11

1. The very high emphasis on achieving National Curriculum related academic skills had led to a tiny-steps, decontextualised and tick-box teaching approach, which, in turn, led to short-term targets, including skills, which generally could not be maintained by the learners. The curriculum was driven by assessment and a great deal of time was dedicated to teaching specific targets taken from assessment criteria which often seemed disconnected from the learners' needs. Whilst there was an acceptance that assessment was a necessity, there was frustration that our learners had to 'fit in' with these systems and the meaningful learning and achievements celebrated by staff and family could not be acknowledged within them.

2. The school's cohort was also gradually changing with an increase in pupils with more complex needs, often with a diagnosis of autism and behaviours of concern. These pupils all had a high level of difficulty in accessing group learning or instruction, and we had already begun to develop smaller class groups for these learners. However, despite the increased opportunity for 1:1 working, the curriculum offered was still based on a traditional model of adapting different (National Curriculum) subject areas or related topics which were delivered as group sessions with pupils seated around a table being asked to engage in desk-top activities.

3. The model was run on the basis of extrinsic reward, where activities which were personally engaging and motivating to individual pupils were offered as a reward for completing the 'work' or just taking part in a lesson led by staff. This concept of 'doing things you don't want to do' had been, of necessity, built into the culture of teaching.

4. Compliance and following a routine became a significant focus, with the success of the lesson often measured not against any learning taking place but against the absence of direct challenges to staff authority.

In 2018, we decided to revise the curriculum across the school, opting for the Equals Semi-Formal Curriculum model (Equals, 2020), which resulted in adopting domains and specialist schemes of work rather than (National Curriculum) subject-specific teaching. We developed a new school vision alongside this, and there was unanimous agreement that the well-being, confidence and independence of every learner should be at the heart of teaching and that preparation for future life should be the key driver of an individualised curriculum. Enjoyment and creativity were also a priority, with staff being excited about being able to offer a different and alternative provision to meet the needs of our unique learners. This subsequently prompted a great deal of discussion about the importance of assessing the potential of individual pupils to ensure curriculum experiences contributed in the best way to maximise meaningful learning.

We next began to consider how to develop provision for these smaller groups of more complex learners. As our tiered pathway model developed, giving a name to this group of learners was extremely powerful. We began to refer to them as 'Informal' learners (that is, those with CLD), and this, in itself, promoted and communicated a concept to teachers and other staff around the needs and provision for these pupils. It also officialised and gave value to an alternative approach which many staff were nervous, unsure or sceptical about.

Now we were beginning to define different curriculum pathways, it was imperative that this did not just become another label for smaller classes, and specifically, not one with negative or limiting associations (such as 'behavioural' or 'sensory' classes as we often hear in special schools). Maintaining a positive focus on the relevant learning that could support well-being and skills for future life has been essential. This linked clearly to the school's newly developed vision and curriculum aims and prompted much debate from staff about what this should look like for these most complex learners.

Asking the right questions

This ongoing debate has led to the following questions, which sit at the heart of the Informal Curriculum approach and continue to drive our pupil progress and planning discussions. We have learnt that the answers are very different for each and every learner and putting personalised strategies in place requires continual reflection and adaptation. The idea of letting the pupils lead has many layers and this is the first: teachers and class teams must take account of the longer-term potential of each learner to develop relevant personalised learning intentions. The delivery of these personalised curricula needs to embrace each learner's needs, preferences and challenges which may often contradict our traditional views of classroom learning, such as sitting at a table and/or being part of a group and/or following direction from an adult.

- What do life skills look like for this group of very complex learners?
- What do they need to reach a state of readiness to learn?
- What will make the biggest difference to their lives, in and out of school, both now and in the future?

Initial observed changes in practice

We encouraged class teachers to begin to make changes in line with their own reflections about the learners in their groups from which the following common themes emerged.

- Many staff began to make causal connections between the demands placed on learners by adults, the disengagement from learning activities and the often-challenging behaviours which resulted.
- Some simple but significant changes to practice were instituted, the essential one being giving pupils choices about whether they participated in activities

or not and accepting that they may disengage and re-engage, sometimes several times during a single session.

- Specific activities and resources which were engaging to individual learners were made available to access throughout the day (rather than just as a reward), and pupil autonomy began to increase.
- This also had the huge additional benefit of enabling learners to go to their preferred activity during moments of stress, thus improving real time self-regulation.

Despite these initial positive steps forward, there were still some challenges in communicating the benefits of changing our approach and yet more questions followed!

- If pupils were not made to comply with the learning activities offered, how would they learn anything?
- What is the role of the staff in this approach if not to direct, support and make decisions about when, where and how pupils access learning or self-regulation activities?
- How do we assess or evaluate the learning taking place without any SMART (Specific, Measurable, Achievable, Relevant and Timely) targets to refer to?

Lessons learnt from lockdown

Kotter et al. (2021) refer to the importance of developing a vision, preparing people for change through creating a sense of urgency, building the right team to implement the change and celebrating successes in the shorter term. This has helped me to understand the necessary stages of making changes and the actions that were needed from me to maintain momentum. Unexpectedly, further changes brought about by the Covid-19 pandemic helped us to cement our vision, drive forward this change as both leaders and staff learnt more about the impact of established routines being completely disrupted and answer some of the questions noted earlier.

During the first lockdown, our school remained open to children of key workers and those in most need. Some of our most complex, 'informal' learners were among this group, and we continued to support them in school without their usual familiar staff, peers and routines. Although the focus was just on keeping these pupils safe and happy during this time (rather than working towards specific individual targets and running class sessions), the impact of this provision was surprisingly positive. We learnt how well these young people could adapt to working with different staff, how deeply and how long they engaged with new or chosen activities as those new to supporting them sought to explore their interests. Signs of anxiety and incidents of challenging behaviour reduced significantly, and some pupils began to thrive in a way we had never seen before. This was particularly evident through communication and interaction skills with an increase in spontaneous communication to make requests, greet and initiate interaction with others.

We got to know and understand our families better and the significant and varied role that school plays for them all. Whilst school is a much-needed source of respite for families, it is also valued as a place of belonging, safety and acceptance for their children. Sadly, many families struggled without this, often referring to the relationships with staff and the access to favoured activities as what was missed most. This close working with families and the positive impact of the different provision in school further cemented and clarified our vision in relation to these most complex learners. The need to develop personalised curricula which value and celebrate the unique characteristics of each pupil, supporting them to lead the lives they want to live, had never been more important.

Next steps

By September 2020, we were able to consider which teams of staff would be most willing to continue to build on the positive progress we had made and embrace the lessons learnt from our lockdown experiences. Ensuring that these staff felt supported to explore and experiment with complete autonomy whilst maintaining a dialogue focussed on pupil progression has been key in developing our provision further. Having a wider, positive team of staff has also helped generate enthusiasm and interest in the work we are doing and fostered staff peer collaboration more naturally. The value of staff peers giving their approval to this new approach cannot be underestimated and prevents it from being seen solely as another management initiative which many in education have become oversaturated with. I have also found it to be crucial that my own knowledge of the curriculum and pedagogy has developed to equip me with the expertise to provide continual support and guidance. This now often results in me asking a series of questions in response to challenges or difficulties in deciding what next steps are most relevant to an individual.

- What have they learnt from what is already in place?
- Where do you see this going?
- What level of support will realistically be needed with this skill into the future?
- Is the learning motivating to the individual?
- How will this help their access to the community?

If we are not truly letting the pupils lead the way by giving opportunities for them to explore, be independent and use those activities which are intrinsically motivating to them, we will never find the answers to these questions. Whilst these learners may never develop functional skills to become completely independent in the community, we want them to be able make *real* choices about the direction of *their* lives. We should strive to develop independence as far as each individual learner is able so that they feel valued, listened to and part of the world around them.

Changing classroom environments

Teachers noted that demanding pupils sit at a table, particularly as a class group, caused many to disengage and resulted in frustration through unmet sensory needs. Through observing the preferences and engagement of learners when offered different environments and activities, the staff have also reported that many learners have a preference for being outside, often regardless of the weather. The informal classrooms in our school now reflect this, having minimal furniture (desks/tables and chairs in particular), space for pupils to move about, large gym balls, trampettes and open, unlocked access to adjoining outdoor areas which are treated as an extension of the learning environment rather than quiet areas or break spaces. We have found that providing pupils with the space and resources to self-regulate and lead their own learning is essential to creating personalised curricula and maximising independence.

Taking teaching and learning into the community

The pupil-led approach has extended beyond the environments of our school. As we have learnt more about what motivates our pupils and what may be possible in overcoming barriers to success beyond school, community visits and outdoor learning opportunities have increased significantly for these groups. We are fortunate to have access to a local nature reserve, community café and supermarket all within walking distance of the school. Facilitating regular visits with small groups or one-to-one support where needed has helped our pupils learn routines and practise interactions which have made a huge difference to their ability to integrate into the community and enjoy favourite activities. We also have a dedicated Forest School teacher who works with individuals and small groups both on and offsite. This is always a popular session where pupils are motivated to use different equipment and resources and develop a range of motor skills along with communication and social opportunities.

The changing nature of teaching

The work that goes on in these classes has developed significantly over time and continues to evolve around the needs and emerging knowledge of the individual learners. Staff now engage with 'reading the room', in being able to share, interact and challenge through learners' personal choices. They are keen to add resources, innovate activities and give pupils the one-to-one time when needed to extend and explore learning. Resources are carefully selected to target individual preferences, making the learning experience offered irresistible.

Music is featured in many aspects of the curriculum to support interaction, social skills, coordination and general engagement, using the *Sounds of Intent* framework (Ockleford, 2008) with its reactive, interactive and proactive template, alongside learners' natural enjoyment and responses to music. Many of our informal learners access one-to-one Music Therapy sessions for different periods throughout the academic year, with individual outcomes being very much in support of our overall aim to give our pupils skills and confidence in having voice and agency within their day to day lives.

Personalised planning; giving teaching back to teachers

If the needs of the pupils are truly the driver for curriculum design, then this should be reflected in personalised planning, rather than just a reflection of where the teacher has pinpointed the pupils' development against some externally set criteria or stage within an academic (often Literacy and Numeracy based) scheme of work. We use MAPP (Sissons, 2018) to support this and have found it to both recognise and capture individual achievements and promote reflection and discussion which drives planning of next steps. In my experience so far, the most helpful aspect of using this tool has been the opportunities to discuss progress in relation to the independence, fluency, maintenance and generalisation of skills. Many helpful considerations have come out of these discussions and very often they have also revealed that the teacher was struggling with where to go next and needed to talk this through. Crucial to success here is to embrace such questions positively and supportively rather than view them as a failure or criticism of the individual teacher.

Our teachers have become used to healthy debate about why they have set a particular learning intention for a given pupil. In fact, I have found I have never discussed teaching and learning so much with my colleagues since implementing this approach. If we find it difficult to explain why a specific learning intention should be set, we go back to what we know about the learner until we find something more relevant and meaningful. This is sometimes difficult when there has been clear progression of skills. For example, a pupil may make progress within the early stages of travel training, and it seems natural to break skills down, adding the next small step each time one is achieved. I have found there is a tendency to add a step merely because the previous one has been achieved, rather than this producing a reflective response on how far the individual learner might go. We always need to be mindful of the individual and their potential. If they will never develop the safety awareness to be independent in the community, should we be setting goals for them to cross *all* roads independently? It requires a significant level of awareness on behalf of the learner to judge the speed, distance and behaviour of vehicles and other pedestrians on many roads. It does not, however, mean that travel training is not a beneficial activity for those with CLD, particularly for a learner who enjoys walking and being out in the community. Learning the routine of following a familiar route and stopping at kerbs or responding to key instructions all help to keep learners safe when out and about and give them greater access to these activities which they enjoy. There are many examples across the curriculum of such skills, and we have learnt to bring learners' potential to the centre of our planning discussions.

Defining progress and positive outcomes

Since committing to adopting the Equals Informal Curriculum, with the support of the right staff to lead it forward, we have observed basic but hugely positive outcomes for our learners. Progress is now captured differently and is far more personalised and meaningful. This includes:

- Sustaining engagement in activities or interaction for longer periods.
- Initiating an activity or interaction.
- Showing more confidence, independence or autonomy within the familiar setting of the classroom.
- Demonstrating self-regulation skills with increased independence.
- Observable improvements in specific skills relating to their individual interests and motivations.
- Increased spontaneity in communicating greetings, requests, choices.
- Independently and appropriately expressing a refusal.
- A reduction in negative behaviours.
- An increased involvement in the local community . . . the list is endless!

Additionally, there have been some observed patterns and themes across the school as a result of this personalised progress.

1. The number of incidents of restrictive physical intervention have significantly reduced. When considering that these incidents occurred predominantly within this group of complex learners, we feel confident in observing a correlation to the change in curriculum approach. Staff and parents report how learners have become more independent and better able to express themselves. Telling us 'no' in an appropriate manner has massive potential for change when learners *know* their communications will be listened to.
2. Several parents have commented on how much happier their child seems and how much it means to them that school is so supportive of their individual challenges. Some have also told us about how they have been able to take their child out or access different activities or situations which they attribute to the personalised work carried out in school. Examples of this include accessing days out using public transport, attending their first big concert, joining family celebrations or simply just being able to walk

around the supermarket. More parents also now reach out to us for support in teaching skills that they struggle with at home and the collaboration around work towards toileting, eating, dressing and personal care is also much improved.

Whilst it must be acknowledged that the capacity of many of these learners to acquire and maintain new skills during the period of one school term (around 3 months) – or even a year – is limited and therefore progress is more difficult to define and capture, the following short case-studies and examples of pupil progress information aim to give a flavour of how learning is personalised to the interests and needs of different learners and the nature of learning intentions within our informal curriculum pathway. It is important to note that not all learning intentions written have led to significant progress (see Nathan's work on 'collecting his own resources' later for example), but this is approached as an opportunity to learn more about the learner or explore what staff can change or adapt to move forward.

Leroy (all pupils' names used in this chapter are pseudonyms)

Leroy joined the school at the age of 11 and has been at Dee Banks for 3 years within Informal class groups. During this time, his communication and interaction skills have developed as his use of sign has increased and become more accurate. He now also verbalises some simple words and can appropriately communicate when he does not want an item or activity. Frequent opportunities for Intensive Interaction (Nind and Hewett, 2001) have also developed Leroy's range of interactions, social skills and ability to initiate interaction with others. Access to a range of different activities have helped towards increasing tolerance of sensory issues such as personal care routines.

The MAPP data that follow show learning intentions and termly progress*:

Learning intention: recognise his sounds are being copied by another (assessed over one term)

Independence	1	2	3	4	5	6	7	8	9	10
Fluency	1	2	3	4	5	6	7	8	9	10
Maintenance	1	2	3	4	5	6	7	8	9	10
Generalisation	1	2	3	4	5	6	7	8	9	10

* *Light grey cells show the child's score at baseline (Time 1)*
Dark grey cells show child's score after having practised the learning intention (Time 2)
Scores of 7, 8 or above show mastery and the child is ready to move to another learning intention

Learning intention: to say 'no' to unwanted items or activities (assessed over one term)

Independence	1	2	3	4	5	6	7	8	9	10
Fluency	1	2	3	4	5	6	7	8	9	10
Maintenance	1	2	3	4	5	6	7	8	9	10
Generalisation	1	2	3	4	5	6	7	8	9	10

Learning intention: respond appropriately to greetings (<u>assessed over one term</u>)

Independence	1	2	3	4	5	6	7	8	9	10
Fluency	1	2	3	4	5	6	7	8	9	10
Maintenance	1	2	3	4	5	6	7	8	9	10
Generalisation	1	2	3	4	5	6	7	8	9	10

Learning intention: to brush own teeth (<u>assessed over one term</u>)

Independence	1	2	3	4	5	6	7	8	9	10
Fluency	1	2	3	4	5	6	7	8	9	10
Maintenance	1	2	3	4	5	6	7	8	9	10
Generalisation	1	2	3	4	5	6	7	8	9	10

Learning intention: develop a small bank of signs for preferred items (<u>assessed over two terms</u>)

Independence	1	2	3	4	5	6	7	8	9	10
Fluency	1	2	3	4	5	6	7	8	9	10
Maintenance	1	2	3	4	5	6	7	8	9	10
Generalisation	1	2	3	4	5	6	7	8	9	10

Nathan

Nathan joined the school at the age of 4 and has been at Dee Banks for 6 years. He experienced some subject-specific teaching during his early years but made little progress in acquiring any formal skills such as reading and numeracy. He enjoys one to one interaction with adults and uses his limited verbal abilities and symbolic understanding to communicate. Nathan had previously progressed through the initial stages of Picture Exchange Communication System (PECS) (Bondy and Frost, 2001) and was able to follow the routine of adding items and attributes from a limited selection to form a symbol-sentence strip. However, the concept of forming new sentences was extremely challenging, and this did not develop into spontaneous communication, nor was it used for a wider range of requests other than those practised when directed by an adult. Since reviewing our approach, learning for Nathan has focussed on increasing independence and autonomy. The following are some examples of learning intentions and recorded progress.

Learning intention: collect own resources for an activity (<u>assessed over two terms</u>)

Independence	1	2	3	4	5	6	7	8	9	10
Fluency	1	2	3	4	5	6	7	8	9	10
Maintenance	1	2	3	4	5	6	7	8	9	10
Generalisation	1	2	3	4	5	6	7	8	9	10

Light grey cells show the child's score at baseline (Time 1)
Dark grey cells show child's score after having practised the learning intention (Time 2)
Scores of 7, 8 or above show mastery and the child is ready to move to another learning intention

Learning intention: initiate familiar self-regulation strategies (assessed over one term)

Independence	1	2	3	4	5	6	7	8	9	10
Fluency	1	2	3	4	5	6	7	8	9	10
Maintenance	1	2	3	4	5	6	7	8	9	10
Generalisation	1	2	3	4	5	6	7	8	9	10

Learning intention: transition between activities outside of the classroom (assessed over one term)

Independence	1	2	3	4	5	6	7	8	9	10
Fluency	1	2	3	4	5	6	7	8	9	10
Maintenance	1	2	3	4	5	6	7	8	9	10
Generalisation	1	2	3	4	5	6	7	8	9	10

Learning intention: make own drink (assessed over one term)

Independence	1	2	3	4	5	6	7	8	9	10
Fluency	1	2	3	4	5	6	7	8	9	10
Maintenance	1	2	3	4	5	6	7	8	9	10
Generalisation	1	2	3	4	5	6	7	8	9	10

Reflections and theoretical viewpoints

Teaching our learners a differentiated National Curriculum drove staff to persevere with conveying skills and concepts which were designed to support academic progress but were hugely challenging for the individual learners. As a school, we now recognise that pupil-led learning within our Informal pathway should not be based on academic models or specific subjects. Most importantly, we have learnt that our curriculum must fit with our learners and not the other way around. It must take account of the characteristics of Complex Learning Disabilities which include often significantly impaired communication and memory, and it must also reflect the personal preferences and needs of our wonderfully unique learners. In this, we have been greatly aided by the Capabilities Approach – see Chapter 4 – (Terzi, 2010; Imray and Colley, 2017; Moljord, 2021) and especially Nussbaum's (2011) coupling of 'what is each person able to do and to be?' with her insistence that it

> is focussed on choice or freedom, holding that the crucial good societies should be promoting for their people is a set of opportunities, or substantial freedoms, which people then may or may not exercise in action: the choice is theirs. It thus commits itself to respect for people's powers of self-definition.
>
> (Nussbaum, 2011, p18, original emphasis)

Staff must accept from the start that the learners may or may not like or engage with offered activities in the way they had hoped, and that forcing, instructing or cajoling learners to take part will not result in meaningful learning but will merely end up as a lesson in compliance. One of the main challenges with this approach is that there can be no lesson-by-lesson, day-by-day or week-by-week guide which teachers had been accustomed to using. It relies on staff adapting to the needs and interests of the learners on an ongoing basis and having excellent understanding of the value of the learning taking place in relation to the specific characteristics of each individual. Being able to identify, evaluate and build on the learning that takes place is the main indicator of how well staff truly understand the aims and benefits of this approach and the meaning of personalised learning.

Conclusion

Hopefully, these case studies and the honest reflection of our journey towards a truly learner-led approach has provided a useful insight into a different view of curriculum and assessment. At Dee Banks School, we believe we are developing the provision that is right for our pupils. We want to offer a place where our children and young people are accepted and cherished as we seek to understand their world from their perspective. We hope that letting them lead the way, giving them real voice and agency, will help to acknowledge and fulfil their current and future potential. Our journey of curriculum development has been an enlightening and liberating experience. It has been a privilege to witness the positive transformation I have observed amongst both pupils and staff who are very proud of the work we do.

References

Bondy, A. and Frost, L. (2001). The Picture Exchange Communication System. *Behavior Modification*, 25: 725–744.

Equals. (2020). *The Equals Multi-Tiered Curriculum Model*. Newcastle: Equals. Available from: www.equals.co.uk.

Imray, P. and Colley, A. (2017). *Inclusion is Dead: Long Live Inclusion*. London: Routledge.

Kotter, J., Akhtar, V. and Gupta, G. (2021). *Change: How Organizations Achieve Hard-to-Imagine Results in Uncertain and Volatile Times*. Hoboken, NJ: John Wiley.

Moljord, G. (2021). Aiming for (What) Capabilities? An Inquiry into School Policy for Pupils with Intellectual Disabilities. *Scandinavian Journal of Educational Research*, 65(6): 1141–1155.

Nind, M. and Hewett, D. (2001). *A Practical Guide to Intensive Interaction*. Kidderminster: BILD.

Nussbaum, M.C. (2011). *Creating Capabilities: The Human Development Approach*. Cambridge, MA: Belknap Press.

Ockleford, A. (2008). *Music for Children and Young People with Complex Needs*. Oxford: Oxford University Press.

Sissons, M. (2018). *MAPP (Mapping and Assessing Personal Progress)*. Newcastle: Equals.

Smith, R.W. and Smith, K.A. (2020). Opportunities and Obstacles to Making Innovation a Priority in Education. *Critical Questions in Education*, 11(2): 167–178.

Terzi, L. (2010). *Justice and Equality in Education: A Capability Perspective on Disability and Special Educational Needs*. London: Continuum.

9 Plan, do, review within a holistic curriculum model

Aimee Robinson

Priory Woods School and Arts College is a state-maintained, all-age (4 to 19) community specialist school situated in Middlesbrough, in the northeast of England, providing a quality, inclusive education for pupils with severe learning disabilities (SLD) and profound and multiple learning disabilities (PMLD). At Priory Woods, we aim to support all of our children and young people to achieve the best that they can through a varied, exciting, dynamic and challenging curriculum in a safe and stimulating environment, both within and outside of school. This is achieved with the dedication of a large school team as well as colleagues in other agencies. As an arts college, we focus on exploiting the arts in all its forms to provide opportunities to develop skills and enrich lives. We recognise that we cannot succeed in our aims alone and value and respect ongoing cooperation with families and other agencies. Our school is a community where everyone is valued and respected; where we have a shared commitment to providing the best learning opportunities possible. We have the highest expectations and aspirations for all of our learners and continually seek to develop to ensure that these are realised.

Priory Woods has been adjudged by Ofsted to be serially 'outstanding'. We believe that one of the reasons for this is that we are constantly seeking to challenge ourselves and move forward; standing still is not an option. As part of this process and partly in response to the Rochford Review (Rochford, 2016) – a central government Department for Education (DfE) led initiative into assessment for those with PMLD and SLD – the school's senior and middle leaders held extended discussions throughout the 2017/18 academic year, which culminated in inviting Equals to deliver whole-school training on developing different rather than differentiated curriculum pathways. This first training day in July 2018, was followed up by a series of in-class observation and coaching support days delivered over a 2-year period, which led towards our confidence in offering a Semi-Formal Curriculum to those learners with SLD.

The school's recognition that significant changes to the curriculum were needed was provided by Equals' pedagogical rationale for pupils with PMLD, CLD and SLD (Equals, 2020). There has to be an acknowledgement of the considerable amount of research around neuro-typical development, but this (as Chapter 3 has presented) had not equated to those with severe learning

DOI: 10.4324/9781003369134-12

disabilities. Nonetheless, we reasoned that, if our pupils consistently start (at the age of 3 or 4) *and* finish (at the age of 19) their academic journeys in a serially 'outstanding' school such as Priory Woods at levels below or, at best, very near to the beginning points of the National Curriculum, we were duty bound to question the validity of the curriculum as well as our teaching of it. After much debate and discussion, we came to the conclusion that linear, hierarchical, subject-specific teaching was of limited value and meaning for pupils who are on the SLD and PMLD spectrums. The Senior Leadership Team therefore looked at the purpose of the curriculum and decided that it needed to be:

- Tailored and relevant to individual learners' needs.
- One in which every learner could succeed.
- Based on each learner's strengths and motivations.
- Engaging, exciting, challenging, thought-provoking and fun.
- Meaningful to the individual learner.
- Aligned to long-term outcomes for learners in preparing young people for life beyond 16.

Even given this clear rationale, the huge changes necessary, have taken time to embed and this has by no means been an overnight transition. Nonetheless, some 5 years on, the vast majority of staff feel comfortable in being able to discuss the intent, implementation and impact behind the curricula we want to deliver and recognise that this is the best fit for our learners.

It was clear that this journey needed real strategic direction and drive due to the huge changes we needed to make. Staffing in our secondary phase was adapted to provide continuity to students, so that we no longer had one member of staff for each subject (English, Maths, Science, etc.) but each broadly age-related class had one teacher and regular TAs assigned to it for most of their learning for the whole academic year. We felt that this would enable us to plan for a more holistic way of working with subject specific headings no longer being needed. We then used the Equals Semi-Formal Curriculum documents to identify our key learning areas of

- Communication.
- Thinking and Problem-solving.
- Self-help and Independence.
- Social and Emotional Needs.
- Sensory and Physical Needs.

In order to trial this new approach to learning, we set up one classroom as an initial Semi-Formal Curriculum base within the secondary phase and we gradually embedded the Equals ethos across the whole school.

Case study

This particular case study focuses on a class of nine 12- to 14-year-old students, all working within the severe learning disabilities spectrum and who, before embarking on their Semi-Formal Curriculum journey, tended to be quite difficult to engage, often presented as passive participants, with limited independence skills, a short attention span and seemingly unaware of how to take ownership of their own learning. The classroom was invariably set up on a 'mainstream' secondary school model, with an adapted National Curriculum being delivered in subject specific lessons. Most classes centred around providing desktop activities, with adults providing input at the beginning of the lesson to explain the content and expectation. Lessons would be based mainly around differentiated National Curriculum subject areas with the main emphasis being on producing a neat and tidy piece of work at the end of it to demonstrate that 'learning' had taken place.

Under our new Semi-Formal Curriculum, we offered instead an individualised approach which allowed staff to develop a 'free-flowing' classroom environment, where a strict timetable is not necessarily followed. That is, if engagement is evident in the activity taking place, it is likely that real learning is also happening; and therefore, why stop the learning just because the timetable says so? Maintaining the flow in this way is just one of the huge advantages of working all week (and all year) with a consistent staff team.

Another major change has been in the elevation of Play as a subject which can deliver many open learning opportunities (Watson and Corke, 2015). For those who are working at the early stages of intellectual development, Play, and playing games,

> are not time out from real work; they are the most intensive developmental work you can do.
>
> (Nind and Hewett, 2001, p66)

Play has the plasticity and flexibility to extend learners' progress through a wide variety of Play types, such as free play, structured play, role play, sensory play, etc., both indoors and out, and these, in turn, can lead directly and holistically into other parts of the Semi-Formal Curriculum, especially Communication, Thinking and Problem-solving and Independence.

At Priory Woods, this was exampled when we decided to adapt a *Plan, Do, Review* approach as a way of structuring the pupils' learning. It is based on the High Scope concept described as

> a way of working with children based on the idea that children learn best from active learning experiences which they plan and carry out themselves. In this way children learn that they are capable, able to make decisions and solve problems about activities which are personally meaningful to themselves.
>
> (www.early-years.org/highscope)

The teaching and learning centres on pupils' motivations and interest, it builds on pupils' prior knowledge, has a clear focus on interactive and active learning and is pupil centred. In practice, this approach allows pupils to receive broad and balanced learning, as it can be modified and adapted to meet all of the learning areas within a Semi-Formal Curriculum. Prior to implementing the *Plan, Do, Review* process, the pupils were given time to explore various types of Play – but especially role play. This gave the adults in the room an opportunity to build a relationship, get to know the pupils and find out their likes and dislikes, giving the pupils the opportunity to spark their own imagination and identify what motivates them. This was achieved through active interaction, with staff immersing themselves in the pupils' play, following their lead and scaffolding the learning through questioning. From this, staff began to observe and evidence the pupils experiencing active learning.

Active learning involves the pupils 'planning' their own learning; they will choose which learning area they want to work in, identify the resources they need, decide if there are any specific language skills they will need, as in, for example, asking a customer a question at a café. This gives pupils' ownership over the learning taking place, and since the decisions they have made are acted upon, they are therefore much more likely to remain on task and be engaged in the process. The staff are also fully involved in this process by taking the opportunity to gauge the learning taking place and the pupils' understanding of the learning environment. This, in turn, reinforces to the pupil that the teacher is interested in them and their learning. The teacher can then observe the pupils learning as they carry out the 'doing' part of the process.

Once the 'doing' part of the process is complete, it is now time for the pupils to 'review' their learning and evaluate the experiences. This may involve pupils explaining that they did not have the correct resources or the number of pupils to successfully play. It allows pupils a chance to discuss their learning, what happened, how they can make it more successful next time, giving teachers an opportunity to assess the learning taking place and how they can facilitate the learning to promote pupil progress. Time and flexibility are needed as the Plan, Do, Review process is a sequence and one which pupils will continually learn from and develop over time.

Setting up

The learning environment was created through the use of role play areas which we call 'working areas'. The teacher's planning is based around these working areas with a deliberate link to careers and preparation for adulthood, given that we were working with a class of 12- to 14-year-olds. For these sessions, the classroom might be seen to be similar to an Early Years classroom, though the Play opportunities leant towards role-play areas likely to support the pupils in their personal learning (adult) journey. These included a café, a supermarket, a hairdresser and a building site. The areas provided real life resources as much as they could in order to give pupils an insight into the real working world.

The working areas were used as an integral part of delivering a pupil-led curriculum model. Within this particular class, it took two academic terms for the pupils to feel confident in planning their own working areas which showed their development and understanding around their learning environments. We recognised that the learners' Play needed to be supported, but this was in the use of facilitating rather than directing techniques. In this way and over an extended time period, the Play of each individual pupil was personally developed throughout the sessions. To maintain high standards of progress for the individual pupil, challenges and tasks were available to ensure pupils reached their full potential (this is completely individual to the pupil and may take some time before these are introduced).

The areas stayed the same for a substantial amount of time, with changes in theme to match the current topic or story. This was dependent upon the pupils' interests and what motivated them. Throughout this process, I recognised that repetition and over-learning were key, and this gave me the confidence to insist that, although some support staff may have felt the same things were being delivered to the pupils week after week, the learners were effectively cementing the experiences and using them to draw on it the next time – and the next time after that. In a Semi-Formal Curriculum, the development of independence, communication and thinking and problem-solving skills is a process which takes time. If the process is right, the product will take care of itself.

In-the-moment planning (an individualised approach to plan, do and review)

Example One. During the summer term, after a group discussion, the class explored the idea of 'Magic', the pupils and staff discussing the learning areas we wanted in the classroom and coming up with a 'Potion Shop', 'Hagrid's Home Corner' and a 'Wizard Creation Station'. The pupils spent time exploring the different areas and immersing themselves in the learning environment. Through role playing as wizards, making different potions and learning about Hagrid's hut, one student began to tell a story about a haunted house. The support staff wrote down the story as the student shared it with his peers. The class really enjoyed the story, and this then took our learning down a completely different path. We learnt the story through actions and signs and encouraged the pupils to mark make in order to sequence the story. In the creation station, the pupils made haunted houses from the junk material, dressed up in the role-play areas and acted out answering the door and finding the ghost. We also made lanterns to see in the dark, and the final plan from the pupils was to showcase this in assembly. We changed this into an 'Enterprise' approach with different students having different job roles, such as making props, the PowerPoint for the assembly and then working together as a team to get it ready for the big day! All the pupils were fully engaged throughout the whole process, which shows the power of allowing pupils to take ownership of their own learning.

Example Two. A working-buddies group was created so that the pupils worked collaboratively with their peers to provide peer support. The class was split into three groups, with one group choosing to work on a café project, their first job being to assign job roles when working in that particular area. After discussion and scaffolding from the teacher, various roles were allocated and the planning began. Pupil A was the waiter, deciding that she needed an apron, a menu and coins. Pupil B chose to be the chef, with his plan including a pan, apron and some food to cook. Pupil C chose to be the customer, deciding that he needed a menu and cups. The member of staff acted as the scribe using a large sheet of A3 paper, though pupils were encouraged to write down or draw their own individual plan if they could. The group then set up the scenario using their plans and various props (such as a proper chef's hat), which had been organised previously, in order to engage in the 'doing' part. This then provided an opportunity for the teacher to make observations and highlight areas of challenge, support and the next steps of learning.

The class remained on-task and carried out what they had planned to do whilst working in the café. However, the customers could not eat their food order, as the waiter did not bring over cutlery, and the chef ran out of milk whilst making a drink for the waiter to take to the customer. The pupils were asked to come over and 'review' their learning, and they quickly identified what had gone wrong and said they needed knives and forks for the customer to eat and that the customer needed to ask the waiter. The chef said he needed to go to the shop to buy more milk. Within that one lesson, the pupils had an opportunity to develop their social, collaborative and communication skills, worked on building memory, showed confidence in their problem-solving abilities and developed their functional play skills.

Offering a holistic approach to learning

One of the main difficulties of differentiating a National Curriculum model is the tendency towards being forced towards a compartmentalised approach to teaching, especially at secondary (post-11) level. The norm of mainstream schools in England is to teach in subjects and to advocate subject specialisation, and many specialist schools (including Priory Woods before our conversion) also still follow that path.

Our Plan, Do, Review classes do, however, really highlight the necessity of regarding learning for those with severe learning disabilities as a holistic experience. The Priory Woods version of Plan, Do, Review comes broadly within the subject of Play but also relates directly to Drama, Thinking and Problem-solving, and Independence. With the inspiration for role play ideas coming from storytelling, we can also see the direct relationship to Communication, especially in the use of Narrative, one of the major elements of Equals' My Communication area of study.

Narratives are the telling by learners of both factual and/or fictional stories. These are not scripted (as in a book) but are derived from memory and repetitive practice. They are usually quite short – a minute or two in the telling – and describe events or relate interests, biographical information, jokes, stories, etc. Narratives are the way we all communicate about our lives – good, bad, funny, sad – to those who matter to us. They are the essential glue of social humanity and their development owes a huge debt to the works of Keith Park (Park, 2010, for example) and especially Nicola Grove (Grove, 2012, 2013, 2014).

It may be that we think of narratives as being long, fictional works, like novels or tales handed down from generation to generation, and indeed, they can be, but for those with severe learning disabilities, narratives are simply a spoken account of connected events. This may take the form of a fictional story, and it is often easier to teach the skills required by introducing learners to this form of narrative to start with, but much more importantly, the narrative skills taught here will allow learners to tell others of the important things that have happened in their lives. For those with severe communication difficulties, this will often be very problematic and without a significant amount of time being spent on the process – often impossible. This makes teaching the art and skill of narrative very, very important.

A story has a beginning, a middle and an end; it has purpose and meaning to both the teller and the listener; it teaches us to listen carefully; it teaches us about structure and about the natural rhythms and flow of language; it teaches us about emotions – fear, excitement, anxiety, heartbreak, happiness, love – in a safe and secure setting, not only other people's (the characters' in the story line) but also our own. Most importantly, however, our ability to tell stories directly both effects and affects our understanding of our own humanity. Sharing our lives with others in this way allows us to relive the happy and exciting and thrilling and gain enjoyment from the interest of others. It allows us to receive a sympathetic ear when bad things have happened and the repeated retelling to lots of different people may allow us to make sense of the event over time. Apart from the cathartic benefits, the very act of relating the narrative can bring an initially overwhelming event into proportion.

Being able to tell our own stories marks us out as special and individual and unique. I have done this; I have value; I am important; I am me. Sharing the sad or pathetic or frightening experiences of our lives allows us to evoke others' sympathy and empathy, put our problems into perspective, receive back the comfort of someone else's similar experience so that we know we're not alone. I am me, but I'm also with others who love me and care enough about me to listen and share in my problems as well as my joys.

So, the experience of acting out the roles of a wizard or a chef because they interest and engage us are not just isolated events in the school calendar but are directly related to the whole process of learning and the connections this enables us to make.

Conclusion

The impact has been astounding and we have seen steps of progress in all areas of learning for all nine pupils. As class teacher, one of the successes of this has been watching the pupils' progress over time within their communication, independence and thinking and problem-solving skills. The pupils in my class have actively taken full ownership of their learning and have been able to direct their own learning by developing and expanding upon their individual areas of interest, motivation and engagement. It has aided the development of the pupils' speaking, listening and communication skills; the pupils have been able to retain information, pass on appropriate information, improve their social skills and be part of dynamic communicative partnerships with both peers and adults. Pupils have built resilience, their confidence growing with their willingness to try things out without the fear of making mistakes. That is, mistakes are inevitably made (how can they not be) but all pupils, to a greater or lesser degree, are now able to accept that mistakes are a central part of the learning process and therefore do not fear making them. The pupils' growth in confidence has helped them work as a team, being more aware of who is around them as they work together towards a common goal. On top of this, staff have observed the transfer of skills from key stage 3 to key stage 4 to Post-16 (that is, from the age of 11 to 19), enabling pupils to embark on a journey that has been individualised to meet their needs and which seeks to promote all the skills needed for life beyond school.

The case study group of students have moved onto Post-16, and some are ready for the next steps into adult life. A few of these students have worked towards their Entry-Level Functional skills; all of the students work in the school's Post-16 Community Café as waiters and earn a wage from this. The holistic journey these pupils have embarked on has given them time to practise and develop skills to an individual level. Even more importantly, they have been given a voice and their agency has been enabled, so they feel confident and valued within school. One of the highlights of adopting this approach came from an ex-student who came back into school and (with the head teacher) observed my lesson, their comments being '*if lessons had been like that when I was at school I wouldn't have spent time out of the classroom. It's good, it's like getting ready to be an adult*'.

References

Equals. (2020). *Pedagogy and Rationale. The Equals Multi-Tiered Curriculum Approach*. Newcastle: Equals.

Grove, N. (2012). Story, Agency, and Meaning Making: Narrative Models and the Social Inclusion of People With Severe and Profound Intellectual Disabilities. *Journal of Religion, Disability & Health*, 16(4): 334–351.

Grove, N. (ed.). (2013). *Using Storytelling to Support Children and Adults with Special Needs*. London. Routledge.

Grove, N. (2014). Personal Oral Narratives in a Special School Curriculum: An Analysis of Key Documents. *British Journal of Special Education*, 41(1): 6–24.

Nind, M. and Hewett, D. (2001). *A Practical Guide to Intensive Interaction*. Kidderminster: British Institute of Learning Disabilities.

Park, K. (2010). *Interactive Storytelling: Developing Inclusive Stories for Children and Adults*. Bicester. Speechmark.

Rochford Review. (2016). *The Rochford Review: Final Report. Review of Assessment for Pupils Working Below the Standard of National Curriculum Tests.* Standards and Testing Agency. Available from: www.gov.uk/government/publications/rochford-review-final-report.

Watson, D. and Corke, M. (2015). Supporting Playfullness in Learners with SLD/PMLD: Going Beyond the Ordinary. In P. Lacey, R. Ashdown, P. Jones, et al. (eds.) *The Routledge Companion to Severe, Profound and Multiple Learning Difficulties* (pp. 365–374). London: Routledge.

10 An introduction to an informal approach

Trish Turner

To explain the journey of forming the curriculum intent and implementation at Brackenfield SEND School in Derby, England, it is first pertinent to explain the context of the school. Brackenfield was an early special school established in 1956, a prefab building resembling a one-story secondary school with a Science lab, Design Technology Workshop, Home Economics room, and later, a computer suite. The cohort, originally with wide-ranging SEND, aged 4 to 16, now consists of learners with severe learning disabilities (SLD) and complex learning disabilities (CLD), aged 4 to 19, typically pupils with additional autism, some non-linguistic, with varying cognitive abilities, though all with significant learning disabilities. Pupil numbers have increased rapidly in recent years from 62 pupils in 2016 to 161 today.

The why: setting the scene and why change was needed

'Blue chair Yusef', was the instruction given to a 6-year-old pupil with CLD several times a day. It was unclear whether Yusef knew what a chair was, let alone what blue was. Brackenfield, like many other Specialist Schools, had, over time, developed a curriculum that represented a watered-down version of the National Curriculum with Numeracy and Literacy at its heart and with the theory that children would progress in a linear fashion. We believed that, though learners would progress slower than their neurotypical peers and their end points would always be lower, the curriculum was fit for purpose. The curriculum came first. The children were then taught the content. This was further reinforced by the traditions imposed upon all learners by a government-approved system of learning, where there was a fundamental belief that literacy and numeracy (and the teaching thereof) underpins all other learning – a theory we ourselves, as teachers, also held as a fundamental belief, having all been trained in the generic teacher training system in the UK.

What this meant was that there were students (not unlike Yusef) who, at 4 years old, were able to count (on a good day) to 3. The next logical step in this linear model would be for them to count to 4. Despite repeated attempts and the use of several different media to facilitate the teaching of this knowledge,

DOI: 10.4324/9781003369134-13

these pupils, at the age of 16, were still only able to count to 3. This posed the question 'why were we expecting pupils to "sit on the blue chair" and learn number when this was something beyond their capability?' and the more important question 'what is it we should be teaching them and how?'.

Though a specialist school, all staff had been trained to teach in the same way – a specific pedagogical model which was target driven for pupils against age-equivalent goals, viz, the Early Years Foundation Stage (EYFS) outcomes and England's National Curriculum. The goal of this curriculum being to prepare the children for the next stage in their education, be that examinations or qualifications required for employment or further/higher education. Beyond that, we did not have any 'specialist' knowledge of how or what to deliver to these young people.

Though we were unsure of *what* we should be doing and *how*, we were certain of three things: children with significant learning disabilities and complex needs:

- Learn differently, so must be taught differently.
- Do not develop in a 'standard' or identikit way, meaning that predicting an end point or target goal, be that short or long term, was nigh on impossible.
- The only inevitability was that all these young people would become adults.

The goal was now clear: to research and find an approach that considered the child first and then best met their learning needs (later described as their holistic needs), preparing them for the inevitable: adulthood.

The What

As a school, we were aware of the work of Dr Penny Lacey (Lacey, 2009, for example), which led us to Imray and Hinchcliffe (2014) and the Equals Curricula (Equals, 2020, for example). Through attending seminars and training events, we metaphorically began 'dipping our toes' into this alternative approach, described by Imray and Colley (2017) as 'process-based learning'.

Following initial research into alternative approaches and curricula materials, it became apparent that our school could (maybe slightly crudely) be divided into two key groups of learners. The first group consisted of those pupils who had severe learning disabilities (SLD) and who would follow a Semi-Formal Curriculum (see Chapter 1). Typically, these are pupils who require an approach which develops **functionality** and **independence**. This is a life-skill-focussed curriculum. In identifying semi-formal learners, we did not look at levels of cognition per se, but more at levels of comprehension and willingness to engage with others; these are pupils who are able to copy an adult and follow instructions. Teaching for these learners is not instructional but is **doing to learn** – doing activities with a high level of repetition to embed learning in long term memory, with an element of naturally occurring or adult-induced sabotage to support the learners' ability to problem solve.

The second group, which this chapter will explore in greater detail, were those who would follow an Informal Curriculum, an approach which supports communication and engagement (again, see Chapter 1). These learners *can* understand instructions but are not necessarily motivated to follow or to copy an adult. Engaging these learners is challenging, since communication is limited, and without engagement and communication, there is no platform to support further learning. Engagement and communication therefore become the core building blocks. For these learners our goal is to develop **choice** and **voice**, enabling them to have agency in their own lives.

The How: the pilot project

Implementation of these two different curriculum approaches was not an overnight journey. It has taken several years to develop staff understanding and change the deep-rooted beliefs and routines they hold from teacher training. The change of approach also had a knock-on effect to all other aspects of the school, from structure of the staffing body to the logistics of the school day and the infrastructure of the school building and facilities. It is fair to say that this is a continuing journey as we respond to current research and through our own trial and error with teaching methods and use of resources and facilities. There is a continuing theme of fitting a square peg in a round hole: why do schools look and function as they do? Partly, as Robinson and Aronica (2015) point out, because they always have done, but this seems also to be strongly related to the prescriptive 'advice' from powerful organisations such as, in England, the DfE and Ofsted. In addition, the constraints of a school building, a 5-day week of 32.5 hours routinely interrupted by registers, breaktime, lunchtime as well as prescribed curriculum content, is not conducive to the development of learners with complex learning needs. The challenge is to reimagine the educational landscape through their eyes and innovate to create a more fitting model.

A trial period was initiated with three classes. These were chosen not just based on the presenting needs of the children but also the skills and attitudes of the staff. These were staff who identified that trying to teach counting to 4 for 14 years or insisting a child sits on a chair to be 'ready to learn' were not effective teaching strategies. They were also open-minded about trying an alternative approach. The staff had attended an Equals (2020) seminar and, with the Equals curriculum documents, implemented the approach which is described later. Initially, this involved taking away demands and being led by the child and their known motivators. The challenge came in extending their learning through these activities, which relied on staff being creative, available for the children and reactive in the moment. From skilled staff who instinctively responded to the children, this worked well. For others, the result was lack of structure and lack of engagement opportunities for the children, which led to the learners essentially roaming or stimming for large periods of the day. It became apparent that staff needed to be cognisant of a range of approaches to support them to effectively deliver an informal approach. These approaches include:

- Intensive Interaction (Nind and Hewett, 1994, for example); and there is an explanation of this approach in Chapter 6.
- Attention Autism (a means of encouraging joint attention). For more information see https://best-practice.middletownautism.com/approaches-of-intervention/attention-autism/
- A range of communication strategies from signing with Makaton (a system of sign-supported speech, based on British Sign Language specifically written for those with learning disabilities) to the use of augmented communication aids such as symbols, objects of reference or TOBIs (true object-based icons).
- Play, specifically Free Play, where the individual learner is enabled and encouraged to both choose what (or who) they want to play with and to take the lead.
- Sensory Exploration (what might be described as 'messy play').
- Physical Exploration, especially trampolines, swings and climbing frames.

Routine and predictability were built through daily routine, usually marked by snack time, lunch time (challenges for those children who use grazing stations constantly throughout the day) and taxi time. The pupils had access to outdoor space, sensory areas, sensory equipment, toilets and kitchenettes within the classrooms. This allowed them to independently get what they wanted/needed or request this from a member of staff through gestures.

As a 'specialist' school of relational practitioners, we have always prided ourselves on listening to the needs and wants of the pupils. What had become apparent was that, prior to the curriculum change, this simply hadn't been happening. Previously, staff had pushed their preconceived ideas of what the pupils wanted/needed/should be doing onto them rather than reading what the children were truly communicating. In reducing demand and allowing the children freedom to access what they desired, early observations indicated that a large percentage of the children opted to be outside, and all pupils were able to sustain activities of preference for prolonged periods of time. The children responded specifically well to water play, sand play, rhythmic drumming and sensory input (specifically proprioceptive and vestibular).

We do not refer to our approach as 'no demand', as there will always be some demand, personal and intimate care, PEG flushes, medicines administration, first aid and home time, to give some examples, but there is no doubt that demand has been massively reduced.

As described, an Informal Curriculum can, without creativity and responsiveness from staff, lead to lack of stimuli for the learners, especially as they are less likely to engage with varied or new stimuli immediately. This may require items and activities to be introduced to pupils several times before they show any interest. It is not uncommon to see a member of staff playing in the messy play, experimenting with paint or climbing on the sensory playground, with the children seemingly paying no attention at all, though it may also be that the children give fleeting attention, coming to an activity with an adult for a brief moment. It is important that the adult welcomes and facilitates the child with the activity for that brief period with the hope they will show preference or start to extend their engagement over time. No task/activity is forced on the children and, though encouraged to participate, children have the freedom to join in or not. It is as important to know what the children won't engage with as what they will; this is, of course, about them communicating preference – sometimes the strongest communication comes when a child does not want to do an activity.

Initial barriers to effective delivery included the following:

- Lack of variety of stimuli and activities, the same known motivators being used day in day out without staff being able to extend learning through these.
- Lack of patience of staff to leave activities out for several days to give pupils the ability to opt in.
- Lack of creativity in finding ways to extend activities further.
- Remaining fixed to a pre-written timetable and cutting activities short even when children were engaging.

To support the removal of these barriers, classes were advised to always have access to preferred items as well as sand and water play, apart from in sessions where there is a requirement for no distractions, such as Attention Autism. Then they might shape activities around a weekly theme as a way of stimulating awe and wonder and as a vehicle to provoke engagement and interaction as well as widening pupil preferences. An example is balloon week.

Monday – the room was filled with hundreds of balloons. The children, on arrival, burst all the balloons.

Tuesday – the balloons were filled with helium and were all on the ceiling without string attached. This prompted the children to interact with the adults in the room to access them, and the activity extended with staff attaching string to the balloons and the children pulling them down and letting them go. The staff then extended again, by tying items to the strings, some of which floated at different heights and some of which weighed the balloons down. By the end of the week, the children were playing and manipulating the balloons, taking care not to pop them.

Other activities on other days included:

- Filling the balloons with water, the children explored these, popping them, throwing them, feeling them, puncturing them and watching the water squeeze out.
- Filling balloons with sand or flour, creating stress-ball-like balloons, the children squeezed these, some popped the balloons to see what was inside, staff hid these under plant pots (along with the water balloons) and the children searched for them.

- Freezing water balloons (embedding preference objects in the ice), these were received in a variety of ways, some children enjoying mouthing or holding them, some, with staff modelling, running them under warm water to reveal the items inside.
- Painting with the balloons, including filling the balloons with paint and popping them. The painting worked best when the floor was covered with big sheets of paper allowing the children to print with the balloons using water-based paint or roll the balloons in the paint and across the paper; as you can imagine, more than just the paper got painted.
- Using modelling balloons to make shapes and link together.
- Filling balloons with glitter and confetti and bursting them (we had lots of glittery staff and children).
- Filling the room full of small balloons and using fans and a leaf blower to blow them around.

Fruit and veg week was interesting. The assumption by staff was that the children would prefer the sweet taste of the fruit. Though they enjoyed mashing and manipulating various fruits, the star of the show was raw white onion. The children seeking sensory input had sought out the onion to mouth and smell. It was such a strong preference in one class, this was then built into their preferred items and enabled class staff to engage the children in further activities such as sensory cooking.

Beyond the themed weeks, the children also take part in a range of other activities such as swimming, trips out into the community and Forest School which, like the classroom environment, is very exploratory. Life extends beyond the school gates, and it is important that the children experience the world around them, with the end thoughts always to prepare them for adulthood. Long-term goals will obviously vary for Informal Curriculum pupils, but it may be something as simple as buying what they want to eat from a shop. They may not get to a point where they are able to navigate around a supermarket independently, know the value of money or how much change they might receive, but this does not mean that they can't go shopping and select what they like to eat. Simple and replicable routines are therefore set up so that:

- Each learner decides what they're shopping for. For learners working on the Informal pathway, this will usually be a single snack item which can be bought for less than £1 but could get more complex if simple meals are being prepared (such as beans on toast for example) in later years, in which case the learner would need a £5 note.
- Having decided what they want to buy, the learner writes out a shopping list and goes to see the school banker, who issues them their £1 coin.
- The learner puts the £1 in their purse and the purse in their backpack, which already holds a shopping bag.
- The learner travels to the shop, learning to be as independent in this process as they can be over time.

- Once at the shop, the learner takes a basket (or a trolley), finds the item, queues at the till, pays the cashier with their £1 coin, takes the change and the receipt, putting these into their purse, puts their purse in their backpack, places the item in their shopping bag and carries the shopping bag back to school. It is important that the learner knows how to shop independently; it is not important that the learner knows how much change they should receive.
- Once back at school, the learner goes to the banker, gives the banker the receipt and change, which the banker then 'banks' into £1 coins again, ready for the next shopping trip.
- The learner can, if they wish, then consume the item they've bought.

Initial outings to the supermarket to familiarise with the setting, the noises, sights, smells, people, etc., can inevitably lead to a different preferred item from the one on the shopping list – or even a trolley full of crisps! It is important that our pupils have agency over their own life, which starts with providing them with the option for choice and, most importantly, enabling them to *know* they can have choice, which may include changing their mind once they've reached the shop. However, having agency does not necessarily equate to doing what one wants because they only have a single £1 coin, which is clearly not enough for a whole trolley full of crisps. These are, then, real learning opportunities, delivered in real time, within a real context and real consequences – in this case, the learner has to stay in budget.

Our delivery also plans for wider engagement and enrichment outside of the classroom. How does a child know if they like the cinema, roller coasters, to play in the snow or on the beach if they have never experienced these things? Why shouldn't our learners have the opportunity to experience these things which may lead to wider fulfilment of their lives?

Planning for learning. The overriding need for all informal pupils is engagement and interaction; however, they do all have individual preferences, needs in the moment and needs going into adulthood. Using the statements from the Preparation to Adulthood Framework (CDC, 2022), we are able to show what we are aiming towards in adulthood for these pupils. We are then able to set learning intentions against the four areas of the framework: Independent Living; Employment; Friends, Relationships and Community; and Good Health. This shapes the priorities for individuals, which are then targeted throughout their daily routine and activities. The Equals Curricula materials are used to inform teaching activities, especially within the areas of Play, Communication and Independent Living.

Evidencing learning. Learning is evidenced through photos, videos and staff statements. Often, learning is best captured via video rather than still photos. Brackenfield uses an electronic platform which allows staff to tag photos and videos against the pupils learning intentions, the EYFS descriptors (DfE, 2021a), the Engagement Model (STA, 2020) and MAPP's descriptors of independence, fluency, maintenance and generalisation (Sissons, 2018). There are also tags for applied literacy and numeracy, though these are not taught as discrete subjects; they are interwoven into all aspects of accessing the world. This allows us to track pupil progress, show their journey through school and also run cross-group/school analysis of pupil progress. Leaders can therefore ensure that classes are providing appropriate coverage; for instance, it may be that children in one class are able to complete their personal learning intentions independently with fluency and maintenance but aren't able to generalise. This, then, would raise the question: are they given the opportunities to generalise, and if they are, are they the right opportunities?

Assessment of learning. Personal learning intentions are assessed through a range of processes, using MAPP. Termly review of assessment and progress (or RAP) meetings are held, where the learning intentions are discussed against the pupils' strengths and needs (long and short term) and the evidence of learning reviewed with the MAPP outcome. The triangulation of this information provides a narrative regarding whether learning intentions are appropriate, too challenging/not challenging enough and the child is provided with the right opportunities to achieve and to prepare for adulthood.

Lessons learnt. Process-based learning is difficult to conceptualise for those who have learnt to teach in a typical way. There is a need to disregard or unlearn how to deliver a 'curriculum-first' approach. Due to the individual needs of the learners, staff are required to adapt to the learner, and this can mean that some staff/pupil combinations will simply never work. Equally, though the fundamental elements of the approach are teachable to staff, it is not possible to replicate an identikit session or lesson to different pupils and expect them to engage or connect in the same way. It is the skill of the practitioner to read the child and respond accordingly and instinctively. In other words, it's all about relational practice, knowing the children and making a connection. A knowledge of the life story and attachment needs of a child is also critical in understanding what their behaviours are communicating and ensuring the right structure for learning is implemented. A child with significant early-years trauma and attachment needs may have the presenting need of an informal learner but will require a much greater level of structure and boundaries to make them feel safe than would be appropriate for typical informal learners.

Parents' perceptions and ambitions for their children can also be a challenge for schools to navigate when moving to this alternative approach. The current education system places such an emphasis on what education *should* be, it is difficult for parents and carers to see beyond the need for Maths and English. Equally, there can be an assumption that we should all want and need friends and interactions with others, with parents often saying 'I just want them to be happy and have friends'. So many of our learners have no want or need for friendships and they do not feature in their version of happiness. An open, honest and supportive dialogue is required with parents around what are the absolute priority needs for their child and how we, as a school, facilitate these. We need to challenge the concept that the teaching of numeracy and literacy in traditional terms is appropriate for *all*, and though there is a need for connection and interaction with others, there is not necessarily the need for friendships as understood in neuro-typical, conventionally developing terms.

Where we are today

Our journey in embedding these alternative approaches is now 5 years in. All students follow a Semi-Formal or Informal approach. We assess against age-related equivalencies for the areas of the Early Years Foundation Stage (DfE, 2021a), Development Matters milestones in numeracy and literacy (DfE, 2021b). This is not intended for target-setting purposes or to identify the next step on a linear set of attainment criteria. It does, however, give a holistic picture of how and at what level a pupil is accessing and comprehending the world around them. A strength and needs assessment is also completed, highlighting priority needs now and into adulthood, as described earlier (thus aligning to a child's Educational Health and Care Plan), and it is from this that a pupil's Personal Learning Intentions are derived. Further contextual information is gained by completing a sensory needs screening, a Speech and Language screening and also running a Journey to Learn profile for each pupil. The Journey to Learn provides information and the narrative around attachment and well-being needs. Based on the holistic picture of the child from the foregoing information, a timetable is built around them targeting their Learning Intentions. Pupils are grouped by similar need and then, where appropriate, grouped into the same timetabled activities, though the need or outcome of the activity for any two pupils is invariably different.

The Informal classes have a weekly immersive theme but always have access to water and sand play as well as the outdoor areas and sensory equipment. The school continues to develop our specialist resources and spaces to support the curriculum.

Staff induction and training is rigorous and requires periods of shadowing as well as reflective discussion. Recruitment is centred around the *right* people who show natural instinct and connection with the children, rather than the right experience. Ongoing training and development opportunities are in place for staff to reflect or further develop their practice. Most importantly, staff are encouraged to meet, to talk and reflect together both about what is working well – but also what is not working.

The What and the impact of change

The impact of changing our approach is, in some circumstances, tangible and, in some, not at all. As mentioned previously, the structure of the school has been impacted, from the design of learning spaces to the addition of specialist equipment. The pupils are happier. A measurement of happiness is not quantifiable, nor are the children able to give us their opinion on their level of contentment; however, the surrounding evidence suggests that happiness has been considerably improved upon. We observe the children to have greater levels of engagement, being able to extend attention for ever-increasing lengths of time and seeking greater contact and connection with staff. Behaviour incidents have plummeted and the need for restrictive physical interventions to prevent harm to themselves or other people have also significantly decreased and are rarely, if ever, employed to support behaviour. Our pupils of all ages experience a level of control they did not have, and this control gives them a level of freedom that was previously denied them. They are now able to engage with a life that they want to lead, rather than having to conform to a life that someone else has chosen for them.

The approach of staff also *feels* different. Staff look to each other for support and are wholly accepting if they struggle to connect and support a child; they do not take this as a criticism of their ability, but instead, are relentless in trying to change tack or find an alternative. A climate of trust and kindness permeates all that happens with the children.

As a leadership team and a school community, this experience and journey has compelled us to challenge our own thinking and preconceptions about social norms; to critically and holistically evaluate what is in the best interest of the learners and families we serve. It has pushed us to completely re-evaluate our purpose as 'educators' of children as well as the process and structure of that education.

Conclusion

Our pupils learn differently; for them, it is not just school but the whole world that is different. We now know that all we thought we knew does not necessarily fit and does not necessarily work for them, so we strive for difference, which, in time, will become the new norm. We no longer consider our 'business' as 'teaching and learning' but as 'learning and teaching'. In every way, we are led and learn by the needs and wants of our young people. This is the very truest model of pupil voice and agency. This may pose a much wider question: in our different model, who is the teacher and who is the learner?

References

CDC. (2022). *Preparation for Adulthood Framework*. Available from: https://councilfordisabledchildren.org.uk/resources-0/preparing-adulthood. Accessed 10 April 2023.

DfE. (2021a). *Statutory Framework for the Early Years Foundation Stage*. Available from: https://assets.publishing.service.gov.uk/government/uploads/system/uploads/attachment_data/file/974907/EYFS_framework_-_March_2021.pdf. Accessed 7 April 2023.

DfE. (2021b). *Development Matters. Non-Statutory Curriculum Guidance for the Early Years Foundation Stage*. Available from: https://assets.publishing.service.gov.uk/government/uploads/system/uploads/attachment_data/

file/1007446/6.7534_DfE_Development_Matters_Report_and_illustrations_
web__2_.pdf. Accessed 7 April 2023.

Equals. (2020). *The Equals Multi-Tiered Curriculum Model.* Newcastle: Equals. Available from: www.equals.co.uk.

Imray, P. and Colley, A. (2017). *Inclusion is Dead: Long Live Inclusion.* London: Taylor & Francis.

Imray, P. and Hinchcliffe, V. (2014). *Curricula for Teaching Children and Young People With Severe or Profound and Multiple Learning Difficulties: Practical Strategies for Educational Professionals.* London: Routledge.

Lacey, P. (2009). Teaching Thinking in SLD Schools. *The SLD Experience,* 54: 19–24.

Nind, M. and Hewett, D. (1994). *Access to Communication: Developing the Basics of Communication With People With Severe Learning Difficulties Through Intensive Interaction.* London: David Fulton.

Robinson, K. and Aronica, L. (2015). *Creative Schools: Revolutionizing Education From the Ground Up.* London: Penguin.

Sissons, M. (2018). *MAPP (Mapping and Assessing Personal Progress): Semi-Formal Model.* Newcastle: Equals.

Standards and Testing Agency. (2020). *The Engagement Model.* Available from: www.gov.uk/government/publications/the-engagement-model.

11 Independence versus interdependence

Exploring the potential of a bioecological learning model for pupils with PMLD

Martin Goodwin and Nathan Taylor

Introduction

The contexts in which we teach pupils directly shape their responses, and create the experience of education for learners. The quality of the environment to enable effective interactions (the proximal) or the resource mechanisms to enable interaction through policy, training, and leadership (the distal), are variable and complex contexts, and these are affected over time. The values, working practices, and procedures at a structural level and policy at a macro level, indirectly and directly influence the ways in which we assess progress (Hayes et al., 2017). The aim of this chapter is to explore conditions that impact on learning for pupils with profound and multiple learning disabilities (PMLD). We focus specifically on the proximal processes that occur in the classroom and explore a bioecological model, rather than furthering the debate that exists in behavioural and cognitive psychology, as there is much debate in these fields (Simmons and Watson, 2014; Imray and Colley, 2017).

Teachers are leaders of learning in the classroom, implementing a curriculum and assessing progress over time. As authors, we were interested in talking to teachers about the potential of proximal processes. Setting aside specific curricula models or assessment schema, we explore interactions with pupils, objects, and symbols in the classroom. We wondered what this reveals about their lived experience of teaching pupils with PMLD and the possibilities for and challenges of re-imaging learning within a bioecological model.

The context

There are different approaches to curriculum design for pupils with PMLD. Schools in England might not realise this – such is the dominance of the national curriculum model – but they do have the freedom to develop their own model based on their overarching vision (Lawson et al., 2015; Ofsted, 2019). Many schools have adopted a curriculum model that may be considered as a sensory curriculum (Longhorn, 1988) or a pre-formal curriculum (Lacey, 2011; Imray et al., 2019). Individual schools have different perspectives on

DOI: 10.4324/9781003369134-14

the notion of inclusion and may decide to organise the learning through national curriculum subjects, while others may opt for schemes of work such as 'my communication' or 'my thinking' to capture the personalised nature of curriculum organisation for pupils with PMLD.

Debates about the optimal approach to curriculum remains contentious (Goss, 2006; Imray and Colley, 2017). The argument for access to national curriculum subjects relies on the belief that a common curriculum ensures equality of entitlement. However, recently, the debate has returned to linear pathways to curriculum development, with schools expected to scope and sequence the curriculum so that skills and knowledge are mapped out over time (Ofsted, 2019). This is incongruous with the assertions made within the Rochford Review (Rochford, 2016) – that learning for pupils with PMLD cannot be pre-determined. Planning of the curriculum in this way fails to recognise the subtlety of responses by pupils with PMLD in specific contexts (Lawson et al., 2015). Moreover, developmentally based curricula centre on differentiation of learners rather than affording their differences and fail to recognise the unique needs of pupils with PMLD. Within this system, declarative knowledge (knowledge of facts and information) is prioritised over procedural knowledge (knowledge of the process), thus devaluing this population (Ten Berge and Van Hezewik, 1999).

Research of learning and curriculum for pupils with PMLD is scarce, which has led to a limited evidence base for school leaders and teachers (Arthur-Kelly et al., 2008; Kossyvaki, 2019). Models of learning are still situated within behavioural and cognitive psychology, and while these are helpful as part of a tool kit to guide teachers' understanding of the processes of learning, especially when they are new to teaching, they remain the dominant models that frame our understanding of PMLD. These are evident in assessment models commonly used in special schools in the UK; for example, Routes for Learning (Welsh Assembly Government, 2020) and The Engagement Model (STA, 2020). These models exist within a wider assessment framework – the special educational needs and disabilities (SEND) Code of Practice (Department for Education and Department for Health-DfE/DoH, 2015) – that incorporates high aspirations, participation and independence for learners with SEND. The notion of participation of pupils with PMLD is beset with practical and ethical complexity. Pupils with PMLD seldom have access to conditions that enable their active participation within their daily lives and have limited support to affect their social conditions (Goodwin, 2019, 2021).

The definition of independence is problematic, as it implies being able to do something without support. Such a limited view of independence poses challenges for its application in assessing pupils with PMLD, as they rely on a very high level of support to engage within proximal processes. Small steps of progress can be challenging, aspirational and achievable. However, care needs to be taken to ensure that the process is meaningful. To enable this, independence can be understood within a model of interdependence (i.e., the dependence of two or more pupils or things). It can be argued that this is implicit within the design structure of Equals Pre-formal Curriculum. Imray et al. (2019, p1) argue 'a pre-formal curriculum provides a structure to ensure that teachers build routines, facilitate change, offer alternatives and observe and guide'.

By setting out the context for the chapter, we have highlighted the tensions that exist between the distal processes (e.g., the Code of Practice, statutory assessment and curriculum) and the proximal processes (e.g., relationships, learning environment and learner profiles) for the teacher of pupils with PMLD. We, the authors of this chapter, work within different settings that apply curriculum models in very different ways. We have been teaching pupils with severe and profound and multiple learning disabilities, including autism, for over 20 years. Neither setting explicitly implements the pre-formal curriculum as developed by Equals; however, we are both influenced by the concept of a pre-formal curriculum. In seeking a commonality, for the purposes of this chapter, we contemplated the conditions for learning, transcending curriculum models and setting aside dominant theories of learning applied in classrooms for pupils with PMLD. We wanted to explore different patterns of learning that co-exist within proximal processes and distal relations. Therefore, we began with the question 'What are the conditions that teachers create to impact on the quality of learning for pupils with PMLD?'

Mclinden et al. (2020, p192) propose a bioecological model as a conceptual framework 'to explore the development of personal agency for learners with multiple disabilities . . . and how this can be sustained through an education pathway'. The bioecological model as developed by Bronfenbrenner provides 'provisional indicators of exercises of agency' (*Ibid*, p195). This model focuses on the empowerment of learners across four proximal processes. These four processes will be defined next and will act as a conceptual framework for a small research study we undertook for the purpose of writing this chapter.

A bioecological learning model

The bioecological model situates the interaction of the person and considers the dynamic relationships that exist within a nested ecology that focuses on Person, Process, Context and Time factors (PPCT). PPCT factors focus on the development of the child (P=person) that is developed through relationships with other pupils and objects (P=proximal relations) in an influencing environment (C=context) over time (T=time) (Hayes et al., 2017).

The bioecological model holistically captures the development of the child within contingent and adverse conditions that impact but also considers the personality, dispositions and available resources of the child and examines how these are encouraged through interdependent proximal processes.

The nature of processes that are undertaken with the person are key to their development. Proximal processes are defined as

> progressively more complex reciprocal interaction between an active, evolving biopsychological human organism and the persons, objects, and symbols in its immediate environment.
>
> (Hayes et al., 2017, p155)

Context is primarily viewed as a nested ecology of levels that impact and influence the person. Within the context, proximal processes and distal relations are considered by how they interact and adjust to each other. The key feature of context is its interdependence in relation to the person, objects, symbols, their shared environment and how they intra-play.

Proximal processes are impacted by the relations, context, distal influences and time factors that structure their lives. Greene et al. (2010, cited in Hayes et al., 2017, p26) suggest that time can be explained in 'micro-time' – what is happening during a particular interaction or activity; 'meso-time' – the extent to which the activities and interactions occur with consistency in the developing child's environment; and 'macro-time' – the historical context for a child's development and the timing of certain events in a child's life.

We propose a model (see Figure 11.1) that highlights the central nature of interdependency in enabling the agency of the pupil. This is achieved through understanding and responding to the profile of the pupil, enabling proximal processes and harnessing the power of context and structures of time so that their development is optimised.

Methodology

The bioecological model provides a different lens to explore the conditions that teachers create to impact on the quality of learning for pupils with PMLD. Six teachers were invited to participate in a short, semi-structured interview (ranging from 45 minutes to 2 hours) to gather their views. In Table 11.1, we provide the teachers' names (pseudonyms given by the authors), the author who interviewed them, the teacher role and whether they worked at the same or different setting as the authors.

Four broad questions resulting from the foregoing model were developed with a range of prompt questions to explore the areas further (see Table 11.2). Teachers were purposely selected from within the chapter authors' professional networks. Each participant was degree educated, and they had a minimum of 1 year as a practising teacher of pupils with PMLD, including early career teachers, experienced classroom practitioners and middle leaders with whole-school teaching and learning responsibilities.

The interviews were audio recorded, transcribed and data was analysed using the Bronfenbrenner's person, process, context and time (PPCT) model

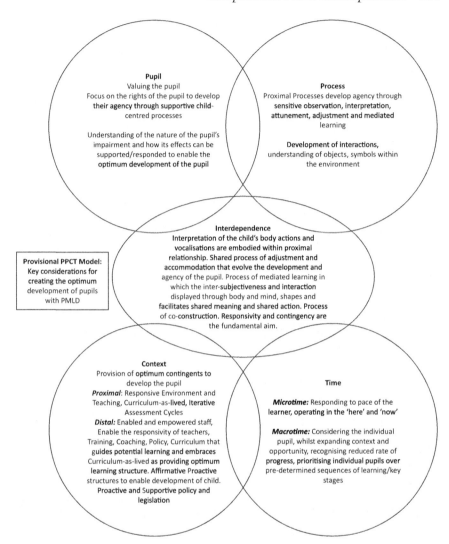

Pupil
Valuing the pupil
Focus on the rights of the pupil to develop
their agency through supportive child-
centred processes

Understanding of the nature of the pupil's
impairment and how its effects can be
supported/responded to enable the
optimum development of the pupil

Process
Proximal Processes develop agency through
sensitive observation, interpretation,
attunement, adjustment and mediated
learning

Development of interactions,
understanding of objects, symbols within
the environment

Interdependence
Interpretation of the child's body actions and
vocalisations are embodied within proximal
relationship. Shared process of adjustment and
accommodation that evolve the development and
agency of the pupil. Process of mediated learning in
which the inter-subjectiveness and interaction
displayed through body and mind, shapes and
facilitates shared meaning and shared action. Process
of co-construction. Responsivity and contingency are
the fundamental aim.

Provisional PPCT Model:
Key considerations for
creating the optimum
development of pupils
with PMLD

Context
Provision of **optimum contingents** to
develop the pupil
Proximal: Responsive Environment and
Teaching, Curriculum-as-**lived, Iterative
Assessment Cycles
Distal: Enabled and empowered staff,
Enable the responsivity of teachers,
Training, Coaching, Policy, Curriculum that
guides potential learning and embraces
Curriculum-as-lived as providing optimum
learning structure. Affirmative Proactive
structures to enable development of child.
Proactive and Supportive policy and
legislation

Time

Microtime: Responding to pace of the
learner, operating in the 'here' and 'now'

Macrotime: Considering the individual
pupil, whilst expanding context and
opportunity, recognising reduced rate of
progress, prioritising individual pupils over
pre-determined sequences of learning/key
stages

Figure 11.1 PPCT Model: key considerations for creating the optimum development of pupils with PMLD

as a conceptual framework (Bronfenbrenner and Morris, 2006). Each author analysed three interviews to capture key themes from within their own networks. The findings from each author were put together to explore the tensions and commonalities that emerged. Two vignettes were developed from the responses gathered within the interviews that the authors felt exemplified the PPCT factors at work within current practice. Next, the findings and discussion are presented together in a dialogue between the two authors.

Table 11.1 Teacher participants

Participant	Interviewer	Role	Setting
Lindsay	Martin	Early Career Teacher	Different setting
Abby	Martin	Middle Leader	Different setting
Deborah	Martin	Teacher	Different setting
Helen	Nathan	Early Career teacher	Same setting
Teresa	Nathan	Middle leader	Same setting
Chantel	Nathan	Middle leader	Different setting

Table 11.2 Semi-structured interview questions

Aspect	Questions
Person	In what ways, if any, does the planning and teaching of the school curriculum value the child?
Process	In what ways, if any, do pupils interact with objects, pupils and symbols in the classroom?
Context	How do you understand the concepts of independence and interdependence in the context of your teaching practice?
Time	Can you tell me about how you develop your class timetable and in what way it maximises the available time for the development of learning?

Findings and discussion

In this section, we discuss the findings from the data alongside theory and practice. Some themes that emerge are congruent while there are also differing views that exist across the two networks of teachers. It was evident that the teachers' own lived experiences of curriculum design and assessment practice influenced their responses to the interviews in different ways.

Nathan: What did you find most striking about the responses of the teachers you interviewed?

Martin: I noticed how participants prioritised interactive learning approaches over a defined sequenced curriculum for driving the development of the pupil (through a pre-determined order of milestones). Interactions were a conduit for shared communication that enable development of thinking and understanding through physicality and other often non-verbal actions.

Nathan: I would agree. It was clear through the responses in my interviews that teachers recognised the conflicts between curriculum design and the ways in which pupils with PMLD learn. How would you reflect on this within a bioecological model?

Martin: Bronfenbrenner describes proximal processes that focus on interaction and relationships with other humans, objects, symbols as

---

Box 11.1 Saeed's vignette as described by Chantel

I have a pupil who did not receive an education for many years. Saeed doesn't have much movement in his wrists or hands. In addition, he has scoliosis. He has very limited vision. With limited movement, he doesn't really get opportunities to experience his body being moved or movement opportunities. I struggled to find a meaningful way for him to engage with activities. Adults would do things for him and to him because they interpreted his responses so well. However, they didn't often step back and see the little things he was doing on his own.

We noticed when he was really enjoying something, one of his fingers would just release ever so slightly. We made him a glove that had little bells on it, the simplest thing; so, when he moved his finger, he would hear the bells jingle. We always worked in a quiet classroom, or he wouldn't hear them. I'm smiling now because it's such a small thing to include in a curriculum. It was a meaningful thing to work on because we've seen it and we've valued it. Soon, Saeed was not only moving his fingers but moving his whole hand. Then he started to move his arm a little bit as well. Now, he can make lots of things happen; for example, by activating a soft pillow switch, he can control a fan or play music.

---

the engine of human development (Bronfenbrenner and Morris, 2006). Despite some systems not providing necessary contingents for optimum development of pupils, the teachers I interviewed persevered with valuing the process of empowering the learner through a process of sensitive observation, interpretation and mediated learning.

Nathan: Yes, I found this too in some of the specific examples that teachers discussed with me. I want to share a specific example from Chantel that she shared with me about her experiences with one of her PMLD learners (who for the purpose of this chapter will be named Saeed). I think it illustrates your point further (Box 11.1).

Martin: Here, the concept of challenge and progress is defined through the process of attunement and adjustment by the teacher, who facilitates the child's development by recognising the emergent agency of the learner; not imposed or standardised expectations of development. Meaning is built through a process of reflection on how the learner interacts within the proximal relationships, objects and symbols within the environment. As Deborah stated, '*symbols should grow organically from that person's interests and motivations*'.

Interactive learning is therefore the powerful nucleus in which meaning is formed, negotiated, shared and extended.

Nathan:　I feel it presents the tensions teachers experience when planning the curriculum. The trend currently is to present a sequenced curriculum. Helen asserted this succinctly in her interview. She reported that the teaching styles and ways in which lessons are taught are based on what the students can engage in, what's relevant to them and real-life concrete experiences which is completely multi-sensory, so that they can access it in a range of different ways.

Predetermining learning by sequencing the curriculum can limit the ways in which the teacher plans for the individual with PMLD.

Martin:　I agree. Whilst developmental areas may provide guidance when utilised as a sequence, pupils with PMLD may not follow typical lines of development. Lindsay discusses the dilemma stating that in theory we're saying that our curriculum values the learner, their individuality and how they learn, but sometimes the curriculum doesn't actually reflect that.

Developmental curricula typically breakdown normative trajectories of development, which fail to consider the impact of impairments and often neglect to recognise the learning priorities of pupils with PMLD.

Nathan:　In what ways do proximal processes support us to think differently about learning, beyond current behavioural and cognitive psychology?

Martin:　We can consider that proximal processes which occur within the microclimate between the pupil with PMLD and the teacher are interdependent of each other. Therefore, interpretation of the pupil's body and vocalisations that are made are embodied within a proximal relationship. The pupil and the teacher are not two separate entities, but mutually exist in a shared process of adjustment and accommodation with each other, within routines, activities with objects, symbols and the environment around them that evolve the development of the pupil.

Nathan:　These embodied interpretations were clear in Helen's reflections of teaching pupils with PMLD. They were incredibly detailed in her discussion of both interactions with objects and pupils. For example, she used phrases such as 'child turns their head very slowly and starts to smile' or 'learner doesn't particularly like wet textured objects . . ., so when he feels something that's wet will start to very slowly just back their hand away'. I found that the participants whom I interviewed reflected on these embodied interpretations consistently. I wonder if there is something more to these inter-pretations than simply stimulus-response causality that might be explored through the bioecological model?

Martin: I believe the term 'interdependence' has much value in reflect-ing the reality of pupils within learning contexts, as it explains the shared reciprocal process of undertaking and participating within routines, experiences through a process of mediated learning in which inter-subjectiveness and inter-action displayed through body and mind, shapes and facilitates shared meaning. Interdependence requires a sensitive approach and a range of skills that, through the proximal process, the teacher contingently deploys in response to the agency of the learner.

Nathan: I think this is very powerful. Is there a specific example within the responses of your interviewees that you feel demonstrates this?

Martin: Deborah described an encounter with a pupil with PMLD whom, for the purpose of this chapter, I will name Mary. The following vignette (Box 11.2) demonstrates how interdependence requires a sensitive approach and a range of skills that, through the proximal process, the teacher contingently deploys in response to the agency of the learner.

Nathan: Interestingly, I feel one of my interviewees extends on this vignette further by suggesting that the importance of achievement is that pupils can interact with their own learning environment when and how they want to within an environment that the teacher provides.

Box 11.2 Mary's vignette as described by Deborah

Mary is a child who appears not to be very responsive. She has limited use of her hands as they are contracted. Also, Mary has a cortical visual impairment. I plan time for her to explore the world within a quiet envi-ronment. When I position her onto a resonance board, she turns her head and moves her fingers. I once put some objects that made sounds near to her hands, and she could obviously perceive that something was there. Whether it was the vibration or the sound, she reached towards the item with her hand. When Mary was lying on her back on the reso-nance board, it appeared that she was sensing vibration through her pelvis from the percussion instrument. Also, it might have been from her heels resting on the resonance board that she could sense these things. Educationally, it's essential that we don't think of anybody as just having a brain and a pair of hands, but we understand how crucial it is that the whole body is involved.

Martin: These examples reveal how teachers have a facilitative and empowering role where they help to scaffold the interaction through a process of co-construction (Bunning, 2009). As such, proximal processes are interdependent, relational processes that are dynamically shaped by both parties and the environment. Furthermore, the way an activity is carried out, the level of choice and control that is promoted through human connection, through which responsivity and contingency become the fundamental aim.

Nathan: I found the participants I interviewed to be more committed to the notion of independence. Through discussion, they asserted different ways of understanding the concept. For example, Chantal argues that as somebody who champions pupils with PMLD, everything we do is about trying to make a difference to their lives in terms of giving them a moment of awareness or learning that they may not have otherwise encountered. I will still use 'towards independence' and phrases like that as a reasonable term because I'm talking about it in the context of that individual and what it means for them.

I think tensions exist in understanding, between the concepts of independence and interdependence. Indeed, another of the participants I interviewed wasn't sure what interdependence means and unsure if it is a helpful concept within their teaching. Chantal believed by developing a consistent environment it was possible to argue that as a teacher her focus was on development of the learner's independence.

Martin: These tensions exist in the literature too. Oliver (1990) notes that disabled pupils perceive independence as having choice and control over their lives; not necessarily being able to carry out skills. Conversely, the notion of interdependence embraces the idea that pupils need support in some or all areas of their lives (Colley and Tilbury, 2020). Reindal's (1999, p354) view is pertinent to enabling the emancipation and responding to the support needs of pupils with PMLD.

When the human condition is viewed as one of interdependency. . . this leads to an understanding of interdependence as 'partnership'. . . independence becomes a two-way responsibility and not solely an individual ability.

Nathan: For me, this is where the proximal and distal processes impact on the conditions for learning. For example, in England, preparation for adulthood is a central tenet of the Code of Practice for SEND (DfE/DoH, 2015). As such, it creates a lack of direction for curriculum design as, post-19, life is uncertain. As in school, life as a young adult and beyond for pupils with PMLD will always involve partnerships with parents, carers, advocates and health professionals. The core and essential standards for pupils with PMLD (Doukas et al., 2019, p34) states that meaningful time 'recognises the need for everyone to participate and be actively engaged in activities personally enjoyed and with pupils they like to spend time with'. I wonder how thinking with the bioecological model might provide a new perspective as proximal relationships are affected in and over time.

Martin: It is a tension I also recognise and appeared in the responses of the teachers I interviewed. Education is viewed as preparation for learners' future lives. Schools stratify time into key age-related stages. It is a classification system in the UK which is made up of four cohorts. The four key stages group pupils chronologically as they progress through compulsory school years. Key stages define learning that should occur and the types of learning opportunities that should be offered. However, the stratification of progression through key stages potentially 'others' pupils with PMLD, as these structures are designed to align to formal curricula. As such, they may not focus on the rights of the child. As Abby explained, 'although the context and opportunities might look a bit different across the key stages, the learning intentions that they're working on are still very individual'.

Nathan: Chantel referred to teaching a 'fragmented' group. This was not meant as a negative term but one which reflects the unique ways in which pupils in her class learn – but also the fact that it is not uncommon to have pupils from more than one key stage within a class. Planning the curriculum over time within chronological structures does not always support teachers to consider the individual learner. Chantel puts it in the following way. 'Pupils don't all do the same thing at the same time. I have a carousel of activities that they will all do over different days. Different learners require a different pace of activity'.

Martin: Time is a key component of the PPCT model. Abby and Chantel talk about time as a multifaceted concept in which Greene et al.'s (2010) representation of 'micro-time', 'meso-time' and 'macro-time' is pertinent, as, within the PPCT model, time and the relations of person, process and context are interdependent. The normative structures of time within education such as through pace of the activity (micro-time), the perceived imposition of different experiences related to age and the organisation of key stages that map out the child's life at school (macro-time) may negatively affect the development of the pupils with PMLD.

Nathan: Indeed. For the pupil with PMLD, adjustment accommodates the right to learn over time and at a significantly reduced rate; this is needed at micro and macro levels. Distal influences, such as educational policy, can disrupt the optimum conditions for learning, as the time needed to support pupils with PMLD positively may be negatively viewed. Currently, we risk inhibiting the natural process that occurs within proximal relations.

Martin: Focussing on the quality of life in the here and now, through quality interactions, is so important for pupils with PMLD. This should be valued within the process of education.

Nathan: The risk is that we lose sight of the importance of education if we do not consider how challenge is conceptualised for pupils with PMLD, beyond engagement. Engagement is an essential ingredient for meaningful learning to occur; however, as Imray (2021, p73) argues, pupils with PMLD must be empowered to 'affect the world'. Mclinden et al.'s (2020, p195) definition of empowered outcomes inspired by Bronfenbrenner's bioecological model is useful. They posit empowered outcomes as

> evidence of measurable levels of individual activity over a specified timeframe that indicates progress and expansion with respect to the child being able to influence the environment to bring about desirable change.

Martin: This makes a lot of sense, as the current prioritisation of declarative knowledge and memory as the key tenet for successful learning (Ofsted, 2019) devalues the importance of using interactive approaches (Collis and Lacey, 1996). It ignores the importance of procedural knowledge for pupils with PMLD. It is essential that the education system values the proximal processes that enable the development of life skills that these pupils imperatively need.

Nathan: Helen and Chantel talked in minute detail about the way they planned their day. The teachers' comments returned my attention to learning in the here and now. They were concerned with planning their timetables that reflected opportunities to learn across different environments acknowledging the ebbs and flows of integrating what might be considered curriculum-as-plan with the curriculum-as-lived (Aoki, 2004).

Martin: Can you explain more about curriculum-as-plan and curriculum-as-lived as it pertains to pupils with PMLD and their teachers?

Nathan: Aoki (2004) talks about the curriculum-as-plan as something that is developed outside of the classroom. In a way, it is abstract. Typically, it is designed by leaders and sets out what the class teacher is expected to teach the pupils in their class. Whereas, curriculum-as-lived is situated in the world of the teacher and pupils through their daily interactions and experiences.

Martin: So, the curriculum-as-lived is about how the teacher and the pupil with PMLD listen and respond (Goodwin, 2013) through a process that is communicative, dynamic, relational and interdependent (Bunning, 2009, cited in Palwyn et al., 2009). Curriculum-as-lived are proximal activities that foster interdependent relationships and enhance the development of shared meaning.

Nathan: Absolutely. It is an ethical and relational approach to understanding the conditions for learning. It resists disembodying learning experiences from the environment. It also relies on the care of the teacher to provide new possibilities to engage and challenge pupils bringing together an understanding of curriculum and the unique learning profiles of each pupil.

Martin: So therefore, the teacher actively listens to a variety of signals, interprets, supports and, through this process, contingently listens and responds. Within the proximal processes, the pupil with PMLD is not passive, but through interdependence, shapes and affects their relations and environment.

Conclusion

To conclude, we return to our initial question 'What are the conditions that teachers create to impact on the quality of learning for pupils with PMLD?'. In our small-scale study, we found that the interviewed teachers revealed significant tensions between systems orientated teaching and specialist teaching. For them, the notion of a sequenced curriculum inhibits agency of the pupils and weakens the responsivity of teachers to enable their development. Through the formation of proximal processes, optimal relations and interactions are fostered and a shared meaning of objects and symbols develop. Time is viewed differently for pupils with PMLD. The trajectory of learning for them is unique, which is consistent with the Rochford Review (Rochford, 2016). Teachers asserted in the interviews that key concepts must be repeated and practised; pupils need more time, disrupting the notion of key stages, as they are normative. The teachers acknowledged the different rates of progress that pupils with PMLD show over an extended period.

Interdependent relations are signified through interactions where teachers are required to contingently and sensitively interact and communicate. Enabling proximal processes requires the de-structuring of standardised curriculum and assessment methods so that the supportive processes that teachers use contingently respond to how pupils with PMLD learn. The principles of the bio-ecological model are consistent with the aim of the Equals Pre-formal Curriculum (Imray et al., 2019). The bi-directional dynamic of process, person, context and time offers a holistic understanding of factors that are conducive in supporting optimum development. Within this model, the agency of the pupil is developed through proximal relations that fundamentally 'understand the development implications' (Mclinden et al., 2020, p195) and is expanded through the harnessing of the lived experience of teaching pupils with PMLD through a process of shared control and responsivity.

We were unable to incorporate the entire breadth of the bioecological model, and we would recommend further research to explore the conditions for analysing the impact of it on development of pupils with PMLD. Moreover, this was a small-scale study conducted in the UK to enrich our views on the topic, and claims may not be representative of a wider range of practitioners within the field. The context of special schools has many impacting dynamics which are complex and highly variable, so further research is needed to expose the mechanisms that optimise or hinder proximal processes.

The bioecological model is an alternative method to articulate elements of effective curriculum design for pupils with PMLD as advocated by the Equals Pre-formal Curriculum (Imray et al., 2019). We believe proximal processes may meaningfully support alternative approaches to understand the development of pupils with PMLD. Through iterative cycles of assessment, the model offers the potential for improved authenticity and the natural development of the learner.

References

Aoki. (2004). Teaching as In-Dwelling Between Two Curriculum Worlds. In W.F. Pinar and R.L. Irwin (eds.) *Curriculum in a New Key: The collected works of Ted T. Aoki* (pp. 159–166). London: Routledge.

Arthur-Kelly, M., Foreman, P., Bennet, D., et al. (2008). Interaction, Inclusion, and Students With Profound and Multiple Learning Disabilities: Towards an Agenda for Research and Practice. *Journal of Research in Special Educational Needs*, 8(3): 161–166.

Bronfenbrenner, U. and Morris, P.A. (2006). The Bioecological Model of Human Development. In W. Damon and R.M. Learner (eds.) *Handbook of Child Psychology; Vol. 1, Theoretical Models of Human Development* (pp. 793–828). 6th edition. Chichester: John Willey and Sons.

Bunning, K. (2009). Making sense of communication. In J. Pawlyn and S. Carnaby (eds.) *Profound Intellectual and Multiple Disabilities: Nursing complex needs.* Oxford: Wiley-Blackwell.

Colley, A. and Tilbury, J. (2020). *Enhancing Wellbeing and Independence for Young Pupils with Profound and Multiple Learning Difficulties: Lives Lived Well.* London: Routledge.

Collis, M. and Lacey, P. (1996). *Interactive Approaches to Teaching – A Framework for Teaching.* London: David Fulton.

Department for Education and Department for Health. (2015). *Statutory Guidance SEND Code of Practice: 0 to 25 Years.* Available from: www.gov.uk/government/publications/send-code-of-practice-0-to-25.

Doukas, T., Fergusson, A., Fullerton, M., et al. (2019). *Supporting Pupils With Profound and Multiple Learning Disabilities: Core and Essential Service Standards.* Available from: www.pmldlink.org.uk/wp-content/uploads/2017/11/Standards-PMLD-h-web.pdf.

Goodwin, M. (2013, Spring). Listening and Responding to Pupils with PMLD – Towards a Framework and Possibilities. *SLD Experience*, 21–27.

Goodwin, M. (2019). Raising the Bar Through a Listening and Responding Approach, *PMLD Link*, 30(1).

Goodwin, M. (2021). Listening and Responding Through Non-Instructed Advocacy. *PMLD Link*, 33(1).

Greene, S., Williams, J., Layte, R., et al. (2010). *Growing Up in Ireland*. National Longitudinal Study of Children: Background and Conceptual Framework. Dublin: Office of the Minister for Children and Youth Affairs.

Goss, P. (2006). Meaning-Led Learning for Pupils With Severe and Profound and Multiple Learning Difficulties. *British Journal of Special Education*, 33(4): 210–219.

Hayes, N., O'Toole, L. and Halpenny, A.M. (2017). *Introducing Bronfenbrenner: A Guide for Practitioners and Students in Early Years Education*. London: Routledge.

Imray, P. (2021). Engagement is Necessary. . . but Challenge is Essential. *PMLD Link*, 33(3): 100.

Imray, P. and Colley, A. (2017). *Inclusion is Dead. Long Live Inclusion*. London: Routledge.

Imray, P., Vazques Navarro, D., Bond, L., Goodwin. M., Bliss, D., Tilbury, J., Croft, E., Green, M., Kelly, M., Purtuk, A. and Lemmon, S. (2019). *Equals Pre-Formal Curriculum* Newcastle. EQUALS.

Kossyvaki, L. (2019). Why is Research Important? Reflections for Professionals and Parents. *PMLD Link*, 31(2): 90.

Lacey, P. (2011). *A Profound Challenge*. Accessed from: https://senmagazine.co.uk/content/education/57/designing-a-curriculum-for-pmld-a-profound-challenge/.

Lawson, L., Byers, R., Rayner, M., et al. (2015). Curriculum Models, Issues and Tensions. In P. Lacey, R. Ashdown, P. Jones, et al. (eds.) *The Routledge Companion to Severe, Profound and Multiple Learning Difficulties* (pp. 233–245). London: Routledge.

Longhorn, F. (1988). *A Sensory Curriculum for Very Special Pupils: A Practical Approach to Curriculum Planning*. London: Souvenir Press.

Mclinden, M., Mccall, S. and Hodges, L. (2020). *Learning Through Touch: Supporting Learnings With Multiple Disabilities and Vision Impairment through a Bioecological Systems Perspective*. 2nd edition. London: Routledge.

Ofsted. (2019). *Education Inspection Framework (EIF)*. Accessed from: www.gov.uk/government/publications/education-inspection-framework. Accessed 13 August 2022.

Oliver, M. (1990). *The Politics of Disablement*. Basingstoke: Macmillan.

Reindal, S.M. (1999). Independence, Dependence, Interdependence: Some Reflections on the Subject and Personal Autonomy, *Disability & Society*, 14(3): 353–367.

Rochford, D. (2016). *The Rochford Review: The Final Report*. Available from: www.gov.uk/government/publications/rochford-review-final-report.

Simmons, B. and Watson, D. (2014). *The PMLD Ambiguity: Articulating the Life-Worlds of Children With Profound and Multiple Learning Disabilities*. London: Routledge.

Standards and Testing Agency. (2020). *The Engagement Model*. Available from: www.gov.uk/government/publications/the-engagement-model.

Ten Berge, T. and Van Hezewik, R. (1999). Procedural and Declarative Knowledge: An Evolutionary Perspective. *Theory and Psychology*, 9(5): 579–720.

Welsh Assembly Government. (2020). *Routes for Learning: Guidance*. Available from: https://hwb.gov.wales/curriculum-for-wales/routes-for-learning#routes-for-learning:-guidance.

12 Pushing the boundaries

Creating a personalised culture with the child at the heart of teaching and learning

Katie Lyon

This chapter aims to provide a practical, honest and reflective account of our journey as a school in ensuring our curriculum and assessment systems meet the individual needs of all our children. The journey has been long, and at times, challenging and is far from over, but what we have created is a culture and practice we are extremely proud of.

Kingsbury School is a primary specialist provision for pupils with severe, complex and profound learning disabilities and has 95 children on roll grouped according to their learning needs rather than by chronological age. Previously, as Deputy Headteacher, I sought to change systems and processes that as a class teacher I found uncreative, prescriptive and irrelevant. There were limited opportunities to celebrate the unique individual progress our children made. Now, as Kingsbury's Headteacher, I am extremely lucky and thankful to have an open-minded, dedicated team who have embraced significant changes with determination, courage and enthusiasm. Without them, this journey would not have been possible.

Sinek (2009) focussed our direction by starting with 'Why?'. Quite simply . . . the key significant word within our journey has been WHY. Why are we doing this? Does it have a positive impact on the child? If the answer is no, then we don't do it.

Intention: Why change?

As a staff team, did we understand our children, and how they learn? Did we understand their developmental age and level of cognitive ability? Did we have the pedagogical understanding? How could we develop 'a distinct and separate pedagogical approach to the learning needs of the most educationally challenging pupils' (Imray and Hinchcliffe, 2014, p1)?

The P Scales (DfE, 2014) gave staff sleepless nights as we relentlessly forced children to try and achieve an irrelevant objective in order to hit our own data-performance-management targets. This was exhausting, frustrating and deflating for staff and led to learning not being meaningful for the children. Children were taught and occasionally learned by rote, but once they walked out of the classroom, struggled to apply their learning or use it effectively in

DOI: 10.4324/9781003369134-15

other contexts. For the majority of children, engagement in Reading, Writing and Mathematics was poor, and those who did engage tended to do so from a desire to conform, as passive learners, rather than from enjoyment and understanding. And why did we make all children sit through formal phonic lessons that had very little impact on their progress?

Our curriculum model was developed around an outdated, linear, subject-specific progress model which placed too much demand on learners, required formal teaching and learning and raised anxiety, which led to lack of engagement, lack of motivation, challenging behaviours and restricted and limited progress, especially for our complex, autistic learners. Through evaluating historical data, it was evident that our curriculum provision and methods of assessing performance were no longer effective in demonstrating our learners' progress. Our curriculum was assessment-driven, where the objective had become to tick sheets rather than enable real learning. Further, behaviour incidents were a daily occurrence and physical restraints were high. Compliance in formal lessons was the expectation – with staff demanding that pupils sit on chairs at tables to complete worksheets or overwrite or copy in exercise books, mainly with physical prompts.

The publication of the Rochford Review (Rochford, 2016) provided an opportunity to create a bespoke, new-generation curriculum and assessment package that would meet the needs of all our children. It allowed us to develop a meaningful and relevant curriculum whilst giving teachers scope and freedom to follow the child's interest and learning style as well as bringing their unique flair to teaching and learning. The journey has not been easy and smooth; it has been long and challenging, with many bumps along the way, but has it been worth it? YES, it certainly has. Our school leaders have had to be brave, resilient and strong in the belief that every decision we make is about the child and not based simply on what we are told we have to do or because other schools do it. Doing something different that doesn't fit the norm is, at times, a lonely and vulnerable place to be and making collaborative links with similar schools and professionals is essential no matter what the distance.

Our curriculum and assessment models have been created through researching excellent, child-centred practice throughout the country. We haven't tried to fit into someone else's model; we have developed aspects that work for our children and personalised it for us. Our model has the child at the heart of everything we do. The Kingsbury Way Curriculum is child-centred and holistic, and assessment is ipsative; that is, assessment is a measure of an individual's progress in relation to their own starting point.

Implementation

Step 1: assessment

Our journey started by questioning our assessment model. We asked ourselves, why are we doing this? Is it having a positive impact on the children?

Upon reflection we realised that our systems did not support the learning of our increasingly complex children. The following provided us with reasons for change:

- Children's Educational Health and Care Plans (EHCPs) and End of Key Stage outcomes needed to be the focus of our assessment systems, not 'off-the-peg' and formulaic published schemas based on projected linear progress.
- Historically, targets had been taught in isolation and not been mastered or generalised, so had very little impact for the child outside the classroom.
- The Rochford Review (Rochford, 2016) and the Ofsted Inspection Framework (Ofsted, 2019), alongside poor internal data from a published assessment framework that no longer reflected individual progress, provided compelling evidence to drive change.
- Our assessment focus needed to change to make our systems about and for the child so that everything we did could have a positive and meaningful impact on their progress.
- The introduction throughout school of Evidence for Learning (EfL), a digital tool for collating data and evidence, was an ideal opportunity to remodel our own assessment schemas and cut down on paperwork.

As the Rochford Review notes,

> existing arrangements for assessing pupils have come to be used as a curriculum, restricting the kind of creativity and innovation that should be used to engage these pupils (with PMLD and SLD) and to tailor teaching and learning to their unique needs. Rather than following the letter of the P scales, it is much more important that knowledge, concepts and skills are acquired in a range of contexts and situations, according to a varied and stimulating curriculum.
>
> (Rochford, 2016, p3)

At Kingsbury, all aspects of school life are now designed to engage and motivate children and provide meaningful learning opportunities. Different curriculum experiences have been designed to meet the needs of all children across the school and personalised plans also form a key part of our curriculum input. A bespoke assessment system is therefore required to support staff to plan the best route for each individual and to capture holistic and ipsative progress in all aspects of development. We now use assessment tools and systems which are driven by our curriculum and specialist approaches to teaching and learning. We have instituted MAPP (Sissons, 2018), an assessment system that celebrates the important lateral progress our children make and which recognises development in areas such as independence and personal and social development. EfL has also proved invaluable in giving us a tool to track the progress and journey of the personalised learning outcomes that link to the progress of expected outcomes from each child's EHCP. Crucially, it has involved parents who help us write meaningful, life-enhancing outcomes, and through the two-way sharing via EfL, we can together look at the development of their children's skills.

As a Senior Leadership Team, we have developed systems that demonstrate accountability of teachers and TAs (teaching assistants) to ensure our children are being challenged and that expectations are high. We reflect on our practice of monitoring and evaluating performance so that our systems are driven by the needs of our individual children and their personalised progress to ensure that we, they and their families are confident that this is the best it can be. Within the first half term of the pupil joining Kingsbury, time is taken to reassess the Long-Term Outcomes on the child's EHCP. The class teacher, alongside the SENCO (Special Educational Needs Coordinator) and parents, discusses these and makes any agreed amendments at the Placement Review. Each child has termly Personal Learning Outcomes (PLOs), linked to the EHCP and based on teacher's pedagogical understanding of child development, further supported by knowledge and awareness of assessment tools such as MAPP and Quest for Learning (CCEA, 2020), an assessment tool specifically designed for those with PMLD. EFL provides a substantial learning journey of PLOs demonstrating progress towards long term outcomes. Parents receive both weekly and termly reports, and pupil progress is reviewed on an ongoing basis throughout the year in the form of in-house and external moderation of judgements. This moderation includes scrutiny of learning journeys – i.e., critical reflection on progress toward learning outcomes, quality of teacher observations and levels of pupil engagement.

Step 2: changing a culture

Gosling and Mintzberg (2003) and Rosenshine's Principle in Action (Sherrington, 2019) helped shape my strategic thinking and allowed me to understand that, for change to be successful, I needed to change an embedded culture within school as well as ensure that my staff team fully understood and supported the changes. Establishing that commonality of purpose has been essential. We have, since, had to work extremely hard to slow down the pace, ensure our communication has been clear, and in turn, empower teachers and TAs to take ownership of these changes. All staff have been given time to learn, practise, evaluate and make changes that benefit the children. We have had to over-learn and repeat training sessions and give time for staff to step back and evaluate the impact and plan ways forward. As a head teacher, I have had to stop worrying about Ofsted (the school inspection service in the UK), be honest with governors and our school improvement partner and do what I know deep down is right for the children.

Developing a 'learning together culture' within school as well as reflecting on our leadership style and approach has made the greatest impact. Adopting a combination of Visionary and Coaching leadership styles (Goldman,

2000) also complement the 'H4 leadership' model (Rees, 2018), describing how Heart, Head, Hands and Health create the right conditions for schools to thrive. Staff, governors and parents needed to understand why change was required and the positive outcomes that change would have for our children, school and family life. In order to create positive change, everyone in the team has been encouraged and valued, ensuring that change was successful and that everyone had ownership and a voice regarding these changes.

Our Learning Together culture has been the key to our success. Dix (2020, p2) states 'getting the culture right is pivotal. . . . The culture is set by the way the adults behave'. I am extremely proud and lucky that my staff team fully embrace and believe in the Kingsbury Way and vision; they have made it come alive and happen. Putting our children at the heart of everything we do has been the golden nugget that has changed our entire culture within school. The whole atmosphere around school has changed; Kingsbury is calm, happy and you feel the love and buzz as you walk through the door. It is about the children; staff morale is the best it has been for years, as everyone has developed the culture and vision and has played their part in developing it. Staff are onboard and talk positively about the impact the changes have had.

Step 3: professional development

The leadership together recognised that changes to the curriculum needed to be embedded before progress could be measured accurately; and, before the curriculum changed, staff needed professional development to move their understanding along. Investing in professional development has been essential. Staff needed to have the pedagogical understanding as to why we were doing what we were doing before it could be implemented successfully. As Wiliam (2017) argues, pedagogy trumps curriculum; indeed, pedagogy dictates curriculum. However, analysis of our practice showed that we didn't really know our children and the developmental levels at which they were working: we used tick sheets from assessment systems to plan our curriculum and just worked through them mechanically. As a team and working closely with Equals, we have spent 4 years learning about child development, play, engagement, total communication approaches and sensory and emotional regulation through the various Equals' Curricula (Equals, 2020). Training has been delivered in a coaching style with staff being fully involved in learning and then in presenting back to one another. The impact has been massive, and our understanding of our children has developed immensely.

Step 4: engagement

The Covid 19 pandemic brought about partial closures and, consequently, small class groups which resulted in being able to creatively spend two terms to get to know our children and develop an understanding of what engages and motivates them. The Engagement Model (STA, 2020) was used informally as an assessment tool, and everything else was put on hold. Teachers were free to teach what they wanted to enable them to re-engage our children. We took this time to deeply understand each child's sensory and communication needs and how they might best be enabled to self-regulate. This resulted in the school's 'This is Me' documents, which provide a detailed picture of each individual. Getting to know the children in this way has been indispensable in developing an effective curriculum.

Step 5: curriculum

Developing the curriculum has been the most challenging part of our journey. Education's starting point should not be about us; it should be about our children, their needs, their aspirations and goals. As Imray and Colley (2017) argue, the majority of our children are unable to engage in subject-specific learning, precisely because of the depth and complexity of their learning disabilities. In line with the recommendations within the Rochford Review (2016) and the SEND Code of Practice (DfE, 2015) and based upon the Equals Curricula, our curriculum has now developed to reflect the four Pathways of Pre-Formal, Informal, Semi-Formal and Formal, supported by a personalised assessment tool in line with their Education Health Care Plans and the engagement model.

The 'Kingsbury Way' curriculum

We are strongly committed to the view that, if a child can't learn the way we teach, we should teach the way they learn. Learning is a two-way process. We provide experiences and opportunities to learn, and by re-visiting skills in different contexts, we ensure that our children not only generalise but also maintain and master skills over time. We pride ourselves on planning opportunities for learning, and through observation and support, we develop and celebrate incidental learning in all situations. All our staff work to engage and motivate children by responding to their interests and nurturing individual strengths. When our children are truly engaged, deep learning and mastery of skills occurs. Engagement is a journey which connects child and their environment to enable learning and achievement.

Our curriculum driver is essentially engagement in learning. This involves ensuring that all children are able to regulate their sensory and emotional needs so that they are ready to learn; once our children engage, then holistic and child-centred learning occurs. We strive to create an environment that is rich and full of opportunities for learning through Play, as learning through Play is a key focus throughout school. Our curriculum model is based around the continuous provision approach similar to an Early Years (neuro-typical) model, but use of the Equals curriculum documents ensures that teaching and learning is always as appropriate and challenging as it can be.

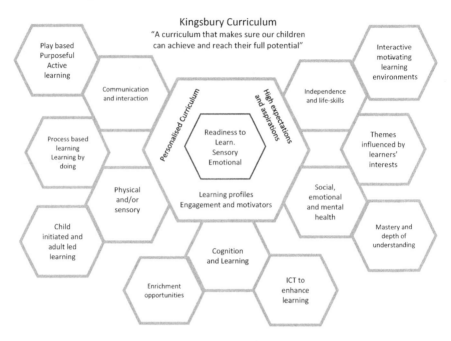

Figure 12.1 Our curriculum is hands-on, engaging, practical and focusses on commu-
    nication, independence, life skills, self-regulation and social and emotional
    skills. This curriculum provides our children with the opportunities to
    develop the lifelong functional skills they will need to make their adult life
    as independent, happy and successful as possible. With children and their
    families at the heart of everything we do, the 'Kingsbury Way' curriculum
    has been developed through a much-valued partnership with home and
    informed by research. We work together to facilitate a curriculum that is
    personalised, challenging, engaging and relevant in order to achieve the
    desired outcomes detailed in children's Education Health and Care Plans.

Accountability

As a staff team, we are confident that what we deliver is right for our children,
and APP, EfL and Quest for Learning have given us the data to fully support
and explain why we do what we do. We work hard to be sure of the child
development levels and play levels of our children; we fully recognise their
barriers to learning; and we are fully aware that some of the children have
'spiky profiles'. As a result, with our current cohort, we do not teach subject
specific lessons; we teach functional skills through a practical and play-based
curriculum, and we can talk confidently to the reasons why. EfL provides evidence for deep-dives demonstrating progress through each pathway directly
linked to areas of EHCPs. Staff talk confidently about early reading, maths and
writing skills and how it is integrated into everything that we do. Although
we do not deliver subject-specific content, we can demonstrate aspects of the

Table 12.1 Kingsbury Curriculum Pathways

Pre-Formal 'Explorers'	Informal 'Sensory Seekers' 'Finders' (EYFS)	Semi-Formal 'Discoverers' 'Experimenters'	Formal 'Adventurers'
Learning to Learn.	A life-skills-based curriculum.	A life-skills-based curriculum.	An adapted National Curriculum emphasising life need.
Learners at very early levels of development. Curriculum that is meaningful to them. Focus: communication and interaction. Physical/sensory. Maximum opportunities to achieve the highest level of independence possible.	Personalised timetables with low demand, access to favoured activities. Nurturing, child-centred approach. Enticing. Play-based, sensory curriculum reduces anxiety and creates an environment for true engagement. Community and life skills. Learners learn how to be rather than having to learn how to do! **Help us to listen better! Learning to be part of society and a community.**	Learners follow a curriculum that is related to their own experiences and interests. Play-based, purposeful, process-based. Learning functional skills. Active learning. Plan-do-review approach. Mastery of skills. Theme-based influenced by learners' interests. Roleplay needs to be functional and real to life.	Theme-based, focussing on meaningful life and independent skills. Learning is linked to practical activities. Mastery and understanding of skills are key. 'Don't teach children to a level of incompetence, all they feel is failure'. Progress is not linear – spiky profiles. DO NOT STRETCH UNLESS YOU ARE ABSOLUTELY CONFIDENT.

National Curriculum within our teaching and learning. Leaders and Middle leaders monitor teaching and learning, ensuring that there is 'Just the Right Challenge' – not lacking ambition but recognising each child's social, emotional and mental health needs as well as their emotional regulation and sensory needs.

Impact

It would take another chapter to evaluate the impact; quite simply, Kingsbury School is a very different place: happy children = happy staff = happy families.

Children

Children are happy, engaged and making individualised, meaningful progress. Behaviour incidents have dramatically decreased, and physical intervention is rarely needed. Children are encouraged to self-regulate. Sensory lifestyles are promoted in everything that we do. Emotional regulation is used daily to assess the demands placed on each individual, and strategies are used to support this. Children love learning; communication has been enhanced; their play skills have developed. Learning is meaningful and independence is developing all the time.

Staff

The staff team is happy, motivated and dedicated. Interactions with children are positive and meaningful. Staff feel that what they are delivering is purposeful and about each individual child, and they are achieving this with a reduced administrative workload. Their understanding of pedagogy has increased dramatically, and they feel empowered, as they own and understand the curriculum they deliver. The team is reflective and always striving to be innovative. Staff enjoy sharing their 'wow' moments each term. We are proud of what we do!

Families

Families are involved in discussing and deciding annual targets. Initially, some parents expressed concerns and challenged the curriculum changes but, through spending time with those parents, personalising the changes for their child and sharing their child's journey, they have come to see the benefits. The vast majority of families fully support the curriculum and see the impact it is having at home and on family life. Families are provided with weekly evidence to demonstrate progress that is meaningful and that they understand, and they, in turn, are able to share evidence of skills being generalised beyond school. The school supports families within the home and offers training.

Final thoughts and advice for headteachers seeking change: a personal reflection on the Kingsbury journey

- Be self-reflective as a leader; develop a coaching style of leadership but maintain high expectations and accountability.
- Listen to staff, take things at their pace and ask them to evaluate and reflect at different stages.
- Staff need ownership – don't do it to them!
- Communicate effectively to ensure everyone is on board and everyone has a clear understanding of the next step, what it looks like and why we need to get there.
- Develop a shared vision and let go of the pacesetting 'do as I do' approach.
- Delegate, be resilient and trust your team.
- Find like-minded leaders and schools – it can get lonely and you need some external moderation and a critical friend who 'gets it'.

- Allow time – it is a very long bumpy journey.
- Be prepared for repetition with staff training.
- Always keep the focus, and don't get sidetracked.
- Be brave, and stick to what you believe in.
- Always ask *why?*
- Invest in professional development for all staff.
- Budget effectively – staff will need money to develop both Play resources and their learning environment.
- All these things will, in the long term, move a collaborative team from 'Good' to 'Great' (Collins, 2001), bringing together an effective team with the children's outcomes at the heart of everything that you do.

References

CCEA. (2020). *Quest for Learning* [online]. Available from: https://ccea.org.uk/learning-resources/quest-learning. Accessed 31 March 2023.

Collins, J. (2001). *Good to Great.* New York: HarperCollins.

Department for Education. (2014). *P Scales: Attainment Targets for Pupils With SEN* [online]. Available from: www.gov.uk/government/publications/p-scales-attainment-targets-for-pupils-with-sen#full-publication-update-history. Accessed 30 March 2023.

DfE. (2015). *Special Educational Needs and Disability Code of Practice: 0 to 25 Years.* Available from: https://assets.publishing.service.gov.uk/government/uploads/system/uploads/attachment_data/file/398815/SEND_Code_of_Practice_January_2015.pdf. Accessed 26 July 2023.

Dix, P. (2020). *When the Adult Changes Everyone Changes.* Carmarthen: Independent Thinking Press.

Equals. (2020). *The Equals Multi-Tiered Curriculum Model.* Newcastle: Equals. Available at www.equals.co.uk.

Goldman, D. (2000). *Leadership That Gets Results.* Boston: Harvard.

Gosling, J. and Mintzberg, H. (2003). *The Five Minds of a Manager.* Boston: Harvard.

Imray, P. and Colley, A. (2017). *Inclusion is Dead: Long Live Inclusion.* London. Routledge.

Imray, P. and Hinchcliffe, V. (2014). *Curricula for Teaching Children and Young People With Severe or Profound and Multiple Learning Difficulties.* London: Routledge.

Ofsted. (2019). *School Inspection Handbook* [online]. Available from: www.gov.uk/government/organisations/ofsted. Accessed 30 March 2023.

Rees, T. (2018). *Wholesome Leadership.* Woodbridge: John Catt.

Rochford, D. (2016). *The Rochford Review: Final Report.* London: Standards and Testing Agency.

Rochford, D. (2020). *The Engagement Model.* London: Standards and Testing Agency.

Sherrington, T. (2019). *Rosenshine's Principles in Action.* Woodbridge: John Catt.

Sinek, S. (2009). *Starting With Why.* London: Penguin Business.

Sissons, M. (2018). *MAPP (Mapping and Assessing Personal Progress): Semi-Formal Model.* Newcastle: Equals.

Wiliam, D. (2017). Learning and Assessment. A Long and Winding Road. *Assessment in Education: Principles, Policy and Practice*, 24(3): 309–316.

Glossary

ASD Autism Spectrum Diagnosis, otherwise referred to simply as autism, and it should be noted that we reject the notion that autism is a disorder. Although a diagnosis of autism is unusual in the PMLD population, it is very common in both CLD and SLD populations. The existence of an ASD may well effect *how* teaching is organised, though the authors in this book are equally concerned with what is being taught and why it is being taught. Several chapters, notably Chapters 1, 5, 7 and 10, question whether our traditional understanding of autism as relating to those who will always need routine, order, certainty and structure (the ROCS of education) is actually the case. That is, is the observed need for ROCS reflective of our shaping the lives of those with autism because it is easier for us, as in, for example, fitting the learner into the curriculum? If such learners were given *real* freedom, choice and agency, would they reject that shaping and be much more able to tolerate uncertainty?

Common Core Curriculum The term used in the USA to describe the broad necessary elements of an academic educational curriculum to which all states might agree in the absence of an agreed national curriculum. The USA, along with other notable countries such as Germany and Canada, does not operate a defined National Curriculum (NC) but leaves it up to each state or province.

CLD Complex Learning Disabilities. A new term (and not to be confused with CLDD as described by Carpenter et al., 2015) coined by Equals to describe learners on the severe end of the SLD spectrum. A fuller description is to be had in Chapter 1.

CYPA Children, young people and adults.

DfE The civil service Department for Education in England.

EHCP Education Health and Care Plan, which, in England, is a means of recognising significant SEND leading to the allocation of additional state funding. At the time of writing, this represents 4% of the whole school population. All children, young people and adults with PMLD, CLD and SLD are highly likely to have an EHCP after the age of 6 and perhaps before, but make up around one and a half percent of the population, or around 40% of those with an EHCP.

Engagement Model   A means of assessing the levels of engagement seen in children, young people and adults with global learning disabilities. The Engagement Model derived from the Engagement Profile and Scale (Carpenter et al., 2015).

Equals   A not-for-profit charity based in England, set up in 1994 to represent the educational interests of children, young people and adults with PMLD and SLD. Equals has, since 2020, published a number of specific *different not differentiated* curricula for CYPA with PMLD, CLD and SLD.

EYFS   Early Years Foundation Stage, which, in England, represents the years from 2 or 3 to 5 or 6, before formal (NC) teaching comes into force and the age of 6. In England, the EYFS Curriculum, a predominantly play-based model, is statutory, though, in the same manner as the NC, it has been written for neuro-typical, conventionally developing learners.

GLD   Global learning disabilities, a generic term occasionally used to collectively describe all those with PMLD, CLD, SLD and MLD. The use of the term indicates that the individual learning difficulties (which make the total learning disability) faced by the individual are permanent rather than a matter of delay and affect all learning.

Governors   are all volunteers (i.e., unpaid) members of the strategic management of every state-maintained school in England and collectively form the school's Governing Body.

Key Stages   – otherwise referred to as KS – represent England's educational age-related organisation. KS1 refers to Years 1 and 2 (aged 5/6 to 7). KS2, Years 3 to 6 (aged 7 to 10/11). KS3, Years 7 to 9 (aged 11–14). KS4, Years 10 and 11.

LSA   Learning Support Assistant, a sometimes-used alternative name for TA.

MLD   Moderate learning difficulties. This term is commonly used in England to describe a level of learning 'difficulty' which is not so profound, complex or severe as that experienced by those with PMLD, CLD and SLD. As this simplistic explanation implies, the term MLD suffers from being inexact and incomplete, with no satisfactory definition existing. Imray and Colley (2017) suggest that the term is meaningless and merely describes the challenges faced by higher functioning people with SLD.

National Curriculum   – otherwise occasionally noted as NC – refers to England's NC, first instituted in 1988 under the Education Reform Act of that year. It is the contention of this book that all national curricula are essentially similar, in that all have been written for neuro-typical, conventionally developing learners, all centre around literacy and numeracy fluency and all describe neuro-typical progress between the ages of 6 and 16.

Ofsted   Office for Standards in Education is England's state-funded but independent inspection body that holds school leaders, particularly headteachers, to account for the quality of the education received by some 9 million or so school-aged children.

PMLD   Profound and multiple learning disabilities, described more fully in Chapter 1.

P Scales   Originally devised in the 1990's as a link between the academic levels achieved by those with profound, complex and severe learning disabilities and neuro-typical academic achievement. There are 8 P Scales ranging from P1, which describes neuro-typical babies shortly after birth to P8, which describes the academic achievement of averagely achieving, neuro-typical 15-year-olds. The P Scales were commonly used as an assessment system by all special schools in England prior to 2016, when the Rochford Review questioned their validity. They have since generally fallen out of favour.

Pre-Key Stage Standards   Were put into place in England by the Rochford Review as an alternative to the P Scales. There are various levels which broadly describe a 'working towards' Year 1 of the NC. The really interesting Pre-Key Stage Standard is Level 6 at KS2, because this describes the upper reaches of the term SLD. That is, if a learner (of whatever age) can independently achieve all of the standards set by Level 6 at KS2, they probably do not have SLD.

Rochford Review   Named after Diane Rochford, who was, at the time, the Headteacher of John F Kennedy School, an all-age (2–19) specialist school in Stratford, east London, and who led the review. The Rochford Review was set up by the DfE to explore the nature of assessment for those with PMLD and SLD in England's education system. Its conclusion was, broadly, that the P Scales were not fit for purpose as a means of comparative assessment for these populations of learners.

SEND   Special educational needs and disabilities.

SLD   Severe learning disabilities, described more fully in Chapter 1.

Specialist Schools   – otherwise known as 'special schools' – are schools that are, in England at least, centrally government funded and whose intake is specifically related to broad types of SEND. Most SLD/PMLD schools in England are all-age (2–19) and will have an intake that will include those with CLD and those with autism.

Specific Learning Difficulties   – known as **SpLD** in England – such as dyslexia and dyscalculia affect one part of learning rather than all learning. There are a number of published books relating to the challenges faced by teachers, but being specific rather than global, they are not the concern of this book.

Teachers   All those who teach, whether they be trained and accredited or not. In this book, at least, TAs are as important to the education of those with PMLD, CLD and SLD as the teacher. Neither teachers nor TAs are required to undertake specific training in order to teach those with GLD. The editors of this book do not understand this 'logic', which largely derives from the notion that all children learn the same way and should therefore be learning the same things. We have not included a chapter about the need for specialisation in teaching qualification, though this might form the basis of our next book!

TAs Teaching Assistants, the term generally used in England to indicate those who support the education of children under the direction of a qualified teacher. TAs are even less well paid and generally offered less training than teachers.

Reference

Carpenter, B., Egerton, J., Cockbill, B., Bloom, T., Fotheringham, J., Rawson, H. and Thistlethwaite, J. (2015). *Engaging Learners With Complex Learning Difficulties and Disabilities.* Abingdon: Routledge.

Imray, P. and Colley, A. (2017). *Inclusion is Dead: Long Live Inclusion.* London: Routledge.

Index

Printed in Great Britain
by Amazon